# Table of Contents

# DEFIANCE!

## The Antichrists of History and their Doomed War Against the Church

Rev. Joseph M. Esper

Queenship

**PUBLISHING COMPANY**
P.O. Box 220 • Goleta, CA 93116
(800) 647-9882 • (805) 692-0043 • Fax: (805) 967-5133
www.queenship.org

**The antichrist faces on the cover**

Starting left to right top row:
Adolf Hilter 1889-1945 AD, *(Page 191)*
Rasputin 1869-1916 AD, *(Page 151)*
Martin Luther 1483-1546 AD, *(Page 85)*
King Henry VIII 1491-1547 AD, *(Page 93)*
Karl Marx 1818-1883 AD. *(Page 145)*

2nd row:
Charles Darwin 1809-1882 AD, *(Page 210)*
Haman (reigned) 485-465 BC, *(Page 4)*
Rameses 1314-1224 BC, *(Page 2)*
Helena Blavatsky 1831-1891 AD, *(Page 173)*
Mao Zedong 1893-1976 AD, *(Page 160)*

Bottom row:
Nero 37-68 AD, *(Page 18)*
Joseph Stalin 1878-1953 AD, *(Page 157)*
Elizabeth I 1533-1603 AD, *(Page 98)*
Vladimir Lenin 1870-1924 AD, *(Page 152)*
Margaret Sanger 1879-1966 AD *(Page 220)*

Library of Congress Number # 2011901645

Published by:
    Queenship Publishing
    P.O. Box 220
    Goleta, CA 93116
    (800) 647-9882 • (805) 692-0043 • Fax: (805) 967-5133
    www.queenship.org

Printed in the United States of America

ISBN: 978-1-57918-400-6

# Foreword

The topic of the "Antichrist" in this book covers man's history from the Garden to the Second Coming of the Lord at the end of time.. From antiquity to the present and the promised future one hidden malevolent figure remains on the scene. He is the deceiver in the Garden, (Gen. 3:1-13), the "Tempter" of Jesus in the desert, (Mt. 4:1-1; Lk. 4:1-13) the "Antichrist" in the first epistle of John (1 John 2:14-15) and in the book of Revelation his battle with the "Woman" and her children (ch. 12) and finally his complete separation and confinement in "the lake of fire and sulphur... forever and ever..." (ch.20.)

The Catechism (#397, 398 ff) speaks of man's disobedience and fall, seduced by the evil one, to be "like" God. All subsequent sin would rise from this disobedience and lack of trust rising from the weakness of man's will and the darkness of his mind prone to sin and openness, conscious or not, to the primal rebel, Satan himself.

It is this history that Fr. Esper brings to our minds and hearts. Can any one today look around and not see the fruits of a history filled with violence, hatred, malice, disobedience and longing of man to become like God. A brief examine of history reveals a seemingly ever growing destructive and proud mind and will of man bringing the world itself to a brink of appalling disaster. The very genes of man's physical body and disposition of the mind is under the probe of science without strictures of moral guidelines.

One thing is certain as we go through the authors presentation: Mary's role is central and through her the final battle against Satan will occur. The complete ultimate goal of mans destiny is Christ presenting those whom the Father had given to Him Not one of them will have been lost. What then does the Father have in store for us?

Fr. Raymond R. Skonezny STL., SSL

# Publishers Foreword

Many faithful Catholics bemoan the fact that the Church today seems to be marked by scandals, a culture of disobedience, the loss of religious vocations, poor or non-existent catechesis, declining Mass attendance, and various other problems. As if that weren't enough, some commentators—including various alleged visionaries and prophets—warn of coming schisms and religious persecutions, even here in the United States. Moreover, modern technology and communications, and the growing power of secularism and our culture of death, may well pave the way for the arrival of powerful political and social leaders committed to the unthinkable: the destruction of the Church. It would seem that Catholics who love the Church have good reason to fear for her survival—but the Bride of Christ has so far weathered every storm and outlasted every adversary.

In her 2000 year history, numerous enemies of the Church have attempted to destroy her—and every one of them has failed, usually at great personal cost. From the perspective of Heaven, the Church is often threatened, but never conquered—and in troubled times, it's more important than ever for Catholics to hold this truth and find reassurance in it. Fr. Joseph Esper's book reminds us of the Church's many victories over her assailants, and demonstrates that—through the power of God—she will continue to triumph over every assault of her foes, including her ultimate historical enemy, The Antichrist himself.

Only God Himself knows when the Antichrist will arrive on earth, and when the end of the world will occur—but there can be no doubt that a severe trial for faithful believers is imminent. The "signs of the times" are all around us—and that makes *Defiance! The Antichrists of History and Their Doomed War Against the Church* a very timely and hope-filled, resource. While it's impossible to predict the exact course of future events, a study of the past reveals the utter reliability of Christ's promise that His Church will never be overcome by evil (cf. Mt. 16:18), and will emerge victorious from every challenge. This reassuring message is needed today more than ever, and Queenship Publishing is happy to have the opportunity to present this book to you.

Claire Schaefer, Publisher

# Introduction

*. . . the Lord knows how to rescue the devout from the
trial and to keep the unrighteous under punishment for
the day of judgment. (2 Pt. 2:9)*

In an article on the topic of the Antichrist published about
125 years ago, a Redemptorist priest named Michael Muller
recounted the story of a train in the Old West traveling at a high
rate of speed one night. The passengers and crew suddenly heard
the sound of something being struck on the track, and though
no one aboard was injured, the train was stopped to investigate.
It was discovered that a large owl had attacked the headlight at
the front the train, trying to extinguish it, and a great bull had
simultaneously charged at the train, trying to derail it. As the two
dead animals were tossed aside, one of the passengers remarked,
"I admire your courage, but condemn your judgment."

Commenting on this unusual event, Fr. Muller wrote,

> *this train may be likened to the holy Catholic Church,
> speeding on her Heaven-sent mission, to lead men to Heaven
> by the light of her holy doctrine. The foolish owl, the enemy
> of light and the friend of darkness, represents Lucifer, who,
> as the Foe of God, and of the light of God's holy religion, has
> always been endeavoring to extinguish the light of the true
> religion. The bull represents the kings and emperors, the
> heretics and members of secret societies, whom Lucifer uses
> to stop, if possible, the progress of the Catholic Church, the
> bearer of the light of faith. Although it is hard, in a certain
> sense, not to marvel at the courage of Lucifer's agents, yet
> we cannot but condemn their judgment, their folly and
> wickedness, in opposing the work of God, and bringing down
> upon themselves the everlasting curse of the Almighty.*[1]

*Centuries earlier, St. Hildegard of Bingen had noted that "The devil performs his craftiness through the work of people," and the 2000 year history of the Church amply illustrates this point. Satan usually doesn't show himself directly (except, perhaps, to those deluded souls willing to worship and serve him), but instead prefers to operate behind the scenes, manipulating weak, sinful, and ambitious men and women in order to further his diabolical plans. Part of the reason he does this is his desire to ape God: just as the Holy Spirit normally works in quiet ways (cf. Jn. 3:8) noticeable only to those who see with the eyes of faith, so the devil likes to set his traps and pull his strings without anyone being aware of it, craftily ensnaring his unsuspecting victims and leading them to spiritual destruction.*

Perhaps the major reason for Lucifer's secrecy, however, is simply that the Lord doesn't allow him to *force* us to choose evil. The devil must respect our free will—and, naturally, his temptations are most effective when we have no inkling of their true origin. God, of course, to avoid overwhelming our freedom, rarely shows Himself to us in a direct manner; He instead works through other people and through the grace-filled events of life as an expression of His loving providence. Satan, on the other hand, as the "father of lies" (8:44), follows a policy of "plausible deniability" in order to deceive the unwary and prevent his victims from repenting of their sins and accepting the divine gift of forgiveness and redemption.

The devil has always made use of willing, and usually (though not always) unsuspecting, agents in his efforts to destroy the Church, tempting and enticing them with promises of earthly power and glory. Moreover, as the great Russian author Feodor Dostoevsky noted, "Whoever has experienced the power, the unrestrained ability to humiliate another human being . . . automatically loses power over his own sensations. Tyranny is a habit, it has its own organic life, it develops finally into a disease."[2]

If Jesus is indeed the "Alpha and the Omega" (Rev. 22:13) and the Lord of history, why is the devil given such great freedom to assault spiritually unaware and defenseless persons in general, and the Church in particular? According to St. Thomas Aquinas, "God, despite His omnipotence and supreme goodness, allows evils He could prevent to exist in the world, if removing them would cause greater good to be lost or greater evil to ensue."[3] That is, the Lord is using Satan's attempts at destroying the Church to bring about her even more glorious triumph. In the words of St. Paul, "We know that all things work for good for those who love God" (Rm. 8:28), and as the popular expression reminds us, "God writes straight with crooked lines."

If evil seems to gain the upper hand at any given time in history, a greater divine purpose is being served—often in the form of a warning to humanity. According to author Michael H. Brown,

> when a society sinned or when the Church needed cleansing God, in His wisdom, gave that society a glimpse of hell. He did this by allowing exposure to the demon. It was a simple truism: sin brought the devil. When a person was living out of tune with the Commandments that person was especially exposed to both attack and deception—the false glamour, the self-importance, the shining elements.[4]

Some 150 years ago, the English convert (and eventual cardinal of the Church) Ven. John Henry Newman recognized a clear link between sin and the rise of Satan's specially chosen servants. As explained by the Jesuit scholar Fr. Vincent P. Miceli,

> in every case of a forerunner of the Antichrist, Newman demonstrates how the apostasy of the people from the true God prepared the coming of these heralds and types of the Antichrist and led to the whole sale slaughter of a religious society. First the people of God in large numbers discarded their sacred religion and then the enemy was allowed to come in. The great apostasy is always the harbinger of the shadows and substance of the Antichrist. The Jews first abandoned God, then came Antiochus; Christians fell away into Arianism, then arose Julian the Apostate and the persecution; the heresies of Nestorianism and Eutychianism destroyed the faith of millions, then came Muhammad. The agnosticism and atheism of the Enlightenment paved the way for the Reign of Terror under Robespierre and the Jacobins.[5]

Jesus had warned that wickedness rushes to fill a spiritual vacuum (cf. Mt. 12:43-35), and in the words of the English poet William Blake, "Man must and will have religion: if he has not the religion of Jesus, he will have the religion of Satan and will erect a synagogue of Satan."[6]

The struggle between good and evil will reach its culmination just before the Lord's Second Coming, but it's been waged with ever-growing intensity throughout history—and we ourselves are unavoidably caught up in it. At the 1976 Eucharistic Congress in Philadelphia, Cardinal Karol Wojtyla (who would become Pope John Paul II two years later) stated:

> We are now standing in the face of the greatest historical confrontation humanity has ever experienced. I do not think the wide circle of American society, or the wide circle of the Christian community, realize this fully. We are now facing the final confrontation between the Church and the anti-Church, between the Gospel and the anti-Gospel, between Christ and the Antichrist. This confrontation lies within the plans of Divine Providence. It is therefore within God's plans and must be a trial which the Church must take up and face courageously.[7]

Lucifer, the original rebel against God (cf. Is. 14:12-15; Rev. 12:7-9), has been unrelenting in his efforts to destroy the Church, and in every era of history has raised up opponents, with varying degrees of arrogance, ruthlessness, or subtlety, to resist and undermine the one True Faith. Jesus warned His disciples to expect to be hated by this world (Jn. 15:18-19)—a hatred motivating entire societies and institutions, in addition to specific individuals. Furthermore, as Michael H. Brown writes, the great beast of Rev. 12 symbolizes

> the spirit of antichrist, and possibly the Antichrist himself. The spirit of antichrist rears its ugly head in every generation, especially at the end of most epochs. When it infuses a person, when it takes someone over, that person, if powerful enough, becomes a forerunner of the Antichrist, an antichrist in miniature.[8]

The more God's Commandments are ignored or flaunted, the more His truth and grace are rejected, and the more His Church is despised and opposed, the greater the power of sin becomes in the world—and thus, a yet stronger role and influence for the servants of Satan. Jesus observed that the children of this world often show great initiative in seeking their own advancement

(Lk. 16:8), and indeed, the devil has never lacked for servants eager to do his bidding.

This book is an attempt to identify the more prominent historical precursors of the Antichrist, and then draw some general conclusions about the character of the person Scripture calls the "one doomed to perdition" (2 Th. 2:3). Many of the figures to be presented here were (or are) important in a military or political sense, but others have also exercised great influence in the fields of philosophy, psychology, science, economics, entertainment, the occult, and even religion.

There are stories of ruthless persecution of the Church, and of subtle—and thus, all the more dangerous—challenges to the Faith. The antichrist's precursors have been motivated by pride, greed, and lust, and also by sincere but misguided religious beliefs. Many of Satan's servants had no idea of whom they were actually serving, but some knowingly and willingly embraced him as their master, only to die in delusion or despair after inevitably being betrayed by him. Some of the characters in this tragic historical drama vehemently rejected the God of Judeo-Christian tradition, while a few more-or-less honestly believed they were working in His Name. The majority of the Church's opponents to be described herein died alienated from God, but several of them sincerely repented at the end—giving us every reason to hope for their salvation.

Only Jesus Christ, the Lamb of God, is worthy to open the scroll containing God's final judgment on human history (Rev. 5:6,9), and it isn't given to us to know in advance when this judgment will occur (cf. Mt. 24:36). However, it is possible for us to find reassurance in regard to our own times by reminding ourselves of the historical storms already weathered by the Church. As early as the late 1st century, St. John could write that "many antichrists have appeared" (1 Jn. 2:18), and even a cursory review of Church history makes his words seem timely for every generation of Christians. Satan continues to sow weeds among the wheat (cf. Mt. 13:38-39), and some of these "weeds" are truly dangerous—but no matter how great their temporary success may be in bringing about a certain degree of hell on earth, their rebellion against Almighty God is ultimately and irrevocably doomed. The Father has made all things subject to Jesus (Eph. 1:22), and as the Bride of Christ (cf. Eph. 5:31-32), the Church will share in His coming victory, with each faithful Christian invited to celebrate the wedding feast of the Lamb (Rev. 19:9).

Christ has not abandoned His people. He assures us not only that He has overcome the world (Jn. 16:33), but also that the gates of hell will never prevail against His Church (Mt. 16:18), and that the Holy Spirit will be with us always (Jn. 14:16), guiding us to all truth (Jn. 16:13) and righteousness. Through the Holy Spirit, we are able to obey St. Paul's exhortation to "rejoice in hope, endure in affliction, [and] persevere in prayer" (Rm. 12:12)—and, after living in this spirit, we will take our place among those who, at the end of time, joyfully acclaim the "King of kings and Lord of lords" (Rev. 20:16).

## NOTES TO INTRODUCTION

[1] "Antichrist," Michael Muller, C.S.S.R. (B. Herder, 1886), as quoted by Emmett Culligan, *The Last World War and the End of Time* (Elbee Press, 1950, 1973), pp. 103-104.

[2] R. Kent Hughes, "Tyranny," *1001 Great Stories and Quotes* (Tynedale, 1998), p. 415.

[3] Rosemary Ellen Guiley, *The Quotable Saint* (Checkmark Books, 2002), p. 78.

[4] Michael H. Brown, *The Last Secret* (Queenship Publishing, 2007), p. 73.

[5] Vincent P. Miceli, S.J., *The Antichrist* (Roman Catholic Books, 1981), p. 109.

[6] Quoted by Fr. Andrew O'Brien in *Make Yourself an Ark!*, Vol. 2 (The American Research Foundation, 1995), p. 15.

[7] Quoted by Stephen Mahowald in *She Shall Crush Thy Head* (MMR Publishing, 1996), p. 11.

[8] Michael H. Brown, *The Day Will Come* (Servant Publications, 1996), p. 282

# Chapter 1

# Antichrists of Antiquity

*Why do the nations rage and the peoples utter folly? The kings of the earth rise up, and the princes conspire together against the Lord and His anointed: 'Let us break their fetters and cast their bonds from us!' He Who is throned in Heaven laughs; the Lord derides them.* (Ps. 21:1-4)

Righteous persons throughout the ages have bewailed the unique sinfulness of their own generation, frequently identifying it as the most iniquitous in history to date—but in fact, human rebellion against God is neither new nor isolated. As the story of Adam and Eve shows, the fallen angel Lucifer wasted no time in leading the first human beings into sin, and after their expulsion from paradise, the original sin of disobedience brought forth a host of other evils. Cain killed his brother Abel out of jealousy, even though the Lord had warned him, "sin is a demon lurking at the door" (Gn. 4:7). The Book of Genesis tells us that within a few generations of the first murder, "When the Lord saw how great was man's wickedness on earth, and how no desire that his heart conceived was ever anything but evil, He regretted that He had made man on the earth" (6:5-6).

The great flood cleansed the world of evil, leaving just eight righteous persons alive—but this respite was only temporary. Satan continued actively opposing God's plan for His creation, and within a relatively short time managed to lead most of humanity into a great sin of pride—namely, the construction of the Tower of Babel, which symbolized men's efforts to achieve redemption (in the sense of reaching up to Heaven) through their own efforts. This grand project suddenly ended when the Lord confused the speech of the architects and workers, but as various language

1

groups thereafter went their separate ways, sinful inclinations accompanied them. The perversity of Sodom and Gomorrah is merely the most vivid illustration of this truth; the devil had no difficulty recruiting willing followers for his diabolical crusade against Heaven.

Every rebellion needs leaders—and this is true even of Satan's war against God, in which the evil one prefers to manipulate his pawns and accomplices from behind the curtains of history. Just as the Lord raises up great saints in His own image, so the devil seeks out, assists, and—for as long as it suits his purposes—protects malleable human beings steeped in wickedness. Over the last several millennia, God's chosen people—first the Jews, and then the members of His Son's Church—have suffered at the hands of ruthless men, ambitious in evil and oblivious to the truth. To set the stage for those who struck at Christ Incarnate Himself, and then persecuted His earliest followers, we must first briefly consider the three greatest persecutors in ancient times of the Jewish people.

## Pharaoh

The word "Pharaoh" is not a proper name, but a title for the kings of ancient Egypt. The Book of Genesis relates how Joseph, the eleventh of Jacob's twelve sons, arrived in Egypt as a slave, but soon won Pharaoh's favor, and was appointed vizier (executive officer, or second-in-command) of the kingdom. Joseph's brothers, who had sold him into slavery, eventually came to Egypt and were reconciled with him, and later his father Jacob came and finished his life there.

The descendants of Jacob's sons multiplied and grew prosperous—but then, according to the Book of Exodus, "a new king, who knew nothing of Joseph, came to power in Egypt" (1:8). Most scholars identify this Pharaoh as Ramses II, who reigned for much of the 13th century B.C. Ramses seems to have been a very cruel and ambitious figure; he came to power by overthrowing his brother, the legitimate ruler, and went about making Egypt into a great kingdom. He was a fierce but impetuous military leader, as shown by his rashness in fighting the Hittites at the Battle of Kadesh (1274 B.C.), where he blundered into a trap. Disaster was averted only through luck, his own bravery, and the indecision of the opposing commander. Afterwards, Ramses reacted in a characteristic manner by personally beheading those generals who had deserted him at a crucial moment in the battle, and declaring the fight to have been a great victory.

Ramses' reign was devoted to expanding his empire by military conquest, erecting impressive monuments, and promoting the use of great luxury at the royal court. These developments required the increasing use of slaves and mercenary troops—trends which contributed to the kingdom's eventual decline.

The little historical information we have on Ramses II fits well with the characterization of Pharaoh we find in the Book of Exodus. The Egyptians, at Pharaoh's command, made slaves of the Hebrew people, or Israelites, forcing them to build cities and fortifications, while oppressing them cruelly; moreover, the king ordered every newborn male Israelite to be murdered. Moses, of course, survived this holocaust, and years later returned at God's command to liberate His people. The remainder of this story is well known; the point to be emphasized is Pharaoh's extreme arrogance and obstinacy: even after witnessing plagues and wonders his own magicians were unable to duplicate, and in spite of great devastation and suffering in his kingdom brought about by his own stubbornness, he foolishly refused to allow the Israelites their freedom. Only after the angel of the Lord struck down the first-born of every Egyptian family—Pharaoh's included—did the Egyptian king finally change his mind and order God's chosen people to depart.

This grudging concession to common sense didn't last for long; Pharaoh was soon filled with regret over losing his Hebrew slaves, and sent his army to pursue them into the desert. As we know, the Lord worked a great miracle on behalf of His people, having Moses lead them through the Red Sea on dry land, and then drowning all of Pharaoh's charioteers and horses when they followed. This event, known as the Exodus, occurred in the 13th century B.C., but the exact date is uncertain.[1]

In regard to the tenth and final plague which finally convinced Pharaoh to release the Israelites, the Jewish people to this day commemorate the Passover each year (recalling how the angel of the lord "passed over" those houses of the Israelites marked with the blood of sacrificial lambs, while striking down the first-born of the Egyptians). Pharaoh, for his part, is remembered as the first of many oppressors who proved no match for the power of the Almighty.

# Haman

Many Jews had been led into exile following the destruction of Jerusalem by the Babylonians in 587 B.C. Babylon, however, was in turn conquered by Cyrus of Persia, who allowed the Jews to return to their homeland and rebuild their city and sacred temple. The Jews thereafter had a favorable attitude toward Cyrus and his descendants, and some of them chose to live within the Persian empire.

The Book of Esther tells the story of a plot against these Jews during the reign of King Xerxes (Ahasuerus) of Persia, who reigned from 485-464 B.C. His vizier, Haman, had a great hatred for the Jews—a hatred which only intensified after Mordecai, a prominent Jew, refused for religious reasons to offer him homage. Determined to take revenge, Haman desired to destroy not only Mordecai himself, but the entire Jewish population of the empire; he convinced the king that his Jewish subjects were plotting against him, and must be exterminated. Accordingly, a royal decree was sent out to the governors of each province of the empire, ordering the Jews there to be put to death on the appointed day.

Mordecai learned of this; wailing aloud, he put on sackcloth and ashes. It happened that his niece Esther was one of many royal wives of King Xerxes, and Mordecai begged her to approach the king and intercede on behalf of her people. The heroine prepared herself with three days of prayer and fasting; then, taking her life into her hands (for it was potentially a capital offense to enter into the king's presence without being summoned by him), Esther approached the king. She found favor with him, and when she asked that he and Haman attend several banquets she wished to provide, he readily agreed. At the first banquet, Esther said nothing about the threat to her people, lulling her enemy into a false sense of security.

In the meantime, Haman ordered a large gibbet to be erected, from which he intended to hang Mordecai. Ironically, when King Xerxes was reminded that he had never properly rewarded Mordecai for saving his life some years earlier, he ordered his vizier to arrange for this. To Haman's great anger and embarrassment, he was forced to walk ahead of Mordecai's horse in the city square, publicly singing his praises. When he returned home in furious shame that evening, his wife—speaking prophetically—said, "If Mordecai, before whom you are beginning to decline, is of the Jewish race, you will not prevail against him, but will surely be defeated by him" (Est. 6:13).

At the second banquet attended by King Xerxes and his vizier, Queen Esther persuasively asked the king to spare her people, and identified Haman as the enemy not only of the Jews, but of the king himself. Xerxes was furious at Haman, and when he momentarily left the room so as to gain control of himself, the disgraced vizier clumsily approached Esther to beg her mercy. Unfortunately for him, the king reentered the room at that moment, and assumed he was witnessing an assault on his royal wife. When a court official happened to mention that Haman had constructed a gibbet with the intent of hanging his enemy Mordecai, Xerxes ordered that Haman be hanged from it himself. The earlier royal decree calling for the destruction of the empire's Jews was rescinded, and the Jewish feast of Purim was established to commemorate the downfall of Haman and the deliverance of his intended victims.

## Antiochus

According to the Jesuit scholar Fr. Vincent P. Miceli, "Prior to the advent of Christ, perhaps the most remarkable shadow of the coming fulfillment of evil in the Antichrist was the heathen, King Antiochus."[2] This great enemy of the Jewish people was one of the kings of the Seleucid dynasty, and the son of Antiochus III, known as the Great. An indication of Antiochus IV's arrogant pride was the title he assumed upon taking the throne himself: Antiochus Epiphanes ("the god made manifest").

According to 1 Maccabees, "There sprang from these [the Seleucids] a sinful offshoot, Antiochus Epiphanes, son of King

Antiochus, once a hostage at Rome. He became king in the year one hundred and thirty seven [175 B.C.] of the kingdom of the Greeks" (1:10). A cruel and eccentric man, he sometimes mingled with crowds and, depending on his mood, freely distributed lavish sums.[3] Antiochus successfully invaded Egypt and plundered its riches; then he turned his attention to the Jews. 1 Maccabees tells us that he

> went up to Israel and to Jerusalem with a strong force. He insolently invaded the sanctuary [of the Temple] and took away the golden altar, the lampstand for the light with all its fixtures, the offering table, the cups and the bowls, the golden censers, the curtain, the crowns, and the golden ornament on the façade of the Temple. He stripped off everything, and took away the gold and silver and the precious vessels; he also took all the hidden treasures he could find. Taking all this, he went back to his own country, after he had spoken with great arrogance and shed much blood (1:20-24).

Wanting a politically unified empire, Antiochus ordered a policy of Hellenization—that is, the adoption of Greek culture. Some of the more "politically correct" Jews eagerly embraced this trend, and built a gymnasium in Jerusalem, while covering over the mark of their circumcision and ignoring Jewish religious and dietary laws. Many others resisted, however, and so Antiochus ordered a severe restriction of Judaism, forbidding the practices of circumcision and abstention from pork. He also outlawed the offering of sacrifices in the Temple, and even worse, had a statue of the pagan god Zeus set up there (2 Mc. 6:2)—the "abomination of desolation."

2 Maccabees describes the bravery of certain Jews who preferred martyrdom rather than to violate the laws of their religion, including an elderly scribe named Eleazar (6:18-31), and a mother and her seven sons, who were put to death in the king's presence, one after the other (7:1-41). Instead of breaking the Jews' spirit, however, the cruelty of Antiochus and his officers inspired further resistance, under the leadership of Mattathias and his son Judas Maccabeus. The Jews, motivated by religious fervor, won a number of great victories over the foreign occupiers, and eventually managed to recapture Jerusalem, and purify and

rededicate the Temple.

As this was happening, Antiochus was engaged in a failed invasion of Persia. While retreating in shame, he learned of the Jews' successful revolt, and, setting out at once for Jerusalem, vowed to take a terrible revenge. However, as Scripture tells us, *the condemnation of Heaven rode with him, since he said in his arrogance, "I will make Jerusalem the common graveyard of the Jews as soon as I arrive there." So the all-seeing Lord, the God of Israel, struck him down with an unseen but incurable blow; for scarcely had he uttered those words when he was seized with excruciating pains in his bowels and sharp intestinal torment, a fit punishment for him who had tortured the bowels of others with many barbarous torments* (2 Mc. 9:4-6).

This sudden agony filled him with a still greater determination to crush the Jews, but after ordering his driver to proceed even faster, he was hurled from his chariot. The scriptural account (which does not make for pleasant reading) triumphantly continues,

*Thus he who previously, in his superhuman presumption, thought he could command the waves of the sea, and imagined he could weigh the mountain tops in his scales, was now thrown to the ground and had to be carried on a litter, clearly manifesting to all the power of God. The body of this impious man swarmed with worms, and while he was still alive in hideous torments, his flesh rotted off, so that the entire army was sickened by the stench of his corruption. Shortly before, he had thought that he could reach the stars of heaven, and now, no one could endure to transport the man because of his intolerable stench* (9:8-10).

We're further told that Antiochus IV, recognizing the supreme power of the God of the Israelites, desperately vowed to change his ways, even to the point of becoming a Jew himself, if necessary, and he sent a flattering letter to the Jews, in which he spoke of his supposed affection for them, while referring to their esteem and good will toward him (2 Mc. 9:19-21)—sentiments which existed only in his self-deluded mind. This insincere repentance did him no good; Scripture records that "this murderer and blasphemer, after extreme sufferings, such as he had inflicted on others, died a miserable death in the mountains of a foreign land" (2 Mc. 9:28). As the Lord had promised Abraham and his descendants, "I will bless those who bless you and curse those who curse you" (Gn. 12:3).

## Herod the Great

St. Matthew's Gospel is the only historical source mentioning the slaughter of the infants of Bethlehem (2:16-18), but such a despicable act of violence, motivated by intense jealousy and paranoia, is entirely consistent with the character and personal history of the man known to us as Herod the Great.

In an era known for ruthless and cunning rulers, Herod stands out, during a reign of over thirty years, for his extreme ambitions and murderous suspicion of those closest to him. The son of an Arabian princess and a Roman-appointed administrator of Palestine, Herod became friends with the Roman Marc Antony—but after Antony's defeat at the Battle of Actium in 31 B.C., he was astute enough to transfer his loyalty to Octavian, who, as the future Roman emperor Augustus, appointed him king and allowed him great latitude in his kingdom. This political success fueled Herod's ambition, but brought him no peace of mind; fearing for his safety, he murdered all the potential Hasmonean (latter-day Maccabean) claimants to the throne, while adopting the role of a "friend of Caesar" and showing himself to be reliably loyal to the Roman Empire. This, of course, aroused the enmity of his Jewish subjects—and when the land was struck by a severe earthquake, a series of droughts, and an outbreak of the plague, Herod was widely viewed as a reincarnation of the hated Pharaoh of Egypt.[4]

Herod was not a Jew himself; his family came from the ancient biblical land of Edom, and so the dynasty he established was scornfully referred to as Idumean. The king at times pretended to observe the precepts of the Judaism, but it was commonly known he had little concern for religion; power and prestige mattered to him more than anything else.[5] Herod's contempt for religious customs and authority was manifested very early in his reign, when he tortured and executed a group of political rebels without any sort of religious trial. This outraged the Sanhedrin (the Jewish religious council), which announced that the king had committed a capital offense under Jewish law, and demanded he appear in person before that body. This was a very serious matter, and the Sanhedrin was used to being treated with the utmost deference by those whom it summoned. Herod, however, appeared before the council in a regal, haughty manner—and before the judges could condemn him, an order arrived from Rome demanding Herod be released without charge;[6] naturally increased his arrogance even further.

After his encounter with the religious authorities, Herod was determined to break any local source of authority other than his own; he ordered the execution of roughly two-thirds of the members of the Sanhedrin (for supposedly meddling in political affairs), and appointed more pliable figures in their places. The king also began appointing and dismissing high priests according to his own whims (even though the position was hereditary)—but when one of his appointees, a young man named Ananelus, actually won the approval and praise of the people, a jealous Herod ordered him drowned in a pool during a great feast he cynically threw in the high priest's honor.[7]

Knowing of his people's hatred for him and fearing rebellion, Herod employed numerous spies and informants, had potential political rivals assassinated (including the grandfather of his wife), and built imposing fortresses in remote areas, should he need a place of refuge. The king was an ambitious builder—not only fortresses and palaces for himself, but a seaport on the Mediterranean (named Caesarea in honor of the emperor), and, in an effort to win the favor of his subjects, a magnificent and much larger version of the Temple in Jerusalem—a project that lasted forty-six years (Jn. 2:20). Even during the building of the Temple, however, his cruelty suddenly erupted. The king had a golden eagle placed over the main entrance as a symbol of Roman authority, but a group of Torah students—offended by the blasphemous image—tore it down and smashed it to pieces. An enraged Herod had them hunted down and then, after a mock trial in a Roman ampitheatre, ordered them burnt alive.

The king's brutality was not limited to his enemies; an increasingly paranoid Herod murdered his brother, two stepsons, and one of his own male offspring (leading the emperor to remark that it was safer to be Herod's pig than his son). The king even executed his wife Mariamme for supposedly plotting against him, though she seems to have been innocent of such charges; later, in his grief, he constructed a magnificent tower in Jerusalem and named it in her honor.

When magi or wise men arrived from the east late in Herod's reign, inquiring about the location of a newborn king, St. Matthew's Gospel tells us that the evil ruler "was greatly troubled, and all Jerusalem with him" (2:3). After consulting with the chief priests, Herod obtained as much information as possible from his visitors, and then sent them to Bethlehem, while deviously pretending to await their report, so that he too might go and render homage. God, of course, thwarted his evil intent by means of an angelic warning given to the magi—and when Herod realized that he himself, in spite of all his cunning, had been outsmarted, he furiously ordered the massacre of all young boys in the vicinity of Bethlehem (Mt. 2:16).

Needless to say, no human being—no matter how evil, violent, and determined—can destroy those who are under God's protection; the Holy Family safely escaped from Herod's clutches. Ironically, his anxiety over Christ's birth was unnecessary; in the words of the bishop St. Quodvultdeus,

> why are you afraid, Herod, when you hear of the birth of a king? He does not come to drive you out, but to conquer the devil. . . . your throne is threatened by the source of grace—so small, yet so great—who is lying in the manger. He is using you, all unaware of it, to work out His own purposes freeing souls from captivity to the devil. . . . But you, Herod, do not know this and are disturbed and furious. While you vent your fury against the child, you are already paying Him homage, and do not know it.[8]

Herod the Great capped his long (37 B.C.– 4 A.D.), evil reign with an attempt to destroy the Source of Life (the only antichrist ever to make this attempt against Jesus in a direct, physical sense); soon afterwards, he paid a fearsome price for his wickedness.

The ancient historian Josephus describes how the king, in a manner reminiscent of Antiochus Epiphanes, became afflicted with terrible intestinal pains; moreover, Herod began suffering from convulsions, severe fever, difficulty in breathing, intolerable itching everywhere on the surface of his body, and the putrefaction of his genitals (which his religious advisors interpreted as divine punishment for ordering some rabbis burnt alive after they had offended him). He tried alleviating the pain by means of mineral baths and being immersed in warm oil, but to no avail; his eyesight began failing, and the stench from his body became almost unbearable. During this period, Herod changed his will at least three times, disinheriting many of his surviving children; the man who trusted no one truly felt he had been abandoned by all.

Unlike Antiochus, who in his dying agony at least made a show of pretended repentance, Herod's hate-filled mind produced one final proof of his wickedness. Knowing there would be great rejoicing as soon as his death was announced, the king had all the illustrious men of the kingdom rounded up and imprisoned, and ordered that they be executed as soon as he had died—that would ensure his death would be accompanied by widespread mourning. As it happened, this horribly deranged order was not carried out. When Herod died soon afterwards, the Jews invited the Romans to come in and take direct control of their nation—for they were terrified that one of the king's sons might succeed him and continue his evil ways.[9]

# Herod Antipas

One of the sons of Herod the Great, Herod Antipas, might be considered in and of himself an insignificant figure—except for two important and unique points recorded in the Gospels: Herod Antipas was the one who ordered the arrest and eventual execution of St. John the Baptist (Mk. 6:17-29), and he was the only antichrist figure in history to see and speak to Jesus personally (Lk. 23:6-11).

Under his father's will, Herod Antipas became tetrarch (a satellite prince) of Galilee (which meant, of course, that Jesus was under his direct political authority). Herod founded the city of Tiberias on the shore of the Sea of Galilee, which he named in honor of the Roman emperor Tiberius—and he curried favor with the emperor by sending him reports on the activities of Roman officials (which may account for the enmity of Pontius Pilate).[10] On a visit to Rome, he met Herodias, the wife of his half-brother

Philip; they fell in love, divorced their spouses, and married one another. Herodias' husband had no objections, but Herod's wife was greatly offended, and fled to her father Aretas, the king of the neighboring land of Nabatea. This marriage caused great scandal among the Jews, and led to public denunciations by St. John the Baptist, who had begun his public ministry of preaching and calling for the repentance of sins.

St. Mark's Gospel tells us that Herodias harbored a grudge against John, and prevailed upon her weak-willed husband to take him into custody. We're informed that "Herod feared John, knowing him to be a righteous and holy man," and while the prophet's words were confusing to him, "yet he liked to listen to him" (6:20). Evidently some embers of conscience still flickered in the king's heart, but—concerned with his worldly position and image—he never allowed them to be fanned into flame. When Herod's stepdaughter Salome performed an exotic dance at his birthday dinner, the king's good sense—never too strong to begin with—deserted him completely; he foolishly promised her anything she wanted. At her mother's instigation, the girl insisted on the Baptist's head—a request Herod did not want to honor, but one he was too weak to resist. The execution took place immediately (6:27); afterwards, a superstitious Herod at first believed Jesus to be John reincarnated (6:16).

According to St. Luke, when Jesus was arrested, Herod happened to be in Jerusalem for the Passover. Hearing that Jesus was a Galilean, Pontius Pilate sensed an opportunity to escape a situation potentially dangerous to his career—so he sent Jesus, under guard, to the king. We read that "Herod was very glad to see Jesus; he had been wanting to see Him for a long time, for he had heard about Him and had been hoping to see Him perform some sign" (23:8). Jesus had earlier referred to Herod as a "fox" (13:32), but in this instance, He remained silent—so the king spoke to Him with contempt and, as a form of mockery, sent Him back to Pilate clothed in a royal robe.

Herod Antipas represents all those influential persons of history who want to see Christ—but only on their own terms. Their motive is curiosity, not a genuine search for truth, and such a motivation does not lead to salvation. Once Herod had allowed

John the Baptist to be executed, even though he knew him to be a righteous man and a true prophet of God, his heart was closed to divine grace—and not even seeing Divinity face to face was enough to make him repent.

In 36 A.D. Herod Antipas was attacked by the neighboring ruler Aretas, still angry over the king's divorce of his daughter. Herod was defeated, but his appeal to Rome to restore his position failed as a result of the death of the emperor Tiberius. Caligula, the new emperor, exiled Herod to Gaul (France) in 39 A.D. Herodias willingly accompanied him there; nothing further is known of them.

# Herod Agrippa

A nephew of Herod Antipas, Herod Agrippa is arguably another minor historical figure—but his life provides a lesson on the folly of actively opposing the working of divine providence. He was educated in Rome and, during the course of a dissolute life there, became a friend of the future emperor Caligula. When he expressed his hope that his friend would succeed Tiberius, the emperor had him arrested; however, Tiberius died six months later, and his friend—now reigning, as Herod had hoped—ordered him set free, and compensated him with a gold chain similar in weight to the one which had held him bound in his cell.[11] Caligula also appointed him king in Palestine; when Claudius became emperor after Caligula's assassination in 41, he confirmed Herod Agrippa's authority and granted him further territories.

The new king made a careful show of observing the Jewish religious rules and customs—but only when he was among them; whenever he ventured outside Palestine, Herod Agrippa lived in accord with his preferred, Hellenistic, culture. The Acts of the Apostles relates that Herod began to persecute the early Church, first ordering the execution of St. James, the son of Zebedee; "and when he saw that this was pleasing to the Jews he proceeded to arrest Peter also" (12:3). St. Peter, of course, was miraculously released from prison by the angel of the Lord, and then took shelter with some of the believers in Jerusalem. We're told that "Herod, after instituting a search but not finding him, ordered the guards [responsible for Peter's custody] executed. Then he left Judea to spend some time in Caesarea" (12:19).

Herod Agrippa died suddenly in 44 during a royal audience; Josephus attributed his death to a ruptured appendix, but Scripture gives a very different explanation:

*He had long been very angry with the people of Tyre and Sidon, who now came to him in a body. After winning over Blastus, the king's chamberlain, they sued for peace because their country was supplied with food from the king's territory. On an appointed day, Herod, attired in royal robes, seated on the rostrum, addressed them publicly. The assembled crowd cried out, "This is the voice of a god, not of a man." At once the angel of the Lord struck him down because he did not ascribe the honor to God, and he was eaten by worms and breathed his last* (Acts 12:20-23).

An earlier king of Israel had torn his robes in distress rather than give even the appearance of letting himself be mistaken for a god (2 Kg. 5:7), but Herod Agrippa accepted the blasphemous flattery of his supplicants—a fatal mistake. Thus, we see that even passively cooperating in Satan's ongoing war against the Lord's divine authority has disastrous consequences. As a Jew—even if a very lax one—Herod Agrippa should have remembered the Lord's commandment: "You shall not have other gods besides Me . . . for I, he Lord, your God, am a jealous god" (Ex. 20:3,5). Unfortunately, the need to walk humbly in God's presence (cf. Mi. 6:8) is a lesson many historical figures chose not to learn.

## NOTES TO CHAPTER 1

[1] Lawrence Boadt, *Reading the Old Testament: An Introduction* (Paulist Press, 1984), p. 163.

[2] Fr. Vincent P. Miceli, S.J., *The Antichrist* (Roman Catholic Books, 1981), p. 108.

[3] John L. McKenzie, S.J., *Dictionary of the Bible* (Macmillan Publishing Co., 1965), p. 37.

[4] Peter Lemesurier, *The Armageddon Script* (St. Martin's Press, 1981), p. 83.

[5] Anne W. Carroll, *Christ the King—Lord of History* (TAN Books and Publishers, 1994), p. 69.

[6]  Shelley Klein, *The Most Evil Dictators in History* (Barnes & Noble, 2004), p. 12.

[7]  *Ibid.,* p. 15.

[8]  *Liturgy of the Hours,* Vol. 1, Second Reading for December 28 (Sermo 2 de Symbolo: PL 40, 655).

[9]  Klein, p. 21.

[10]  McKenzie, p. 356.

[11]  *Ibid.,* p. 355.

## Chapter 2

# The Roman Emperors

*I saw a woman seated on a scarlet beast that was covered with
blasphemous names, with seven heads and ten horns. . . .
Here is a clue for one who has wisdom. The seven heads
represent seven hills upon which the woman sits.
They also represent seven kings. (Rev. 17:3,9)*

King Nebuchadnezzar of Babylon was upset by a disturbing
dream, one which none of his royal advisors could interpret.
The prophet Daniel, however, enlightened by God, was able
to describe the dream and explain its meaning. The statue seen
by the king in his dream, made of gold, silver, bronze, and iron
mixed with clay, represented four kingdoms, each succeeding one
another in turn—though a stone hewn from a mountain without
being touched by human hands struck the statue, causing it to
collapse (Dn. 2:31ff).

St. Jerome identified these four kingdoms as the Babylonian,
the Medo-Persian, the Greco-Seleucid, and the Roman. Many
biblical scholars now question the validity of this "traditional"
interpretation, but no convincing reason for rejecting it has been
proposed.[1] That the stone represents the Church and, in a sense,
its founder Jesus Christ, is made clear by Daniel himself, for as he
told the king,

*In the lifetime of those kings [of the fourth empire] the God of
Heaven will set up a kingdom that shall never be destroyed or
delivered up to another people; rather, it shall break in pieces
all these kingdoms and put an end to them, and it shall stand
forever. That is the meaning of the stone you saw hewn from
the mountain without a hand being put to it, which broke in
pieces the tile, iron, bronze, silver, and gold (2:44-45).*

The only "kingdom" established during the time of the Roman Empire that still exists on earth is, of course, the Catholic Church. Because of her divine origin and spiritual power, no earthly power can overcome or withstand her—but this certainly doesn't mean the Church is exempt from suffering and persecution. Jesus had warned His followers, "If they persecuted Me, they will also persecute you" (Jn. 15:20), and the evidence of the past 2000 years plainly vindicates His words. Worldly rulers who seek unwarranted power over their subjects are greatly threatened by a Church whose authority and focus are not ultimately of this world. Indeed, as Cardinal John Henry Newman remarked, "The instance cannot be found in the history of mankind, in which an anti-Christian power could long abstain from persecution."[2]

Individual believers sometimes find themselves on the front lines of Satan's unrelenting assault; the evil one incites his servants to employ both violence and ridicule against Christians, hoping either to frighten or embarrass them into abandoning their faith. That's why the great Catholic apologist G. K. Chesterton noted, "A man who has faith must be prepared not only to be a martyr, but to be a fool."[3] This observation calls to mind St. Paul's teaching that "The message of the Cross is foolishness to those who are perishing, but to us who are being saved it is the power of God" (1 Cor. 1:18).

Not only does God confound the "wisdom" of the world; He also overturns or invalidates its strength (cf. 1 Cor. 1:25) by giving His children the power to endure all things for the sake of His Name—and in the process, the community of believers becomes stronger than ever. According to St. Thomas Aquinas,

*The Church has proved ever indestructible. Her persecutors have failed to destroy her; in fact, it was during times of persecution that the Church grew more and more; while the persecutors themselves, and those who ... would destroy [the Church}, are the very ones who come to nothing. ...*[4]

Speaking specifically of the Roman Empire's persecution of the Church, St. Augustine noted, "The martyrs were bound, imprisoned, scourged, racked, burned, torn apart, butchered—and they multiplied."[5] When the Jewish Sanhedrin sought to execute the apostles for preaching in the Name of Jesus, the Pharisee

Gamaliel cautioned them, "If this endeavor or this activity is of human origin, it will destroy itself—but if it comes from God, you will not be able to destroy them" (Acts 5:38-39). Following Gamaliel's advice to exercise tolerance would also have been a useful policy for the Roman authorities, for their efforts to destroy the Church, spread out over a period of almost three centuries, proved utterly futile.

The Book of Revelation speaks of Babylon the Great, a harlot drunk on the blood of martyrs (17:5-6); the coded reference to Rome is easily understood by the clue which mentions "seven hills upon which the woman sits" (17:9), for Rome is the city of seven hills. While the practice of Christianity was technically illegal for most of the first three centuries of the Church's existence—putting Christians at potential risk from government officials, local authorities, and hostile pagan mobs—there were long periods of relative peace, or benign neglect, on the part of imperial Rome. At other times, however, official policy was more rigorously enforced—and it happens that there were seven emperors in particular who stand out in their efforts to persecute or even destroy the followers of Jesus.

# Nero

More than any other figure in ancient history, Nero was associated in the minds of many Christians with the Antichrist. The Romans themselves (at least the upper classes) came to despise him for his unbalanced and tyrannical ways. According to one historian,

*He was a perverse, cross-dressing exhibitionist who murdered his mother, brother and wife and anyone else who stood in his way. His cruelty, violence and grotesque appetite for self-indulgence brought the Roman Empire to the brink of political and financial ruin.*[6]

A megalomaniac who commissioned a 100 ft. high statue of himself, Nero was sexually perverse; he was guilty of rape and sodomy, and even married a boy who attracted him—after first having him castrated. He executed one of his wives, and kicked another to death; another wife, however, won his favor—perhaps because she helped him invent strange or bizarre sexual games.[7] Narcissism was perhaps an occupational hazard for Roman emperors, but Nero took it to an extreme. He evidently had a deep psychological need to be the constant center of attention, and indulged himself by writing and performing poetry, requiring the nobility to attend his singing performances, engaging in chariot races (which, of course, he always won—for the other drivers didn't dare face the consequences of embarrassing the emperor), and performing on stage. Nero always preferred playing the role of a murderer—and usually ended up literally stabbing his victim to death, to the horror of the audience. On at least one occasion, however, he let himself be victimized on stage—not by a pretend murderer, but by one of his homosexual lovers, who ravaged him in front of everyone, much to the disgust of the Romans.[8]

The combination of Nero's enormous ego and unlimited power eventually drove him insane—but he was still capable of recognizing danger and responding with a cunning sense of self-preservation. Popular sentiment attributed the fires which destroyed half of Rome in 64 to the emperor's desire for "urban renewal" (i.e., a massive expansion of the imperial palace). Needing a scapegoat to divert public anger, Nero and his henchmen accused the Christians, who were widely perceived to have strange and even sinister beliefs and practices. Nero's persecution, though local (as opposed to empire-wide) in nature, "stamped itself forever upon the memory of the Church by reason of its fiendish cruelties as well as its distinguished victims"[9] (namely, Saints Peter and Paul).

The 1st c. Roman historian Tacitus wrote in his *Annals*:

*Nero had self-acknowledged members of this sect arrested. Then, on their information, large numbers were condemned— not so much for their arson as for their hatred of the human race. Their deaths were made a farce . . . so that despite their guilt and the ruthless punishment they deserved, there arose a sense of pity. For it was felt that they were being sacrificed to one man's brutality rather than to the public interest.[10]*

Tacitus, obviously no admirer of the Christians, noted that Nero managed to deflect public anger away from himself and onto his defenseless victims (though the historian wrongly believed them

19

to be guilty of the crimes attributed to them).

Many Christians were taken to a stadium used for public entertainment—and here the emperor outdid himself in cruelty. The followers of Jesus were attacked by wild beasts, or forced to portray the role of murder victims in grotesque plays—and, of course, their deaths were not make-believe. All the while, the Roman populace roared in approval. Nero even took his torture of the Christians one step further: some of them were soaked in pitch, and then set aflame to serve as living (and dying) torches for the emperor's outdoor evening parties.[11] The policy of appeasing the mobs with "bread and circuses" proved wildly successful, and long after Nero's death, many of the members of the lower classes (in contrast to the nobility) remembered him with fondness.[12]

Nero, like many tyrants, was highly superstitious. After becoming emperor in 54, he became increasingly alienated from his mother Agrippina, and five years later had her murdered. (As the emperor's men approached her with drawn knives, Agrippina bared her abdomen and told them to strike the womb that had brought Nero into the world.) For the remainder of his life, Nero felt himself to be haunted by her ghost,[13] and even tried to have occult practitioners from Persia exorcise it. Nero's guilt didn't stop him from having his wife Octavia murdered in 62. That same year, a bronze statue of the emperor was struck by lightning and destroyed; soon afterwards, the city of Pompeii was severely damaged by an earthquake, and Mt. Vesuvius—the volcano which would destroy the city completely in 79—began rumbling.

In the face of these heavenly portents, Nero became increasingly paranoid, and ordered the execution of large numbers of senators, army officers, and aristocrats—which, of course, solidified the growing opposition to the emperor. According to the Roman historian Suetonius, Nero had been told by his astrologers that in the end he would be deserted by all the world.[14] In 66 Halley's Comet appeared. That was also the year of the Jewish revolt against Rome, and it was Nero's army which besieged Jerusalem and eventually destroyed the city and its Temple (though only after the emperor's death). As one author notes, "Nero's persecution of the Christians at Rome lasted three and-a-half years, and the Jewish war, which overcame the Jews, lasted the same period."[15] This same period of time is mentioned in Scripture, not coincidentally, in regard to the persecution to be waged by the great beast in Revelation (13:5).

When Tigellinus, Nero's previously-faithful henchman, deserted him, the emperor knew his cause was hopeless. In his madness, he spoke of poisoning all the members of the senate and burning the city of Rome to the ground,[16] but as the army turned against him, he was forced to flee. When his enemies were on the verge of overtaking him, Nero took his own life (supposedly lamenting, "Oh, what a great artist perishes in me!"). According to Tacitus, "during the civil wars which immediately followed Nero's death, a report that Nero was alive still, and actually on his way to the province of the East, excited general alarm through Acacia and Asia."[17]

Nero, of course, was truly dead, but his memory continued to exercise a strong grip on Christian consciousness; for a long time to come, many leaders and members of the Church considered him the embodiment of evil. A strange footnote to Nero's story arose over 1000 years after his death. Demonic activity, including unearthly howling and shrieks, became so intense at the site of his tomb in Rome that Pope Paschal II called for three days of prayer and fasting. Following this spiritual preparation, a tree which had grown over Nero's burial place was cut down, and his tomb itself was dug up and his remains scattered—bringing an end to the haunting.[18]

# Domitian

Like the Pharaohs of Egypt, Roman emperors were sometimes officially granted divine status upon their deaths; indeed, the dying words of Vespasian, one of Nero's successors, were recorded to be "Woe is me! Me thinks I'm turning into a god." Several of the emperors, however, claimed this status for themselves during their lifetimes—including Caligula, Nero, and most notably, Domitian (r. 81-96). This, of course, was something no follower of Christ could ever acknowledge; as one commentator notes, "If Nero posed like a god, an emperor like Domitian expected to be addressed as one. Christians accordingly viewed the emperor as Antichrist because he usurped the worship due to God and thus reenacted the sin of Satan."[19]

Domitian, who called himself "Master and God," demanded to be recognized as such—and those who refused or even hesitated did so at the risk of their lives. As one historian notes, the Book of Revelation, "with its denunciations of idolatrous, persecuting Rome as the scarlet woman drunk with the blood of saints, may reflect the tension of the churches in Asia Minor at this time."[20] The state of the emperor's mind can be gauged from the fact that, early in his reign, he spent hours each day catching flies, and then stabbing them with a sharp pen; he also amused himself with other cruel and perverse practices.

A legend states that in 94 the emperor, curious as to the origins and beliefs of the Christians, had the surviving relatives of Jesus brought from Judea to Rome, where he questioned them about this so-called messiah; finding them harmless, he set them free.[21] If the legend is true, something must have soon changed Domitian's attitude towards the Christians, for a persecution broke out in Rome, targeting Christians, along with other persons (including aristocrats) who had aroused the emperor's suspicion. According to the 4th century Church historian Eusebius,

*Many were the victims of Domitian's appalling cruelty. At Rome great numbers of men distinguished by birth and attainments were for no reason at all banished from the country and their property confiscated. Finally he showed himself the successor of Nero in enmity and hostility to God. He was, in fact, the second to organize a persecution against us.*[22]

St. Clement, the fourth bishop of Rome, or pope, was martyred during Domitian's persecution. Some time before this, Clement had written:

*We must look upon all things of this world as none of ours, and not desire them. This world and that to come are two enemies. We cannot therefore be friends to both; but we must resolve which we would forsake and which we would enjoy.*[23]

Clement and other committed Christians were willing to put God's Kingdom first, even at the cost of their lives. As one historian notes,

*If Juvenal's satire is true, that even to talk with Domitian about*

*the weather was to cast hazards for your life, how real was the peril of those who through allegiance to Christ disdained to ascribe to a suspicious madman the divinity on which he laid such stress!*[24]

Not every intended victim of the deranged emperor actually suffered martyrdom, however. An aged St. John, the only apostle still alive, was arrested and brought before Domitian; because he refused to denounce his faith, the offended "god" ordered him to be boiled alive. When the apostle miraculously emerged from the pot of boiling alive and unharmed, a frightened and superstitious emperor instead ordered him exiled—and it was while there, on the barren island of Patmos in the eastern Mediterranean, that John wrote the Book of Revelation.[25] (Many scriptural scholars doubt the apostle himself wrote the last book of the Bible. No matter which Christian named John wrote it, however, Rev. 1:9 makes it clear his testimony on behalf of Christ was the reason for his exile to Patmos.)

Soon after his failed attempt to execute St. John, Domitian himself was struck down. His increasingly erratic and dangerous behavior prompted a conspiracy against him—in which his own wife Domitilla joined—and soon afterwards, the mad emperor was slain by his wife's steward.

# Decius

Rome was founded in 753 B.C., and so the city's millennial celebrations were held in 247. Emperor Philip the Arab, who in his role as pontifex maximus (high priest of the Roman civil religion) led the cultic celebrations, was himself well-disposed toward Christianity (and was commonly believed to be a Christian himself). Nevertheless, the Christians had, for religious reasons, abstained from participation in the public ceremonies—and when the empire began experiencing rebellions, mutinies, and barbarian invasions the following year, many pagans believed their gods were expressing anger at the "atheists" (as Christians were often designated) and demanding punishment. As the Christian theologian and scholar Origen noted in 248, popular sentiment was becoming increasingly hostile to the Church.[26]

In 249, Philip the Arab was killed in battle by Decius, a rebellious general, who thereupon claimed the imperial throne. Wanting to strengthen the empire's discipline and political unity, and knowing that repressing Christianity would be a popular policy, he issued a decree requiring all citizens to offer sacrifice to the Roman gods. A pragmatist at heart, Decius wasn't seeking at first to make martyrs of the Christians, but when he encountered a young Christian named Celerinus who steadfastly refused to give up his faith, he decided sterner measures were needed.[27] After having Celerinus killed, Decius, who was wary of the influence and authority of the holy Bishop of Rome, St. Fabian, quickly ordered him arrested and executed (for as one contemporary Church leader noted, the emperor feared Fabian more than any potential rival to the imperial throne[28]). The persecution in Rome which followed was so severe that the Roman clergy didn't dare elect Fabian's successor as long as this particular emperor was in power.

Christians had been persecuted throughout much of the Church's early history, but these assaults were generally of brief duration and of limited geographic scope; Decius' persecution was the first one enacted throughout the entire empire.[29] Early in 250, after St. Fabian's martyrdom, an edict was sent out ordering provincial governors and magistrates to ensure all citizens—particularly Christian religious leaders—publicly offered a pinch of incense in honor of the gods and the genius of the emperor. Some Christians, including several bishops, apostasized, or denied their faith, especially those who had become prosperous in worldly terms;[30] others, like St. Cyprian, Bishop of Carthage, and St. Dionysius of Alexandria, went into hiding. A large number of Christians became confessors, that is, believers who were imprisoned for their faith in Christ—for instead of killing the followers of Jesus outright, Decius preferred, whenever possible, to have them recant their faith as a result of torture and imprisonment.[31]

As it happened, however, there were also many martyrs during the Decian persecution. In Africa, seventeen imprisoned Christians died together of thirst and hunger. In Bithynia (in modern-day Turkey) Saints Lucian and Marcian (who had been practitioners of black magic, but who converted after their spells proved powerless against a Christian maiden) were arrested; after refusing to renounce their faith, they were burned alive. In Egypt, an old man named Julian, and a boy of fifteen named Dioscuros, were executed in front of a bloodthirsty mob. When another prisoner brought before the tribunal appeared to be wavering in his commitment to Christ, five soldiers there, themselves secret Christians, signaled to him to remain firm; when the officials noticed this, the five freely admitted their membership in the Church, and joyfully went to their deaths.[32]

The theologian Origen was arrested and tortured on the rack; he survived the experience, but died of his injuries a few years later. In Sicily, the virgin St. Agatha was put to death for her faith in 251 (though the legend that she was denounced as a Christian by a Roman senator after she rejected his marriage proposal is probably apocryphal). Many other Christians, whose names are known only in Heaven, also died for their faith; speaking of their sacrifice, St. Cyprian said, "Precious is the death which has purchased deathlessness at the price of one's own blood, which has received a crown from God for the supreme act of valor."[33]

The severity of the persecution varied from place to place throughout the empire, and by the summer of 251 it had died down almost entirely—not because of any change of heart on Decius' part, but because the emperor's attention was diverted by barbarian incursions on the northern frontier. Decius died in battle against the Goths that August, due in part to the treachery of Gallus, one of his officers. This ended a severe trial by fire for the Church—but the respite would be brief.

# Valerian

The usurper Gallus came to power after the death of Decius—just as the former had violently seized the imperial throne from Philip (bringing to mind Our Lord's warning in Mt. 26:52 that those who live by the sword die by the sword). Gallus resumed the persecution of the Church in 252, and St. Cornelius, the successor to St. Fabian as Pope, was arrested and sent into exile. Soon afterwards, however, Gallus died, and was succeeded as emperor by Valerian in 253, who had been an important official under Decius.

At first Valerian seemed favorably disposed to the Christianity,[34] but in 257 he decreed a new persecution of the Church. By edict of the emperor, noble Romans were not allowed to become Christians, and Christians themselves were forbidden to hold assemblies (forcing them to gather secretly for Mass). Even more ominously, bishops and clergy were to be tracked down, seized, and put to death; Valerian hoped that, lacking their shepherds, the sheep would abandon their faith and return to the worship of traditional Roman gods.[35]

In Africa, St. Cyprian was taken into custody, put on trial, and executed. In Rome itself, Pope St. Sixtus II and several companions were arrested while gathered for Mass in a catacomb; they were immediately executed by the sword. The deacon St. Lawrence, a Church administrator, was spared just long enough to collect and turn over the Church's funds to the prefect of Rome; he instead gave away all the money to the poor, whom he declared to be "the Church's treasure." His martyrdom immediately followed.

Valerian's persecution, though a painful and heavy blow against the Church, proved no more effective in destroying it than that of Decius, and his fate proved to be even more ignoble than his predecessor's. Like Decius, Valerian had to face barbarian incursions, though by this time, the Roman legions were enfeebled by the plague. Though in his sixties, Valerian personally led the army against Persian invaders in the East—where his own military incompetence, along with an act of betrayal, led to his capture by the enemy.[36] The Persians were willing to ransom the humiliated emperor, but Valerian's son Gallienus—quite content to rule in his father's stead—made no efforts to obtain his release.

For the remaining six years of Valerian's life, Sapor, the Persian king who had conquered him in battle, mockingly clothed the captive emperor in royal purple, but also had him chained and dragged from his stirrup. Sapor treated Valerian as a slave, using him as a step when he mounted his horse. When the Roman finally died, his body was stuffed with straw and hung as a trophy in a Persian temple.[37]

# Diocletian

Gallienus, whether from genuine human decency, a desire to disassociate himself from his father, or simple superstition, retracted the decrees Valerian had issued against the Church, and restored to it the right to assemble and even hold property. Thus, the Church had several decades of peace, which lasted until the onset of what became known as the Great Persecution.

When Diocletian assumed the imperial throne in 284, he found an empire in serious decline, and he attempted vigorously—though somewhat unsuccessfully—to solve its many problems. Believing the empire to be too large for one man to rule, he divided it into two parts—East and West—with each half to be ruled by an Augustus (emperor) and a Caesar (a second-in-command, having the right of succession); he himself chose to rule as emperor in the more prosperous East. Diocletian was originally tolerant of all religions, including Christianity, and in fact, his own wife and daughter were catechumens, as were quite a few of his court officials.[38]

Eventually, however, various influences turned the emperor against the Christians. The Church was still unpopular with leading elements of Roman society; the Greek philosopher Hierocles, for instance, warned Diocletian that Christianity is not "like the cult of Mithras [an important pagan god]. The followers of Mithras never spoke against the gods. But the Christians consider our gods to be demons, unholy spirits, and claim that only the Hebrew rebel they worship is the one true god."[39]

An even more sinister influence upon Diocletian was Galerius, the soldier he had appointed as his Caesar in the East. Galerius kept urging the emperor to persecute the Christians. Diocletian was reluctant to agree, but it was very important to him to keep his designated successor happy, lest the empire be dragged into another destructive civil war, so he issued a series of edicts reinstating the some of the earlier proscriptions of Valerian (which his son Gallenius had repealed), but without condemning Christians to death. However, two fires at the imperial palace in a two week period—which Galerius blamed on the Christians, but in fact may have been his own doing—finally convinced Diocletian to unleash the full force of the imperial government against the Church.[40]

Early in 303, the emperor ordered all Christian churches to be destroyed and all copies of their Scriptures to be burnt. Christians were purged from the army, and no longer had legal recourse to Roman courts—putting them at the mercy of their enemies; many times individual Christians and Church property were attacked by angry mobs. It was also official government policy that Church leaders be seized and put to death. The persecution—which was pursued more vigorously in the East than in the West—was so violent at one stage that Diocletian actually had medals struck which claimed "Christianity is at last extirpated."[41] However, while many individual believers were killed, the Faith continued to live, to the bewilderment of the emperor. Two of his own palace officials refused to renounce their beliefs and offer a pinch of incense to the gods, even after Diocletian—because of his long association with them—personally pleaded with them to do so. When they insisted that they were faithful servants, but could not acknowledge any God but Christ, the emperor sent them off to be tortured and beheaded.[42]

Some of the better-known victims of the Great Persecution include St. Lucy (martyred in Sicily in 304), St. Agnes (executed in Rome by being stabbed in the throat), St. Anastasia (put to death in Sirmium, a Roman city in the Balkans), St. Philomena (a teenage girl killed after reputedly rejecting a marriage proposal from the emperor himself), and the brothers and physicians Sts. Cosman and Damian (martyred together in Syria).

One of the more inspiring stories of martyrdom involves St. Genesius, a pagan actor performing on stage in Rome in front of Diocletian himself. In a play mocking Christian beliefs and practices, he underwent a pretend baptism, but a miracle of grace occurred: Genesius was suddenly converted to Christianity.[43] When he began praising God, the audience laughed appreciatively, but they were stunned into silence when he then rebuked the emperor and called upon him to repent. An angry Diocletian thereupon had the actor-turned-apologist tortured and executed.

Another significant story involves the Spanish deacon St. Vincent, who was arrested, along with his bishop, Valerius, by a magistrate named Dacian. The two Christians would not deny Christ, and their sufferings during imprisonment only seemed to make them stronger in the faith. Dacian had Valerius exiled, and concentrated his efforts on breaking Vincent—but repeated tortures could not induce him to apostasize. A frustrated Dacian had the torturers themselves beaten for their failure; then changing tactics, he promised to release Vincent if only the deacon would hand over the Church's liturgical books. When Vincent refused, and happily endured further torture, he was thrown into a particularly filthy cell, where he promptly converted the jailer to Christianity. Dacian could only weep with rage. Soon afterwards, Vincent—in the presence of Christian friends finally allowed to visit and minister to him—died peacefully.

This account of St. Vincent's suffering epitomizes Diocletian's failed war on the Church: just as the magistrate Dacian grew increasingly frustrated, so the emperor came to a growing awareness that—contrary to his earlier expectation—he could not prevail against the Christians, a conclusion reinforced when his own palace in the city of Nicomedia was struck by a thunderbolt and destroyed.[44] The emperor seems to have undergone a psychological collapse,[45] made worse by his declining health. Allowing Galerius to reign in his stead, he withdrew from public life. According to one historian, "Diocletian, broken with disappointment and sickness, had already starved himself to death. He had seen the Church which he had tried to crush arise from the contest with still greater strength. The Empire was defeated; the Galilean had conquered."[46] It would be several more years, however, before Diocletian's successor was forced to acknowledge this truth himself.

# Galerius

Galerius had inherited his hatred of Christianity from his mother Romula, a pagan priestess who had despised the Christians ever since they had rejected her by fasting and praying instead of joining in her occult rituals. As soon as he had the opportunity, Galerius intensified the Great Persecution. As one author notes,

> The retirement of Diocletian (1 May 305) removed from the persecutors all restraint. . . . A fifth edict appeared even more stringent than the previous. The fallen idols were to be re-erected, all households were to sacrifice, and, lest there should

*be any escape, all goods for sale in the markets were to be*
*polluted with libations [sacrificial offerings to the pagan gods,*
*making them inedible for Christians]. For two years it rained*
*blood. In some towns the streets were strewn with fragments*
*of corpses.*[47]

Emperor Galerius had virtually dictatorial power in the East,
but in the West an elderly man named Constantius was on the
throne. Galerius tried to exploit the situation by appointing
Severus, a man beholden to him, as Caesar in the West, while
holding Constantius' son Constantine hostage in the East. However,
Constantine—a brave and resourceful young man—managed to
escape from custody and return to his father's side; the following
year, when Constantius died, the army in the West ignored Severus
and proclaimed Constantine as Augustus. Galerius was furious,
but was unable to do anything about the situation—and then,
against his wishes, he was also forced to end his persecution of
the Church.

In 311 the emperor was struck down by a terrible disease, in
which it seemed his body was being eaten away by an ulcer.[48]
Galerius, like many persecutors of the Church, was prey to
superstition; fearing the God of the Christians was punishing him
for inflicting a persecution upon them, he issued an insincere edict
of toleration:

*In this extraordinary document, wrung from a man by the*
*terrors of the unknown, Galerius tried to dupe the Christians*
*and their God into remitting for him the punishment of his*
*cruelties. He had only persecuted, he maintained, to "bring*
*back to a good disposition the Christians who had abandoned the*
*persuasion (sectam) of their own fathers" and "the institutions*
*of the ancients." He confessed that he had failed to induce his*
*victims "to display due reverence for the gods, or pay heed*
*to the God of the Christians." So the edicts are rescinded; in*
*return the Christians were expected "to pray to their God for*
*our recovery."*[49]

Galerius' feigned conversion was no more effective than that of
King Antiochus Epiphanes several centuries earlier; the emperor
died in agony a few days later.

Galerius was succeeded in the East by Licinius, while

Constantine ruled in the West—but the latter was forced to defeat a rival named Maxentius. On the night before the decisive battle of Milvian Bridge, fought outside Rome in 312, Constantine saw in a vision a cross in the sky with the words *In hoc signo vinces* ("in this Sign you will conquer"). The emperor ordered his army to adopt the Christian Cross as its standard, and after a successful battle in which Maxentius was killed, entered Rome in triumph. The following year he and Licinius issued the Edict of Toleration, or Edict of Milan, which declared, "We therefore ordain that anybody—including the Christians—may observe the faith of their sect and cult,"[50] thereby at long last legalizing the existence of the Church.

In the East, Licinius also had to overcome a rival; his Caesar Maximin sought to usurp the throne and reinstitute a persecution of the Christians. Noting Constantine's earlier success resulting from the help of the Christian God, Licinius—though a pagan—had his troops recite a prayer to the Supreme God (though in words avoiding any direct reference to Christ or the pagan gods), asking for victory in battle.[51] The emperor received the triumph he desired, but failed to draw the proper conclusions from his success and Maximin's defeat. Some years later Licinius reneged on his promise:

> He purged believers from his government, demanded sacrifice to pagan gods, burned churches, and sent Christians to slave labor, torture, and death. Like so many rulers to come, Licinius saw the Church as a barrier to his absolute power.[52]

This situation, of course, gave Constantine the opportunity to defend the Church while at the same increasing his own power. In 323 his army, invaded the East and, still using the Christian Cross as its standard, decisively defeated Licinius; afterwards, Constantine reunited the entire empire under his direct rule.

Two years later Constantine convoked the Council of Nicea to resolve the Arian controversy (which will be described in Chapter 3). On Good Friday the emperor himself addressed the assembled bishops in a classic oration; in the words of one historian,

> The speech moved to its climax, the power of prayer, the fates of the Christians' persecutors and the rewards for service like Constantine's, rendered (he said) to Christ and God alone. . . . He hinted at Antioch's ill-judged support for the "tyrant"

*whom his hearers could recognize as Maximin, ruler in the East. Addressing the deceased Maximin, he moved to a broader contrast between pagan superstition and the Christian faith. The rewards of the imperial persecutors were visible in their recent fates. Decius had died in the "Scythian plains," making Roman arms the mockery of nomads. Valerian had been flayed alive by the Persian king, who had dried his skin and kept it as an "eternal trophy" at the Persian court. Courtiers had murdered Aurelian in Thrace, while Diocletian had been driven mad by guilt for murdering so many Christians. Nicomedia still told how a thunderbolt from God had struck and burnt down Diocletian's palace.*[53]

Never again would the Roman empire use direct violence against the followers of Christ—but one final imperial challenge to the Church remained.

## Julian

As a six-year-old boy, Julian witnessed the brutal murder of his father and several other family members by the imperial guard. He blamed Emperor Constantius for the crime—and because the emperor advertised himself as a devout member of the Church, Christianity was forever discredited in Julian's mind.[54] He himself was raised as a Catholic (as Christians were also called), but, as soon as it was safe to do so, formally renounced his religion and embraced paganism (and is thus known to history as Julian the Apostate). So determined was he to reject his religious upbringing that he actually scraped his forehead with a stone, as if to remove the skin that had been touched by the waters of baptism.[55]

The young Julian was fascinated by paganism, and as a student in Ephesus he sought out a pagan priest who promised to initiate him into occult mysteries. The two descended into a dark underground cavern, reputedly the home of demons able to forecast one's future. During the descent, Julian began encountering fiery apparitions and hearing strange and terrifying sounds; feeling himself surrounded by evil, he made the Sign of the Cross—and the demonic manifestations ceased. In the words of Julian's contemporary St. Athanasius,

*In the very presence of the fraud of demons and the imposture
of the oracles and the wonders of magic, let him [the Christian]
use the Sign of the Cross which they all mock at, and but
speak the Name of Christ, and he shall see how through Him
demons are routed, oracles cease, and all magic and witchcraft
is confounded.*[56]

Unfortunately, Julian failed to draw the obvious conclusion;
having regained his courage, he continued downward. When evil
spirits reappeared, he again drove them off with the Sign of the
Cross, but his occult guide convinced him that only by abandoning
Christianity could he find the esoteric knowledge and power he
craved.[57]

Julian combined his interest in the occult with the study of pagan
philosophy—but when he went into revolt against Constantius, he
sought popular support by pretending to be an orthodox Catholic.
Following the sudden death of Constantius in 361, Julian came to
power, and began demonstrating his true religious allegiance. It
was now politically impossible to outlaw Christianity—let alone
implement a violent persecution of the Church—but Julian did
everything in his power to reintroduce and promote the practice
of paganism. This effort proved to be a complete failure; in the
words of one commentator,

*His religious opinions were an adolescent mishmash of neo-
Platonism, abject superstition . . . and personal vendetta. In its
totality, Julian's religion likely appealed to no one but himself.
His ultimate legacy was to thoroughly discredit the paganism
he hoped to restore.*[58]

Nevertheless, there were those who could be persuaded, by
bribes or threats, to resume the practice of paganism. Even in
such ceremonies, however, warnings from Heaven were present
for those willing to see them. On one occasion Julian

*accordingly repaired to the [pagan] temple, attended by all his
court, among whom was a Christian page, who had a short time
previously been admitted to the Sacrament of Confirmation.
Everything being ready for the sacrifice, the Emperor ordered
the priests to commence the sacred rites. They endeavored
to do so, and raised their knives to strike the victim prepared
for the sacrifice; but what was their astonishment when they*

*found themselves unable to proceed! Their knives became suddenly blunted and incapable of inflicting a wound; while, to add to their consternation, the fire on the altar was suddenly extinguished. Thereupon the presiding priest exclaimed: "Some unknown power prevents our sacrifice. There must be some Christian present, who has been baptized or confirmed." The Emperor, on hearing these words, immediately ordered a search to be made, when behold! one of his own pages stood forth and addressed him. . . . "I invoked the sacred Name of Jesus, and the demons no longer had any power." At these words, the Emperor, who, though an apostate through malice and self-interest, knew well the power of the Name of Jesus, was struck with terror, and, fearing the Divine vengeance, retired from the temple in confusion.*[59]

Despite the obvious power of Christ, Julian stubbornly persisted in his attempts to undermine the authority of the Church. He decided to order the rebuilding of the Temple in Jerusalem; not only would this win the favor of his Jewish subjects, but—perhaps more importantly, in Julian's mind—he would discredit Christ as a prophet, for He had foretold that, following the Roman destruction of Jerusalem, not one stone of the Temple would remain standing upon another (Mt. 24:2). However, this ambitious project was doomed to failure. A series of violent earthquakes interfered with the work; in one instance, a tremor resulted in the collapse of a portico, killing a number of workmen. As a contemporary witness recorded,

*But though Alypius [the foreman] pushed the work forward energetically, and though he was assisted by the governor of the province, frightful balls of flame kept bursting forth near the foundations of the temple and made it impossible for the workmen to approach the place, and some were even burned to death. And since the elements persistently drove them back, Julian gave up the attempt.*[60]

This failure only seemed to deepen the emperor's hatred for Christ and His Church. He wrote a polemic called *Against the Galileans* (a title he used to disparage the Christians, as it implied that Christianity had obscure and insignificant origins); in it, he claimed that the Old Testament prophecies were merely fables,

Jesus (the "Galilean") was nothing more than a charlatan who managed to deceive His ignorant and gullible followers, and the Christian religion was an historical absurdity.[61] (Julian did, however, grudgingly acknowledge the Church's charitable activity; this, he claimed, explained Christianity's popularity—and in order to counter it, he said, pagans would have to surpass Christians in this regard.)

In 363, while Julian was preparing for a military campaign against Persia, a Christian soldier was taunted by his pagan comrades, who referred to Christ in a derogatory way by asking, "Where is your Carpenter now?" Without hesitation the Christian replied, "He is making a coffin for your emperor."[62] This prophecy was soon fulfilled, for during the army's retreat after an unsuccessful invasion of Persia, Julian was fatally wounded in battle. Some accounts have him accusing his favorite pagan god of betrayal with his dying words: "Helios, thou hast ruined me!" However, another (and probably more reliable) tradition states that Julian took some of the blood flowing from his wound and flung it into the sky, while exclaiming, "Galilean, Thou hast conquered!"[63] Regardless of the actual circumstances, Christians widely interpreted Julian's death as an expression of divine judgment.

Thus, with the demise of the last of the great imperial enemies of Christianity, Daniel's prophecy was fulfilled: God had indeed "set up a Kingdom that shall never be destroyed or delivered up to another people; rather, it shall break in pieces all those kingdoms and put an end to them, and it shall stand forever" (2:44). The Church, which began as a tiny mustard seed, grew into the largest of plants (cf. Mt. 13:31-32); without any semblance of worldly power or the use of violence, it triumphed over the greatest empire yet known to history, while in the process transforming and redirecting the course of Western civilization. Not only was Satan's attempt to crush the Church by means of the imperial power of Rome a failure, but Rome itself became the earthly headquarters for the Kingdom of God. This new reality, however, also brought with it many new challenges.

## NOTES TO CHAPTER 2

1  Desmond A. Birch, *Trial, Tribulation & Triumph* (Queenship Publishing, 1996), pp. 483ff.

2  Paul Thigpen, *Quotes from the Saints* (Servant Publications, 2001), p. 162.

3  G. K. Chesterton, *Heretics* (John Lane Company, 1905), p. 97.

4  Thigpen, p. 39.

5  *Ibid.*, p. 141.

6  Miranda Twiss, *The Most Evil Men and Women in History* (Barnes & Noble, 2002), p. 21.

7  H. W. Crocker III, *Triumph: The Power and the Glory of the Catholic Church* (Three Rivers Press, 2001), p. 24.

8  Michael Vincent Boyer, *The Hollywood Culture War* (Xlibris Corporation, 2008), p. 513.

9  Herbert B. Workman, *Persecution in the Early Church* (Oxford University Press, 1906, 1980), p. 83.

10  As quoted in Raymond E. Brown and John P. Meier, *Antioch & Rome* (Paulist Press, 1983), p. 99.

11  Anne W. Carroll, *Christ the King—Lord of History* (TAN Books and Publishers, 1994), pp. 85-86.

12  Twiss, p. 30. The author notes that for years afterward, "flowers were put at his burial place and funerary busts of him were commissioned. Even his edicts were treated with special reverence, as though he was still alive and would soon return to take vengeance on his enemies" (ibid).

13  *Ibid.*, p. 24.

14  James J. L. Ratton, *Antichrist: An Historical Review* (Burns and Oates, Ltd., 1917), p. 95.

15  *Ibid.*, p. 97.

16  Twiss, p. 30.

17  Ratton, p. 95.

18  Michael H. Brown, *The Last Secret* (Queenship Publishing, 2007), pp. 71-72. According to Mr. Brown, Paschal "asked the faithful to assemble with axes and picks in order to chop down an infamous walnut tree that had grown on Nero's tomb and was supposedly the habitat for evil spirits. The pope assured his workmen that as they destroyed it they would be under the mantle of Mary. Paschal himself took a swing or two at the tree and soon it was felled, along with every tree, bush, and shrub on that unlucky hill. The hill was left barren. And lastly they dug up Nero's tomb, casting its dust to the wind and the bone into the Tiber. From what I can gather, that was the end of the haunting. The date was March 13, 1099, and soon after a chapel was erected there in Mary's honor" *(ibid)*.

# The Roman Emperors

Christopher Nugent, *Masks of Satan* (Christian Classics, 1983, 1989), p. 40.

[20] Henry Chadwick, *The Early Church* (Penguin Books, 1967), p. 27.

[21] Robin Lane Fox, *Pagans and Christians* (Alfred A. Knopf, Inc., 1986, 1989), p. 433.

[22] As quoted in Crocker, p. 26.

[23] Jill Haak Adels, *The Wisdom of the Saints* (Barnes & Noble, 1987), p. 27.

[24] Workman, p. 84.

[25] Carroll, p. 88.

[26] Chadwick, pp. 117-118.

[27] Fox, p. 454.

[28] Michael Walsh, *An Illustrated History of the Popes* (St. Martin's Press, 1980), p. 32.

[29] St. Cyprian of Carthage, who went into hiding during the persecution of Decius (and who died as a martyr under the emperor Valerian), wrote several years later that God had allowed this assault on the Church for three reasons: (1) Christians could not spiritually withstand an extended period of political peace and material prosperity; (2) they had fallen into materialism and worldly concerns, and (3) as a result, they lost their zeal for the faith. Cf. Birch, pp. 299-300.

[30] Commenting on this situation after the persecution had ended, St. Cyprian observed, "Their property held them in chains . . . chains which shackled their courage and choked their faith and hampered their judgment and throttled their souls. . . . If they stored up treasure in Heaven, they would not now have an enemy and a thief within their household. . . . They think of themselves as owners, whereas it is they rather who are owned: enslaved as they are to their own property, they are not the masters of their money but its slaves"—as quoted in Randy Alcorn, *Money, Possessions, and Eternity* (Tyndale House Publishers, 1989, 2003), p. 416.

[31] Workman, p. 98.

[32] *Ibid.,* p. 99.

[33] Rosemary Ellen Guiley, *The Quotable Saint* (Checkmark Books, 2002), p. 168.

[34] Richard P. McBrien, *Lives of the Popes* (Harper San Francisco, 1997), p. 48.

[35] Workman, p. 102.

[36] Crocker, p. 39.

[37] Workman, p. 102.

[38] *Ibid.,* p. 106.

[39] Crocker, p. 40.

[40] Carroll, p. 97.

[41] David F. Burgess, *Encyclopedia of Sermon Illustrations* (Concordia Publishing House, 1988), p. 180.

[42] Crocker, p. 41.

[43] Rev. Francis Spirago, *Anecdotes and Examples for the Catechism* (Roman Catholic Books, 1903), p. 165.

[44] Fox, p. 652.

[45] Carroll, p. 97.

[46] Workman, p. 113.

[47] *Ibid.*, pp. 110-111.

[48] Carroll, p. 98.

[49] Workman, p. 111.

[50] Carroll, p. 99.

[51] Crocker, p. 50.

[52] *Ibid.*, p. 54.

[53] Fox, p. 652.

[54] Abbot Giuseppe Ricciotti, *Julian the Apostate* (TAN Books & Publishers, 1960), p. 42.

[55] Very Rev. Canon G. E. Howe, *Stories from the Catechist* (TAN Books & Publishers, 1922, 1989), p. 165.

[56] Guiley, p. 44.

[57] Ricciotti, p. 41.

[58] Crocker, p. 69.

[59] Howe, pp. 311-312.

[60] Ricciotti, p. 225.

[61] *Ibid.*, pp. 232-233.

[62] Burgess, p. 35.

[63] Ricciotti, p. 254.

*Chapter 3*

# Enemies of the Church—
# Within and Without

*Children, it is the last hour, and just as you heard
that the Antichrist was coming, so now many antichrists
have appeared. Thus we know this is the last hour. They
went out from us, but they were not really of our number;
if they had been, they would have remained with us. Their
desertion shows that none of them was of our number.*
(1 Jn. 2:18-19)

The Church's triumph over the Roman Empire had many
profound implications, and these were by no means limited
to religion. Constantine began relying upon Catholic bishops
as his political advisors and administrators (even as he himself
increasingly meddled in ecclesiastical affairs), and politics and
religion became ever more intertwined in the decades which
followed. Moreover, once Christianity was declared the official
religion of the state, ambitious men began looking upon the Church
as an avenue for political, social, and economic advancement.

As it became easier and, from a secular perspective, more
advantageous to be known as a Christian, the overall spiritual
fervor of the Church inevitably declined. This condition prompted
some committed Christians, such as St. Anthony of Egypt and other
"Desert Fathers," to go live apart in the wilderness as hermits so
as to escape the "corruption" of the world—and this desire for
spiritual purity and holiness later aided the growth of Christian
monasticism.

Even though political "victory" over imperial Rome did not
bring about the Kingdom of God on earth, the Church's influence

changed or transformed society for the better in many ways. Human sacrifice was outlawed, as were bloody gladiatorial contests (though not without some controversy), women were treated with more dignity than ever before, and slavery largely disappeared. As one scholar notes, "The uniqueness of the Christian Middle Ages [the foundations of which were laid during the last years of the Roman Empire] has in fact been seen in its being the first complex civilization of history that was not built upon a base of slave labor."[1]

At the same time Catholicism was growing in influence, however, new challenges arose. By the beginning of the 5th century it was readily apparent that the empire, at least in the West, was in a serious state of economic and military decline. This point was driven home with dramatic emphasis in 410 when Rome was sacked by the barbarian Visigoths under their chieftain Alaric—the first time in 800 years that enemy forces had entered the city.

This previously-unimaginable disaster, which shocked and terrified much of the civilized world, prompted pagan philosophers to blame Christianity for the empire's misfortunes: if only Rome had remained faithful to the gods who had traditionally protected the city, they claimed, all would be well. In response, St. Augustine wrote his massive tome *The City of God* (which took thirteen years to complete). The Bishop of Hippo (a city in North Africa) insisted that Rome wasn't punished for being Christian, but for failing to repent of her sins.[2] Furthermore, he said, the Lord God controls the unfolding of human history; societies are blessed to the extent they seek to live in accord with His Will.

This undeniable truth doesn't mean, however, that innocent and even holy Christians are spared from suffering in times of turmoil and danger. The barbarian tribe known as the Vandals, foolishly invited into North Africa by an imperial official seeking vengeance after being forced into dishonorable retirement, devastated the province; cities and churches were destroyed, and large numbers of faithful and clergy alike were put to the sword. St. Augustine had tried without success to prevent the disaster; he himself died of a fever in 430 as the Vandals were besieging Hippo. The Church had withstood the violence of Roman persecutions; it would also survive, at great cost, the onslaught of barbarian invasions.

# Attila

When the Roman Empire lost its military dominance over the various barbarian tribes, it was forced to adopt a new strategy: allowing some tribes to settle within its frontiers (helping create a buffer against the more warlike barbarians), playing off one tribe against another, bribing potential invaders to go elsewhere, and creating alliances (sometimes through politically-arranged marriages). However, Attila, the highly intelligent leader of a warlike tribe known as the Huns, wasn't so easily manipulated. According to a contemporary description, Attila

*was a man born to shake the races of the world, a terror to all lands, who in some way or other frightened everyone by the dread report noised abroad about him, for he was haughty in his carriage, casting his eyes about him on all sides so that the proud man's power was to be seen in the very movement of his body.*[3]

A monk gave him the title "the Scourge of God"—an appellation that seems to have pleased him—and he certainly did his best to live up to his fierce reputation. One of the reasons for this was strategic: many cities and towns surrendered to him without a fight, simply because they had heard what happened to those who dared to resist. Attila was aware of the benefits involved in projecting a ruthless image, and he encouraged violent behavior and atrocities on the part of his warriors. As one historian writes,

*In his late thirties, Attila attacked and decimated the city of Naissus; in fact, the riverbanks became so littered with human bones that for years after no one would enter the city because of the stench of death. Attila enjoyed the apocalyptic scenes his men caused. He had a habit of fiercely rolling his eyes, in order to inspire greater terror in his victims.*[4]

Over one hundred different towns and cities were captured and looted by the Huns, and many thousands of defenseless men, women, and children perished at their hands. Churches and monasteries were destroyed, monks and virgins slain, and the graves of saints desecrated. Legend states that when the Huns encountered the virgin St. Ursula returning from a pilgrimage to Rome, the barbarian chieftain was so smitten by her beauty that he proposed marriage—and when she refused, he ordered her and her numerous companions killed.

Attila's personal life was equally violent and depraved; he and his brother had originally shared the position of ruler of the Huns, but he murdered him in 445 so as to assume full power himself. A polygamist, Attila was credited with fathering over a hundred children, and is actually believed to have practiced cannibalism by eating two of his sons, after one of his wives served them to him roasted in honey.[5]

The Huns rampaged through Gaul (modern-day France), but were checked in the Battle of Châlons by a combined army of Romans and barbarians (all of whom feared Attila more than each other). The city of Paris was also spared from a Hunnish attack—through the leadership of the virgin St. Genevieve. She promised the residents of the city that if they did penance, God would protect them from harm; when the city leaders expressed doubt, she told the women, "Let the men flee if they want to, if they are incapable of fighting. We women will pray so hard that God will surely hear our prayers!" Genevieve's guarantee was honored by Heaven; the Huns did not attack as they had planned[6] (and centuries later the holy virgin was honored by being declared the patron saint of Paris).

In 452, the Huns invaded Italy, where they first destroyed the city of Aquilea, and then marched on Rome. The empire's western armies were unable to stop him, and the emperor—who was little more than a figurehead—stayed out of harm's way in the fortified city of Ravenna. Believing nothing could stop him, Attila boasted that "the total conquest of Italy was to be his crowning work of destruction."[7] However, God had other plans; Attila was never to set eyes on Rome.

Historians debate the exact reason for this. Some claim the Huns were weakened by a plague, and therefore unable to continue; others suggest Attila's superstitious nature came into play. A contemporary historian, Priscus, wrote that "Attila's mind had been bent on going to Rome. But his followers took him away and reminded him that the last person to conquer Rome, Alaric the Visigoth, had not lived long after the event."[8] Further factors, such as polluted water and a shortage of food, are also said to have influenced his decision to turn back. However, the most important factor was a spiritual one.

Pope St. Leo I, knowing it was up to him to turn aside the Huns, prayed and fasted, then set out to meet Attila while he was still far to the north of the city. Upon encountering the barbarian leader, the Pope convinced him to spare Rome and depart from Italy. As one author states,

> It seems plain that the Scourge of God was finally deflected because God heard the prayers of St. Leo and inspired his words. Two results followed from this. First, those diehard pagans who had been complaining that the barbarians had come because of the substitution of Christianity for the worship of the gods of Rome were answered. Christ, not Jupiter, had saved Rome, in the person of his vicar—a point St. Leo hammered home with the hammering of Jupiter's statue into another shape. Second, the destiny of Europe was not to be a province of Asia [the homeland of the Huns], the tributary of a great Empire of the steppes; that fate would befall Russia and many other states under Mongol rule, but the West had a different future.[9]

When Attila's servants afterwards inquired why he had agreed to the Pope's request that he avoid any further looting or bloodshed, the warrior king supposedly explained that, as Leo was speaking, a heavenly figure stood over him protectively, brandishing a sword—and Attila was terrified that he'd be killed unless he did as the Holy Father asked.[10]

The following year, Attila took another bride—a beautiful German woman named Ildrico. According to legend, she had vowed revenge upon the one who had slaughtered so many of her countrymen. The man who had wrought such great death and destruction didn't survive his wedding night; either he was stabbed to death by his new bride, or an artery burst, causing the Scourge of God to drown in his own blood.[11] As Scripture says, "when the wicked perish, there is jubilation" (Prv. 11:10), and indeed, the news of Attila's death brought joy and relief to the terrorized peoples of the empire.

The fact that Leo had successfully intervened on Rome's behalf, while the emperor hid behind the walls of Ravenna, greatly increased the prestige of the papacy, and as government authority broke down still further in the West, the Church filled the vacuum. Bishops took steps to protect their people from danger, and arranged the feeding of the poor and hungry; popes defended the rights of the people and of the Church from distant emperors in the East, and sought to spare the land from further threats of violence. (A few years after dissuading Attila, Pope Leo convinced the Vandals merely to loot Rome, and not massacre its inhabitants, as was their normal practice.[12])

When the barbarian invasions swept away the remnants of imperial authority in the West, and threatened to destroy civilization itself, it was the Church which preserved culture and learning, while offering a degree of shelter to the common people. According to famed historian Will Durant (himself an agnostic),

> *The basic cause of cultural retrogression was not Christianity but barbarism; not religion but war. The human inundations ruined or impoverished cities, monasteries, libraries, schools, and made impossiblethe life of the scholar or the scientist. Perhaps the destruction would have been worse had not the Church maintained some measure of order in a crumbling civilization.[13]*

Catholic monasteries in particular helped save the learning of past centuries from those who had no appreciation for learning, art, beauty, or other cultural achievements.

The Church also helped restore a degree of order to society by sending missionaries to Christianize the barbarians. A striking example of the Church's civilizing influence involves Clovis, king of the barbarian tribe known as the Franks. Like Attila fifty years earlier, he sought to capture Paris—but St. Genevieve, now in her seventies, once again rallied the inhabitants. Their situation eventually became desperate due to the lengthy siege that followed, but the saint personally escaped, filled twelve boats with grain and supplies, and managed to bring them back to the city. Clovis, knowing he was beaten, gave up; Genevieve, knowing the ways of Divine Providence, prayed for his conversion.

This miracle of grace happened, due to the holy influence of Clovis' new wife, Clotilda, and of St. Remigius, Bishop of Reims—along with the king's success in battle after praying to Jesus Christ. Clovis consented to receive baptism in 496, and—contrary to his expectation—his warriors agreed to follow their master's example. This event marked the beginning of Catholic France.[14]

Each political success brought new challenges for the Church, and some of them proved to be quite dangerous. In addition to continuing threats from barbarian tribes such as the Alemanni and the Lombards, Vikings conducted destructive raids throughout much of Europe, destroying churches and shrines and killing scores of monks, religious, and believers. Furthermore, pagan priests in various lands—such as the Druids in England and Wales—fought the Church, sometimes violently; Catholic priests were murdered in occult rituals, and Church property was wrecked.[15]

In spite of the violence and disorder of the so-called Dark Ages, the Church managed to survive and even overcome every worldly challenge the evil one raised up against her. Satan, however, as a "murderer" and "the father of lies" (Jn. 8:44), also had a quite different tactic to employ against Christianity, one which he would use to great effect: raising up enemies from within the Church itself.

# Heresy

Referring to the numerous heresies, schisms, revolutions, and persecutions that have afflicted the Church during her 2000 year history, the Jesuit scholar Fr. Vincent Miceli noted, "The devil and his antichrists never give up, nor will ever give up, as long as the time of man's trial and pilgrimage on earth lasts."[16] Heresy is a particularly valuable weapon in Satan's arsenal, for if he can get believers to deny or distort a teaching of the Church, the truths of salvation are obscured and the influence of Catholicism is weakened.

According to the great Catholic apologist Hilaire Belloc,

*The denial of a scheme [of religious belief] wholesale is not heresy, and has not the creative power of a heresy. It is the essence of heresy that it leaves standing a great part of the structure it attacks. On this account it can appeal to believers and continues to affect their lives through deflecting them from their original characters.*[17]

In other words, heresy is a "stealth attack" on religious faith. From the devil's perspective, direct assaults on the Church are often counter-productive (as when persecution by the Romans simply made Christianity stronger than before); therefore, Satan uses his agents—quite often without their awareness—to undermine the Church from within, leaving enough religious teaching and practice untouched to avoid, if possible, alerting his intended targets.

Philosophies, rationalism, and other systems of worldly wisdom are quite useful in this regard; that's why St. John Chrysostom warned, "Poor human reason when it trusts in itself substitutes the strangest absurdities for the highest divine concepts."[18] One such absurdity is the heretic's belief that he is actually preserving the truth, rather than obscuring or rejecting it. The heretic

*will never see himself in the role of heretic. No heretic throughout the centuries of Christianity ever did. Heretics either pretended to be still within the Church even though they held opinions diverging widely from the Church's teachings, or they declared that they alone were representatives of true and unadulterated faith and that the Church had left the path of Her founder which they, the heretics, had to rediscover.*[19]

Christ's Church has suffered greatly from heresies and dissent over the centuries, just as Scripture foretold: "For the time will come when people will not tolerate sound doctrine but, following their own desires and insatiable curiosity, will accumulate teachers and will stop listening to the truth and be diverted to myths" (2 Tm. 4:3). Nevertheless, as St. Augustine proclaimed,

*This is holy Church, the one Church, the true Church, the Catholic Church, fighting against all heresies; she can fight, but she cannot be conquered. All heresies are expelled from her as if they were dead branches pruned from the vine; she herself, however, remains fixed in her root, in her vine, in her charity. The gates of hell shall not prevail against her.*[20]

Jesus, "the way, the truth, and the life" (Jn. 14:6), has given His Church "the Spirit of truth" (Jn. 14:17) to guide her to all truth (Jn. 16:13)—and this means heresies and their founders, no matter how influential, dynamic, and popular, cannot hope to prevail.

## Early Heretics

Early Christians—particularly the Church Fathers—had a

great abhorrence of heretics, for they were viewed as thieves and robbers who, instead of entering through the gate, climbed into the sheepfold elsewhere so as to harm the sheep (cf. Jn. 10:1). It was widely believed the curse of God was upon them; St. Polycarp, for example, upon learning that the heretic Cerinthus was in the public bathhouse in Ephesus he had just entered, fled for his life, fearing the building might collapse on such a notorious enemy of the Gospel.[21]

In that particular instance, Cerinthus avoided divine judgment, but the fate of heretics was often an unhappy one. Mani, the 3rd c. Persian prophet who founded the religion of Manichaeism (which ensnared Augustine until his conversion to Christianity), was brutally imprisoned and tortured by the king of Persia. After he died, the king ordered a burning torch to be thrust through his corpse to make sure he was truly dead; then his head was mounted over the city gates.[22] The heretic Sabellius was excommunicated around 217, and is believed to have died unreconciled to the Church;[23] the antipope Novatian, however, may have suffered martyrdom during Valerian's persecution[24] in the middle of the 3rd c. (presumably demonstrating his repentance by the shedding of his blood).

Novatian's denial of the Church's authority to forgive lapsed Christians (those who denied their faith in a time of persecution) was echoed by Donatus a century later, who insisted that clergy who betrayed the faith were no longer capable of administering the sacraments.[25] Efforts to reconcile his followers to the Church were unsuccessful; indeed, some of the Donatists resorted to violence, forcing the imperial government to suppress them. Donatus himself died in exile (prompting his followers to declare him a martyr[26]). Death in exile was also the fate of the 5th century heretics Nestorius (who had been excommunicated and removed as Bishop of Constantinople for denying that both a divine and a human nature exist together in the one Person of Jesus Christ) and Pelagius (who denied the necessity of divine grace for salvation).

Pelagius, a British priest, came to Rome and developed for himself a reputation as a holy and important theologian, and he conducted an ongoing correspondence with Saints Jerome and Augustine. However, "From his letters these holy men soon discovered his real character; under the mask of piety they discovered a depth of hypocrisy; and under an imposing language, frightful errors of doctrine, against which they judged it necessary to caution the Faithful."[27] Influenced by pagan philosophies, Pelagius denied the realities of original sin and concupiscence, the resurrection of the body, and the necessity of Christ's saving death and resurrection.[28] Pelagius was eventually banned from Rome and Palestine, and may have died in an Egyptian monastery.[29]

One of the more bizarre heresies (and one of the more tragic fates for a heresy's founder) was Montanism, which originated in Asia Minor in the latter part of the 2nd century Montanus believed a heavenly Jerusalem would soon descend upon a local village, and he and his disciples Prisca and Maximilla preached the need for extreme acts of penance, for—they claimed—only original sin could be forgiven (through baptism), not those personal sins committed after birth.[30] The Montanists even succeeded in converting the Church Father Tertullian to their cause. Finally, however,

> their arrogance reached the blasphemous height of declaring that the Holy Ghost had descended upon Montanus and his followers in a higher and fuller manner than upon the Apostles at Pentecost, enabling [them] to teach things higher than they, nay, even than Christ Himself. . . . One prophetess indeed declared that Christ had appeared to her under the form of a woman, and women as well as men appeared as officials in the revivalistic orgies before Montanist altars.[31]

According to the contemporary author Apolinarus of Hierapolis, "But by another kind of death Montanus and [his prophetess] Maximilla are said to have died. For the report is that, incited by the spirit of frenzy, they both hung themselves; not at the same time . . . and thus they died, and ended their lives like the traitor Judas."[32] Also, Theminson, Montanus' accomplice and appointed successor, was supposedly "carried into the air by a devil, flung down, and so died."[33]

Arguably the most notorious heretic of all, however, arose early in the 4th century, and his heresy threatened the unity of the Church more than any other event in the first millennium of her existence.

# Arius

St. Ignatius of Antioch had warned his flock, "Avoid heretics like wild beasts; for they are mad dogs, biting secretly."[34] Developing this point further, he added,

> Keep away from strange fare, by which I mean heresy. For those people mix Jesus Christ with their teachings, speaking things unworthy of belief. It is as if they were giving a deadly poison mixed with sweetened wine, so that the unsuspecting victim readily accepts it and drinks his own death with fatal pleasure.[35]

Ignatius was speaking of heresy in general; St. Anthony of Egypt referred to the heresy of Arius in particular when he warned,

> Do not defile yourselves with the Arians, for that teaching is not from the apostles, but from the demons, and from their father, the devil; indeed, it is infertile, irrational, and incorrect in understanding, like the senselessness of mules.[36]

The modern mind may wonder why the Church considered one man and his teaching so dangerous; however, as Hilaire Belloc explained,

> The Arian attack [a denial of Christ's divinity] proposed a change of fundamental doctrine, such that, had the change prevailed, the whole nature of the religion would have been transformed. It would not only have been transformed, it would have failed; and with its failure would have followed the breakdown of that civilization which the Catholic Church was to build up. . . . its underlying motive was a rationalizing of the mystery upon which the Church bases herself: the mystery of the Incarnation. Arianism was essentially a revolt against the difficulties attaching to mysteries as a whole though expressing itself as an attack on the chief mystery only. Arianism was a typical example on the largest scale of that reaction against the supernatural which, when it is fully developed, withdraws from religion all that by which religion lives.[37]

In other words, if the Church had failed to resist the teaching of Arius (and thereby rejected divine revelation on the nature of Christ), she would have become merely a human institution, and condemned herself to irrelevancy at best, and eventual destruction at worst.

Belloc's description of Arius, a presbyter (priest) from Egypt, is revealing:

> There was a great deal of ambition in him, such as you will find in all heresiarchs [originators of heresy]. There was a strong element of rationalism. There was also in him enthusiasm for what he believed to be the truth. His theory was certainly not his own original discovery, but he made it his own; he identified it with his name. Further, he was moved to a dogged resistance against people whom he thought to be persecuting him. He suffered much from vanity, as do nearly all reformers.[38]

As Scripture says, "pride is the reservoir of sin" (Sir. 10:13); it was pride that led to Lucifer's downfall (cf. Is. 14:12-15), and the devil uses this same vice—in some ways, the most dangerous of the Seven Deadly Sins—to ensnare further victims.

When Arius began preaching his belief that Jesus, though greater than all creation, was merely a created being Himself, unequal to the Father in power and dignity, the bishop of Alexandria tried to reason with him privately, but he would not cease his activities. A regional council of North Africa bishops then excommunicated him, but Arius—too enamored of the celebrity status he had attained—would not disappear from the scene. "With so much popularity at his back, not only among laypeople—including seven hundred women, self-proclaimed holy virgins, who campaigned on his behalf—but among Eastern clerics, he knew that he could successfully mount a rhetorical army to challenge the supremacy of the Catholic Church."[39]

Arius skillfully exploited his opportunities to advance his cause; as one author states, "He used his very persuasive gifts of oratory and writing, his reputation for learning, his handsome person, his genius for making and flattering friends, even his ability to bring fine theological problems within the understanding of the people through the medium of popular songs."[40] The heretical priest managed to gain a powerful ally in the influential bishop Eusebius of Nicomedia, who, as a friend of Constantia, the sister of the Emperor Constantine, soon became the real leader of the Arian party. As St. Jerome remarked, "Arius, intent on leading the world astray, began by misleading the Emperor's sister." According to the great defender of orthodoxy St. Athanasius (who was himself exiled five separate times for his opposition to Arianism),

> *Eusebius and Arius, like serpents coming out of their holes, have vomited forth the poison of this impiety; Arius daring to blaspheme openly, and Eusebius defending his blasphemy. He was not, however, able to support the heresy until he found a patron for it in the Emperor. . . .*[41]

Constantine, the great protector of the Church (though he himself delayed receiving baptism until he was on his deathbed), was concerned the Arian controversy threatened the political unity of his empire, so he convened the Council of Nicea in 325 to resolve the issue one way or another. Under the guidance of the Holy Spirit, the Council formally condemned Arianism and declared that the Son is "consubstantial" or "of the same substance" as the Father (*homoousios* in Greek).[42] However, this formal and definitive Church teaching (recited by Catholics each weekend at Mass in the Nicene Creed), though ratified by Pope Sylvester I, did not end the controversy.

Arianism continued to grow in popularity and influence, and over the next ten years Arius' allies—including many bishops in the East, along with some members of Constantine's own royal court—prevailed upon the emperor lift the heretic's excommunication and restore him to full membership in the Church. During an interview, Arius deceived the emperor by pretending to accept the decrees of Nicea, and Constantine thereupon ordered that he be allowed to receive Communion in the cathedral of the imperial capital of Constantinople the following Sunday.[43] Alexander, the saintly bishop of the city, protested, but the emperor brushed aside his concerns—so the saint appealed to a higher authority.

Writing many centuries later, St. Alphonsus Liguori gives a thorough, and somewhat graphic, description of what happened next:

> *Saint Alexander, grieved to the heart, went to the church accompanied by only two persons, and prostrating himself on the floor, with tears in his eyes, prayed to the Lord: "O my God, either take me out of the world, or take Arius, that he may not ruin Your Church." Thus Saint Alexander prayed, and on the same day, Saturday, at three o'clock, the Eusebians were*

*triumphantly conducting Arius through the city, and he went along, boasting of his reestablishment, but when he came to the great square the vengeance of God overtook him; he got a terrible spasm in his bowels, and was obliged to seek a place of retirement. A private place near the square was pointed out to him; he went in and left a servant at the door. He immediately burst open like Judas; his intestines, his spleen, and his liver all fell out, and thus his guilty soul took her flight to her Creator, deprived of the communion of the Church. When he delayed too long, his friends came to the door, and on opening it, they found him stretched out on the floor in a pool of blood in that horrible state. This event took place in the year 336.*[44]

We might wonder at the severity of divine judgment in Arius' case, but we must remember the all-important issue at stake: Arius denied the divinity of Christ, and if Jesus were not both fully human and fully divine, redemption could not have been accomplished. (The first humans had sinned, and so justice demanded that a human being atone for sin—but the offense against divine dignity was so great that only God could accomplish the miracle of redemption. Thus the necessity of the Incarnation; the God-man entered our world to save us from our sins.)

Arianism was a demonic assault on the Church, for had the heresy prevailed, it would have lost for humanity the gift of salvation purchased by the blood of Christ—and beginning with Judas, Satan has always used (and discarded) his servants in the pursuit of this goal. As for Arius himself, the words of St. Cyprian—spoken in a different context some eighty years earlier—serve as a fitting epitaph: "He cannot be united to Christ, who preferred to imitate Judas rather than Christ."[45]

# John XII

Unlike certain bishops (e.g., Donatus, Nestorius, and Eusebius of Nicomedia) and priests (e.g., Sabellius, Arius, and Pelagius), no pope has ever formally taught heresy—but more than a few have acted in a way that brought confusion or discredit, and sometimes great sorrow and tribulation, to the Church. In addition to numerous saints and even several great historical leaders,

Catholicism has also been led by pontiffs whose serious failures constitute undeniable proof that the Holy Spirit continues to guide and protect the Church—for her continued existence, in spite of sometimes disastrous leadership, has often seemed nothing less than miraculous.

Many of St. Peter's successors have harmed the Body of Christ through their human weakness, demonstrating folly, stubbornness, incompetence, poor judgment, and an over-reliance on the power and values of this world. Indeed, some—through their secular and political failures—seemed determined to validate Jesus' observation that "the children of this world are more prudent in dealing with their own generation than are the children of light" (Lk. 16:8).

Because of Our Lord's promise that the gates of hell would never overcome the Church (Mt. 16:18), it is theologically impossible for a pope to propose or promote religious error—but that is no guarantee a particular Vicar of Christ won't act in a scandalous or seriously sinful manner. Sadly, a number of popes were guilty of grave moral failings following their accession to the throne of Peter. Two of them in particular, separated by more than 500 years, stand out in notoriety: John XII and Alexander VI.

Rome in the 10th century was dominated by several influential families, and the patriarch of one of them, Alberic II, was responsible for the election of four different popes.[46] On his deathbed, he appointed his illegitimate son Octavian as his successor, though he required the nobility of Rome to promise that, should the reigning pope die, Octavian would be elected to the papacy. Unfortunately, when the pope did in fact die a year later, the nobles kept their promise.

When Octavian came to power in 955, he was only eighteen years old; he took the name John XII as an expression of his papal authority, though he continued using his birth name in his capacity of prince of Rome. Twenty-three popes so far (including one antipope) have used the name John (more than any other papal name). It would not be much of an exaggeration to say that John XII manifested more deliberate sinfulness than his twenty-two namesakes combined. Not only did he neglect his duties as both pope and prince by encouraging mob rule, violent factions, and public crime within the city of Rome (all of which his father had vigorously stamped out); his personal immorality was appalling. John appointed Church officials in exchange for bribes, ordered a priest who had criticized him to be castrated, and was allegedly guilty of incest and of raping nuns.[47] As one historian notes,

> In his relationship with the Church, John seems to have been urged toward a course of deliberate sacrilege that went far beyond the casual enjoyment of sensual pleasures. It was as though the dark element in his nature goaded him on to test the utmost extents of his power, a Christian Caligula whose crimes were rendered particularly horrific by the office he held. Later, the charge was specifically made against him that he turned the Lateran into a brothel; that he and his gang violated female pilgrims in the very basilica of St. Peter; that the offerings of the humble laid upon the altar were snatched up as casual booty.[48]

As if these crimes weren't enough, John called upon pagan gods to help him win at gambling (to which he seems to have been addicted), and on one occasion even toasted the devil during a night of drinking and carousing.[49] In addition, John rewarded his mistresses not with gold, but with lands; he made one of them the governor of several cities, and also gave her sacred religious vessels from St. Peter's itself. So disgusted were the bishops of France that, in a council which threatened to break away from the authority of Rome, they demanded, "Where is it written that the innumerable company of the priests of God, scattered over the earth and adorned by learning and merit, should be subject to monsters devoid of all knowledge, human and divine, and a disgrace to the world?"[50]

The devout Saxon king Otto the Great, first of the Holy Roman emperors, drove John from power in an attempt to rescue the Church from scandal and corruption, though John regained the papacy for a time during the political infighting which followed. Not surprisingly, the pope's death came as the result of violence: he was caught in the act of adultery, and beaten so severely by the outraged husband that he died of his injuries a few days later. Salacious tongues soon transformed this account into a morality tale in which the aggrieved husband was actually "the devil himself, come to fetch home his most faithful servant."[51]

# Alexander VI

Of all the disreputable pontiffs of the Renaissance and pre-Reformation papacy, Alexander VI surely ranks first in notoriety; one scholar calls him

*arguably the most infamous successor to the throne of St. Peter, described by the Florentine historian Francesco Guicciardini as "more evil and more lucky than perhaps any pope before him." [Cardinal Rodrigo Borgia] enjoyed a decidedly unreligious life, fathering numerous children and earning a sharp rebuke from Pope Pius II. His favorite mistress was the Roman aristocrat Vannozza Catanei by whom he would sire four children: Juan, Cesare, Lucrezia, and Jofre.*[52]

Belloc laments, "When all is weighted, Alexander VI was a source of enormous scandal to the Church, and his life and character shook and cracked the edifice of Papal Prestige. He only reigned eleven years. But those eleven years were of lamentable and permanent effect."[53]

Alexander had used bribery to acquire the papacy in 1492, and then devoted himself to advancing the fortunes of his family. Cesare was made a cardinal of the Church at age eighteen. Juan, however—whom the pope planned to make king of Naples—was murdered, with his body throne into the Tiber River. (Cesare, with whom Juan had dined a few hours earlier, was widely suspected of the crime.) A distraught pope ordered his son's body to be dragged from the river—causing cynical Romans to remark that Alexander had finally become a fisher of men.[54]

For a time, the pope was so shaken by his son's murder that he gave serious thought to reforming himself and the Church—but he soon tired of these spiritual efforts, and devoted himself instead to helping Cesare make war on the nobles of Rome. This effort against the enemies of the Borgias frequently involved the use of murder (especially by poison) on the part of both father and son.

During the unusually hot summer of 1503, Alexander's cousin, Cardinal Giovanni Borgia, suddenly died—alarming the pope, who was approximately the same age and equally overweight. As he looked out a window of the Vatican Palace, Alexander remarked, "This is a bad month for stout people." At that very moment, an owl flew through the window and dropped dead at his feet—an omen which naturally terrified the pope.[55]

Soon afterwards, Alexander and Cesare both became desperately ill, as did the cardinal with whom they had dined a few days earlier (leading to rumors of an attempted poisoning gone wrong). Cesare—whom Niccolò Machiavelli would later use as his model in writing *The Prince*—recovered, only to die three years later in battle (with his last words reputedly being "I die unprepared!"). Alexander, however, steadily declined. As one historian describes,

> *Alexander entered his death agonies. Rumors of supernatural activities made their rounds, for no man could believe that such a pope was making his exit in a natural manner. Servants swore that they overheard the dying man pleading with an invisible companion for a little more time—he had sold his soul to the devil who had promised him a pontificate of exactly eleven years and one week. [In the words of a contemporary author:] "The devil was seen to leap out of the bedroom in the shape of an ape. And a cardinal ran to seize it and, having caught it, would have given it to the pope. But the pope said, 'Let him go, let him go. It is the Devil.' And that night he fell ill and died."[56]*

There is, of course, no way of proving any sort of pact between the devil and the Borgia pope—but there is no doubt that his legacy was a shameful one, weakening the prestige and authority of the Church and making her far less able to respond effectively to the challenges Martin Luther and his supporters would pose a mere fourteen years later. In terms of scandalous behavior, Alexander VI may have been the worst pope of all; however, even he—like other unworthy pontiffs, before and after him—never fell into heresy, a truth helping illustrate the reality of papal infallibility.

A former Evangelical who converted to Catholicism, David Currie, notes that Catholic belief in papal infallibility is similar to Evangelical belief in the infallibility of Scripture, and then explains:

> *When the pope, as head of the Church, proclaims doctrine, he*

*will not be mistaken in his teaching. This does not mean he cannot make mistakes concerning other topics. This does not mean his teaching will be as good as it could be. This does not mean he will always have the wisdom or courage to teach the truth when he should. What it does mean is that the teaching that is done will never be in error (heretical).*[57]

Papal infallibility doesn't guarantee the successor of St. Peter will be a holy or honorable man; it simply means that even the worst of popes—someone like John XII or Alexander VI—will never be able to formally teach doctrinal or moral error (even if, for some misguided or perverse reason, it were his desire to do so). Jesus had declared that Peter and his successors would have the power of binding and loosing (Mt. 16:19), and that the Holy Spirit would help them remember and proclaim all His teachings (Jn. 14:26)—and because Our Lord never goes back on His word (cf. Heb. 13:8), it is impossible for even the most unworthy pope to mislead the faithful.

There are numerous examples from early Church history showing that while the bishops or patriarchs of the other major ecclesiastical sees of Antioch, Alexandria, and Constantinople often fell into heresy, the bishops of Rome never did so.[58] Even an immoral, ambitious churchman like Vigilius, who, having helped murder Pope Silverius to clear the way for himself, became pope in 538 with the assistance of the empress—to whom he promised to promote the heresy of Monophysitism, which she favored—found himself unable to teach doctrinal error. Once on the papal throne, Vigilius informed the empress that as pope, he could not teach Monophysitism or support those who did—knowing full well the danger involved in defending orthodoxy. As David Currie relates, Vigilius

*was guilty of both simony [obtaining ecclesiastical office through bribery] and murder, yet God forgave him and provided him the grace to endure his own martyrdom. While saying Mass in Rome, Vigilius was arrested by the emperor's men and deported to Constantinople. He never saw Rome again before his death, ten exceedingly difficult years later. At no point after becoming pope, however, did Vigilius teach the heresy embraced by the empress and most of the Eastern*

*Church. Jesus had kept His promise. The gates of hell skulked away empty-handed — the trophy had eluded it again.*[59]
Barbarians and invaders may wound the Church, but never destroy her; heretics may divide the Church, but never overcome her; bad popes may scandalize the Church, but never prevent her from fulfilling her mission. Because Jesus is her Lord, the identity of her enemies ultimately doesn't matter; through Christ's grace and protection, the Church's victory is assured.

## NOTES TO CHAPTER 3

[1] Christopher Nugent, *Masks of Satan* (Christian Classics, 1983, 1989), p. 45.

[2] H. W. Crocker III, *Triumph: The Power and the Glory of the Catholic Church* (Three Rivers Press, 2001), p. 87.

[3] Diane Moczar, *Ten Dates Every Catholic Should Know* (Sophia Institute Press, 2005), pp. 25-26.

[4] Miranda Twiss, *The Most Evil Men and Women in History* (Barnes & Noble, 2002), p. 34.

[5] *Ibid.*, p. 35.

[6] Moczar, p. 27.

[7] Sister Catherine, M.I.C.M., *Our Glorious Popes* (Loreto Publications, 1955), p. 38.

[8] Twiss, p. 40.

[9] Moczar, p. 31.

[10] Sister Catherine, p. 39.

[11] Twiss, p. 40.

[12] Crocker, p. 91.

[13] Will Durant, *Caesar and Christ* (MJF Books, 1950), p. 79, as quoted in Thomas E. Woods, Jr., *How the Catholic Church Built Western Civilization* (Regnery, 2005), pp. 9-10.

[14] Moczar, p. 41.

[15] Michael H. Brown, *The Last Secret* (Queenship Publishing, 2007), p. 51.

[16] Vincent P. Miceli, S.J., *The Antichrist* (Roman Catholic Books, 1981), p. 131. Fr. Miceli quotes Jean Ousset's list of the different heretical or schismatic individuals and groups afflicting the Church during her history. This list includes: 2nd century – Gnostics, Docetists, and Montanists; 3rd century – Manicheans; 4th century – Eutychians, Donatists, and Arians; 5th century – Monophysites, Nestorians, and Pelagians; 6th century – SemiPelagians; 7th century – Menethelites; 8th century – Iconoclasts; 9th century – Iconoclasts;

10th century – practitioners of simony and other abuses; 11th century – Berengarians; 12th century – Albigensians, Waldenses; 13th century – Albigensians; 14th century – Wycliffe; 15th century – the "Great Schism," in which there were two antipopes at one time; 16th century – Luther, Calvin, Zwingli, and Henry VIII; 17th century – Jansenists, Rationalists; 18th century – Jansenists, Quietists; 19th century – Modernists, Old Catholics; and 20th century – Neo-Modernists, and followers of Teilhard de Chardin. From Jean Ousset, "Dark Disorder Within the Church," *Christian Order* (January 1974), pp. 19-33.

[17] Hilaire Belloc, *The Great Heresies* (Sheed and Ward, 1938; TAN Books & Publishers, 1991), pp. 3-4.

[18] Ronda De Sola Chervin, *Quotable Saints* (Servant Publications, 1992), p. 54.

[19] Rudolf Allers, *What's Wrong With Freud?* (Roman Catholic Books, 1941), pp. 202-203.

[20] Paul Thigpen, *Quotes from the Saints* (Servant Publications, 2001), pp. 38-39.

[21] Matthew Bunson, *Our Sunday Visitor's Encyclopedia of Catholic History* (Our Sunday Visitor, 1995), p. 188.

[22] Geo. Widengren, *Mani and Manichaeism,* trans. Charles Kessler (Weidenfeld and Nicolson, 1961), p. 41.

[23] Bunson, p. 740.

[24] *New Catholic Encyclopedia* (Catholic University of America, 1967), "Novatian," Vol. X, p. 534. Novatian, a theologian in Rome during the persecution of Decius, opposed the election of St. Cornelius as successor to the martyred St. Fabian, and set himself up as an antipope. He and his followers were excommunicated in 251. During times of persecution, of course, the Romans made no distinction between orthodox and schismatic Catholics.

[25] Crocker, p. 38.

[26] W. H. C. Frend, *The Donatist Church* (Claredon Press, 1952), p. 181.

[27] Very Rev. Canon G. E. Howe, *Stories from the Catechist* (TAN Books & Publishers, 1922, 1989), p. 87.

[28] Thomas Colyandro, *The Judas Syndrome* (St. Benedict Press, 2010), p. 54.

[29] Richard M. Hogan, *Dissent from the Creed* (Our Sunday Visitor, 2001), p. 116.

[30] Bunson, pp. 570-571.

[31] M. L. Cozens, *A Handbook of Heresies* (Sheed & Ward, 1947), p. 25.

[32] www.answers.com, "Montanus."

[33] *Catholic Encyclopedia*, on-line version, "Montanus."

[34] Jill Haak Adels, *The Wisdom of the Saints* (Barnes & Noble, 1987), p. 111.

[35] Thigpen, p. 115.

[36] Adels, p. 111.

[37] Hilaire Belloc, p. 11. Belloc elaborates on the threat Arianism posed to Catholicism:

> *Had this movement for rejecting the full divinity of Our Lord gained the victory, all our civilization would have been other than what it has been from that day to this. We all know what happens when an attempt to simplify and rationalize the mysteries of the Faith succeeds in any society. We have before us the now ending experiment of the Reformation, and the aged but still vigorous Mohammedan heresy. . . .*
> *Such rationalistic efforts against the creed produce a gradual social degradation following on the loss of that direct link between human nature and God which is provided by the Incarnation. Human dignity is lessened. The authority of Our Lord is weakened. He appears more and more as a man—perhaps a myth. The substance of Christian life is diluted. What began as Unitarianism ends as Paganism* (pp. 27-28).

[38] *Ibid.*, pp. 26-27.

[39] Crocker, p. 52.

[40] Sister Catherine, p. 14.

[41] *Ibid.*

[42] Bunson, p. 410.

[43] Crocker, p. 61.

[44] Sister Catherine, p. 24.

[45] *Liturgy of the Hours*, Vol. 3, Second Reading for Friday of the Eleventh Week in Ordinary Time (CSEL 3, 284-285), p. 378.

[46] Matthew Bunson, *The Pope Encyclopedia* (Crown Trade Paperbacks, 1995), p. 194.

[47] Brown, pp. 55-56.

[48] E. R. Chamberlin, *The Bad Popes* (Dorset Press, 1969), p. 43.

[49] Bunson, *Pope Encyclopedia*, p. 194.

[50] Chamberlin, p. 59.

[51] *Ibid.*, p. 61.

[52] Bunson, *Pope Encyclopedia*, pp. 13-14.

[53] Hilaire Belloc, *How the Reformation Happened* (TAN Books and Publishers, 1928, 1992), p. 31.

[54] Bunson, *Pope Encyclopedia*, p. 14.

[55] Chamberlin, pp. 201-202.

[56] *Ibid.*, p. 203.

[57] David B. Currie, *Born Fundamentalist, Born Again Catholic* (Ignatius Press, 1996), p. 90.

[58] *Ibid.*, pp. 92-94. Mr. Currie's book includes a chart providing a side-by-side

comparison of the bishops of Rome and those of the three other major sees. Many times bishops of the latter fell into heresy or schism; the popes never did so.

[59] *Ibid.*, p. 96.

# Chapter 4

# Christianity vs. Islam

*This is how you can know the Spirit of God: every spirit that acknowledges Jesus Christ come in the flesh belongs to God, and every spirit that does not acknowledge Jesus does not belong to God. This is the spirit of the antichrist that, as you heard, is to come, but in fact is already in the world. (1 Jn. 4:2-3)*

In its "Declaration on the Relation of the Church to Non-Christian Religions" (*Nostra Aetate*), the Second Vatican Council affirmed, "The Catholic Church rejects nothing of what is true and holy in these religions," for their doctrines and moral precepts "often reflect a ray of that truth which enlightens all men" (n. 2). Therefore, the Council invited Christians, "while witnessing to their own faith and way of life, [to] acknowledge, preserve and encourage the spiritual and moral truths found among non-Christians, also their social life and culture" (n. 3).

Speaking specifically of Islam, the document continued,
> *The Church has also a high regard for the Muslims. They worship God, Who is one, living and subsistent, merciful and almighty, the Creator of Heaven and earth, Who has also spoken to men. They strive to submit themselves without reserve to the hidden decrees of God, just as Abraham submitted himself to God's plan, to whose faith Muslims eagerly link their own. Although not acknowledging Him as God, they worship Jesus as a prophet, His virgin Mother they also honor, and even at times devoutly invoke. Further, they await the day of judgment and the reward of God following the resurrection of the dead. For this reason they highly esteem an upright life and worship God, especially by way of prayer, alms-deeds and fasting (n.3).[1]*

Many Muslims are known for their great love of Our Lady, and for their own high moral standards. Indeed, when one of the alleged visionaries of Medjugorje inquired as to which of the inhabitants of the region—a land filled with devout Catholics—was closest to God, Mary supposedly revealed that an elderly Muslim woman was in fact farthest along on the path of holiness.[2] Moreover, Our Lady of Medjugorje allegedly stated that while not all religions are equal, all people are equal in God's sight, and added, "You are not true Christians if you do not respect other religions."[3]

Genuine respect, however, must be a two-way street, and there are ominous signs that at least some prominent and influential Muslims do not respect the West's Christian heritage and democratic values. As one author, Walid Shoebat (himself a Muslim terrorist before his conversion to Christianity), notes,

*The renowned Muslim scholar Mawlana Sayid Abul Ala Mawdudi from the Indian subcontinent stated: "Islam is not a normal religion like the other religions in the world, and Muslim nations are not like normal nations. Muslim nations are very special because they have a command from Allah to rule the entire world and to be over every nation in the world."[4] According to Mr. Shoebat, even many Western, so-called moderate Muslims regularly express such beliefs. Abdullah al-Araby in his book The Islamization of America cites a very frightening letter from one Catholic Archbishop to the Pope as he describes his speech during an interfaith dialogue. An excerpt from his letter recounts that during the meeting, an authoritative Muslim figure stood up and spoke very calmly and assuredly, "Thanks to your democratic laws, we will invade you, thanks to our religious laws, we will dominate you."[5]*

In his book *God's War on Terror: Islam, Prophecy and the Bible*, Mr. Shoebat makes what many would consider an outrageous (or at least, highly politically incorrect) claim: militant Islam will itself be a direct manifestation of the spirit of the Antichrist; he asserts that "all the references in the Bible to nations that God proclaims His war against in End-times . . . are Muslim."[6]

Could such a bold charge be true? Might devout Muslims, willing to give their lives in the name of Allah, actually be fighting against God and His Son's Church? Certainly this claim would not have sounded outrageous to many Church leaders and theologians throughout history. Muhammad—revered by all Muslims as the Prophet—was often viewed by Christians as a precursor of the Antichrist. For instance, Dante's *Inferno* placed Muhammad in the lower regions of hell, and as one author describes, "There he receives everlastingly some of the worst punishment that hell has to offer. A gash from throat to anus causes his intestines to hang between his legs. Many of the damned are so horrified by the mutilated Muhammad spectacle that they forget momentarily their own torment."[7]

Other Catholic authors shared this extremely negative opinion of Muhammad. In his 1632 book *De Antichristo* ("Concerning the Antichrist"), Dominican friar Tommaso Campanella identified the Muslim Prophet as a precursor of the Antichrist because of his denial of Christ's divinity,[8] and a similar judgment was expressed by the 19th century convert Ven. John Henry Newman. In the words of the Jesuit scholar Fr. Vincent Miceli,

> *Newman presents the false prophet Muhammad as a third historical shadow of the Antichrist [the first two being Antiochus Epiphanes and Julian the Apostate]. This shadow began his imposture about 600 years after Christ and his armies tore at the soul and body of Christ in the fierce religious wars they waged against the Church.*[9]

Who was Muhammad: a divinely-inspired religious leader, a fraud or antichrist figure, or a well-meaning but misguided individual? His name means "the praised one,"[10] and for over 1300 years he has indeed been praised (though not worshipped) by countless millions of people—but is this praise merited?

## Muhammad

In 610 a forty-year-old Arab caravan trader or merchant named Muhammad emerged from a cave, claiming the angel Gabriel had appeared to him and revealed that he was a prophet and messenger of the one true God; indeed, (though he himself was a pagan), his role was to be the final prophet in the Judeo-Christian tradition.[11] Some years later, Muhammad foresaw the spread of Islam (a word meaning "submission") throughout Arabia, but apparently had no concept of it as a worldwide religion.[12] Islam was intended to convert Arabs from their paganism—by means of force, if necessary. One historian writes,

> *At first, Muhammad had little success, but soon his movement grew. Muhammad the prophet also became a military leader, and in 630, captured Mecca. The new religion spread as quickly as Christianity had, but with a big difference. Whereas Christianity had spread by persuasion, Islam was spreading by force. Christ had allowed His enemies to kill Him; the prophet Muhammad, armed with a sword, wasn't about to take that chance.*[13]

While it can be argued Muhammad was deeply spiritual and sincere in his beliefs, and perhaps even in some ways a holy man, he—like every human being—falls far short when compared to Christ. As one author explains,

> *Christ was the epitome of the perfect man, without an evil thought or act, always ready to forgive, whereas Muhammad, especially during the last 10 years of his life, often manifested the basest qualities of mankind. He was full of suspicious thoughts and often quick to put his thoughts into action, sometimes massacring people either with his own sword or having others do it for him.*[14]

Muhammad himself recognized his underlying mental or emotional instability; after his supposed vision of Gabriel, he told his wife Khadija, "I am afraid of becoming mad . . . I see all the signs of madness in myself." Furthermore, at times he feared he was possessed by an evil spirit (a jinn), and was tormented by thoughts of committing suicide.[15]Prophets in the Judeo-Christian tradition sometimes felt profoundly unworthy or conflicted over their divine calling (cf. Mk. 1:7; Jer. 20:7-9), but never to the extent experienced by Muhammad—who, unlike Isaiah who saw the Almighty Himself (Is. 6:1), merely encountered one of the Lord's angels.

Scripture tells us that "Jesus Christ is the same yesterday, today, and forever" (Heb. 13:8), but this unchanging commitment to the truth was apparently not always the case with Muhammad—at least in regard to his teaching:

> *According to tradition, at one point, in an effort to patch things up with the Quraysh [his own tribe], Muhammad conceded*

*that there were three pagan deities . . . to whom one could look for intercession with Allah. Later realizing that it was in fact Satan who had led him to these thoughts, Muhammad then insisted that the supporting verses in the developing Qur'an [also rendered Koran] be withdrawn.*[16]

This degree of doctrinal flexibility seems somewhat convenient or self-serving—especially in light of the Christian belief in the immutability of God's word, and the sinfulness of tampering with it (cf. Rev. 22:18-19).

Muhammad's moral standards and behavior were at times highly questionable. He admitted "that two things in the world, women and perfume, attracted him—so much so that, flushed with success, he departed from his own laws and claimed his privilege as a prophet in pursuit of the former"[17] (in contrast with the attitude of Jesus, Who came to serve and not be served). Ignoring his own teaching that a man might have only four wives, Muhammad himself had at least fifteen, and perhaps as many as twenty-five—the youngest of whom, Aisha, was only seven years old when given to the Prophet in marriage (and only nine when the marriage was consummated).[18]

When a Samaritan village rejected Jesus, He responded not by summoning fire from Heaven to destroy it (as two of His apostles wanted), but by calmly setting out for a different village instead (Lk. 9:52-56). The Prophet, however, had few qualms about using violence to promote his version of truth. When peaceful methods failed in converting the Meccans to Islam, Muhammad felt himself justified in waging a holy war—though just how holy it actually was is seriously open to question. As one scholar notes, "The whole life of Muhammad after his flight to Medina was one continued scene of butchery and rapine. He and his associates and followers plundered every caravan of its valuable commodities."[19] Even a sympathetic biographer admits,

*Once the Prophet had arrived in Yathrib in September 622 he began to establish a theocratic community. From this secure base he began to wage war against the non-believers. There should be no mistake about one point in particular: the Prophet was the aggressor in the conflict, even though his forces were much weaker than those of his adversaries. He wished to*

*convert the Meccans to Islam; they essentially wanted to be left
in peace with their wealth and their pagan deities.*[20]
A further illustration of Muhammad's cruelty can be seen in
his treatment of a woman who confessed to being a prostitute: the
Prophet condemned her and participated in her execution, himself
throwing the first stone—a marked contrast to Jesus' response to the
woman caught in adultery (Jn. 8:3-11).[21] Moreover, one historian
states that after his rejection by the Meccans, Muhammad "also
showed a great deal of ill-will to any person or group that did not
accept him or the things he did, no matter how evil they were.
At times he wantonly had people killed and massacred. This
disposition stayed with him to the end of his life."[22]

On his deathbed, Muhammad overheard two of his wives
talking about the beautiful decorations they had seen in a Christian
cathedral. This upset him so much he shouted, "The Lord destroy
the Jews and Christians. Let His anger kindle against such as turn
their prophets' tombs into places of worship." He also reacted
angrily when the women tending him tried to make him take some
medicine; perhaps fearing an attempt to poison him, he ordered
them to drink it themselves—which they did.[23]Muhammad's last
recorded words were a curse upon Jews and Christians,[24] in contrast
to Christ's words of forgiveness toward His executioners and His
expression of trust in God (Lk. 23:34,46).

# Islam: A Judeo-Christian Heresy?

It would seem the primary reason Muslims share many
similar beliefs with Jews and Christians is that Islam is actually
a Judeo-Christian heresy. Muhammad wanted his new religion
to appeal to Jews and Christians, so he borrowed many of their
Scriptures and religious teachings (though sometimes without a
full understanding of the doctrines involved).[25] As one historian
notes,

> *Some of the later Fathers of the Church considered Islam a
> Christian heresy. In fact, Islam was strikingly similar to the
> other Christians heresies that had been popular all over the
> East. The Arians also had denied the divinity of Christ; they
> would agree with the Koran that Jesus is not to be worshipped*

*as God. The Nestorians denied Mary the title Mother of God.
And the Montanists believed that God continued to send new
revelations through new prophets.*[26]

The great Catholic historian and apologist Hilaire Belloc
insisted,

> *Mohammedanism [Islam] was a* **heresy:** *that is the essential
> point to grasp before going any further. It began as a heresy, not
> as a new religion. It was not a pagan contrast with the Church;
> it was not an alien enemy. It was a perversion of Christian
> doctrine. . . . It differed from most (not from all) heresies in this,
> that it did not arise from within the boundaries of the Christian
> Church. The chief heresiarch, Mohammed himself, was not,
> like most heresiarchs, a man of Catholic birth and doctrine to
> begin with. He sprang from pagans. But that which he taught
> was in the main Catholic doctrine, oversimplified.*[27]

The primary oversimplification, of course, was a denial of the
Incarnation (God-made-man). Muhammad acknowledged Jesus
as the greatest of all the prophets, but insisted He was only a man;
this dismissal of Catholic teaching also involved a rejection of the
Trinity, along with the Eucharist, the Mass, and the need for an
ordained priesthood.

Further theological difficulties arise in the Qur'an's misuse of
Scripture, which it frequently quotes but sometimes distorts. For
instance, it claims that God made His covenant with Abraham's
son Ishmael (claimed by the Arabs as their ancestor), rather than
with Isaac (a Jewish patriarch).[28] Also, the Qur'an emphatically
denies that Jesus died on the Cross: "They killed Him not, nor
crucified Him. But it was made to appear so."[29] Moreover, in
Jn. 16:7 Jesus speaks of the "Comforter" or "Advocate" He will
send, but "All Muslims accept that this 'Comforter' is the Prophet
Muhammad. Just as John the Baptist prophesied the coming of
Jesus, so did Jesus alert the world to the Prophet Muhammad."[30]
As one scholar notes, "From the inaccurate and sometimes greatly
distorted account of the Christian faith that Muhammad provides
in the Qur'an, it appears more likely that he received the outline
of the Christian teaching by the adherents of various heterodox
Christian sects in Arabia itself."[31]

In addition to these theological difficulties, the Qur'an has been shown to contain some two dozen grammatical errors, along with many foreign words—seemingly contradicting Islam's claim that the angel Gabriel dictated it "in perfect Arabic."[32] Furthermore, the Qur'an mentions twenty-two prophets (prior to Muhammad) by name, including Adam, Noah, Abraham, Moses, and Jesus—and claims that all of them were Muslim.[33]

Theological controversies of this sort can have major cultural and historical consequences; according to one author, "Islam illustrates another important fact of religious life—that heresy builds on heresy just as protestant division begets protestant division. For the lands that fell to Islam—from North Africa, to Visigothic Spain, to the eastern possessions of Byzantium—were the areas most profoundly troubled by the earlier Arian heresy."[34] Arianism, however, involved little physical violence; the same was not true of Islam.

# Historical Instances of Islamic Violence and Persecution

A thorough recounting of historical acts of Muslim violence against Christians (and also, it must be admitted, of some Christian violence against Muslims) is beyond the scope of this book; however, a brief summary can be given.

During the era of widespread Islamic conquest and expansion which began soon after Muhammad's death in 632, many Christian churches and Jewish synagogues were destroyed throughout North Africa and the Middle East (including the Church of the Resurrection in Jerusalem).[35] Muslims also claimed the right to confiscate churches and convert them into mosques (as with Hagia Sophia in Constantinople)—a precedent still considered valid today.[36] Moreover, conversion to Islam was sometimes forced upon Jews and Christians.[37] As one historian notes,

*the extreme pressure exercised by the threat of death, enslavement, deportation, destruction of one's home, and payment of tribute for which some lacked the means could well be summed up in the word "forced." Furthermore, parents who were unable to come up with the tribute money could have their children seized or become slaves themselves; either prospect was probably enough in many cases to produce at least outward acceptance of Islam. There are records of Christians in eighth-century Armenia and Syria being herded into churches and burned to death because they would not apostasize; elsewhere they were tortured, which often resulted (surprise!) in "conversion." In Spain in later centuries, the story was the same: perhaps thousands of Spaniards who refused to apostasize were martyred, while the whole Jewish population of Granada—some three thousand—was massacred in 1066.[38]*

Those Christians and Jews who chose to pay tribute rather than convert were reduced to *dhimmi* or "protected" status, a form of second-class citizenship sometimes involving even fewer rights than those possessed by slaves.[39] Dhimmis had to pay a land tax to their masters, a poll tax (mainly used to finance *jihad*, or the subjugation of other Jews and Christians), were forced to wear special clothing (making their second-class status easily recognizable), and were forbidden to display the Cross or other religious symbols in public.[40] As one scholar notes, Muslims "sometimes boast of the *dhimmi* protection they accorded non-Muslims. But this protection begs an important question: From whom and from what are *dhimmis* protected? . . . the protection they receive is from zealous Muslims desirous of harming of killing them."[41]

Slavery was an important feature of Islamic society. According to one historian,

*Muslims were by no means the only people to have slaves during the Dark and Early Middle Ages, but they turned the institution into an extensive and organized labor system that endured into modern times; in parts of Africa and Asia it apparently still exists today. Men were taken for labor, the women for exploitation by individual soldiers or within a ruler's harem.[42]*

More European Christians were enslaved over the centuries by Islam than the total number of black Africans sent as slaves to North and South America combined.[43] Sometimes conquered cities or regions were required to provide a yearly quota of slaves; this later developed into a particular despicable custom practiced by the Turks called *devsirme*, or "boy tribute." Parents were forced to surrender some of their sons, who were forcibly converted to Islam and trained for diplomatic or military service in the Ottoman, or Turkish, empire. (These soldiers were known as Janissaries.)

It's estimated that "between half a million and a million Christian boys, mostly in the Balkans, were victims of this brutal system from its inception until its abolition in 1848, and this does not include the numerous other slaves taken by the Turks."[44] In the 13th century, the Church actually founded a religious order to ransom Christians enslaved by Muslims: The Order of Our Lady of Mercy, or Our Lady of Ransom (popularly known as the Mercedarians).[45]

Muslim occupation of the Holy Land from the 7th century onward meant that Christian pilgrims, in addition to facing a long and difficult journey, also faced the very real prospect of persecution and even martyrdom. Sometimes they were allowed to come and go peacefully; on other occasions, they were the victims of Muslim violence. For instance, a large group of German pilgrims in 1064 refused on principle to carry arms or defend themselves when attacked; as a result, only 2000 of the original 7000 survived.[46] A few decades earlier, in 1009, a fanatical sultan named Hakim

> launched the most intense persecution of Christians in the East since Diocletian's reign of terror in the late third century. He demolished all the beautiful churches in Jerusalem, including the massive Church of the Holy Sepulchre, which was left a forlorn ruin. Hakim soon tired of his persecution. . . . Once again, pilgrims were allowed to flock to Jerusalem, though now the Muslim rulers charged them an admission fee at the gate. . . . But this respite lasted only for a short time. When the Turks—who were recent converts to Islam—captured Jerusalem, they brought with them a fanaticism even worse than Hakim's. They enslaved the Christians of Palestine and viewed foreign pilgrims as nothing more than infidel pests.[47]

As one scholar notes, "two-thirds of the world's Christian lands had fallen to the Muslim sword. By 1095 it was clear that, unless Christians united to halt the aggression, the remaining Christian lands would soon be overrun."[48]

# *Jihad* in History

Many early 7th century Arabs had become Muslim only as a way of avoiding violence at the hands of Muhammad and his followers, and when the Prophet died, so did their commitment to Islam. However, Muhammad's successor, Abu Bakr, decreed that apostates from Islam were subject to death, a policy he ruthlessly enforced.[49]

Abu Bakr also continued the Prophet's policy of spreading Islam by force—though he and his successors, in contrast to Muhammad's original understanding of his mission, soon expanded into non-Arabic lands. This is the origin of *jihad*, or holy war. Islam has always made a distinction between *Dar al-Islam* (the Land of Islam) and *Dar al-Harb* (the Land of War). The former refers to those lands populated by Muslims and ruled by Islamic law; the latter is the domain of non-Muslims, or infidels, who may be conquered by any or all acts of warfare and violence.[50] Several centuries passed before Christians made a concerted effort to resist this aggression—an organized response known to history as the Crusades.

One British authority on Muslim history stated, "For the Muslims in general the Crusades were little more than a frontier incident—a continuation of the kind of fighting that had been going on in Syria and Palestine for the last half century."[51] However, many people today wrongly consider the Crusades as nothing more than an unprovoked and unjustified act of Christian or European aggression:

> *History has largely bypassed the Muslim attacks on and invasion of Europe that lasted from the seventh to the twentieth centuries, but has remained transfixed on the Christian Crusades to the Holy Land that lasted only from the eleventh to the thirteenth century. We could say that the historical perspective is greatly out of focus.[52]*

The Crusades, far from being aggressive wars against peaceful Muslims, were "a belated military response of Christian Europe to over three centuries of Muslim aggression against Christian lands, the systemic mistreatment of the indigenous Christian population of those lands, and harassment of Christian pilgrims."[53]

*Jihad* has had a far greater and more lasting effect on history than the Crusades ever did; moreover, "The Crusades primarily sought to regain lost territories, whereas the Muslims, even after the Crusades, wanted [to] occupy Europe in order to Islamize it" (the reason Bosnia, Kosovo, and Albania are largely Islamic today).[54] Atrocities were committed by both sides during the Crusades (as were acts of chivalry and compassion); the level of Christian violence, however, rarely approached that systematically practiced by victorious Muslim armies in their wars of conquest. For instance, when the city of Constantinople fell to the Muslims in 1453,

> *several thousand Christians sought refuge in St. Sophia [the cathedral of Hagia Sophia] before Mahomet II (the Ottoman caliph and sultan) gave his troops license to wield their scimitars. They then massacred 4,000 refugees, raped women, and slaughtered them as well. Then Mahomet ordered a muessin [herald] to mount the cathedral's pulpit to give the church formally to Allah. In addition, 50,000 inhabitants were taken away as slaves.*[55]

For several centuries, fear of *jihad* led to the frequent use of this prayer throughout the churches of central and southern Europe: "From the fury of the Mohammedans, spare us, O Lord."[56] Even the relative decline of Islamic military and economic power compared to the emerging nations of modern Europe didn't completely eliminate the threat of religious persecution and ethnic cleansing, as evidenced by the fate of the Christians of Armenia just one century ago:

> *By the end of 1916, the anti-Armenian measures exercised by the Turks "were virtually complete." Thus, of the almost 1.9 million Armenians in the Ottoman Empire before World War I, about one million were killed (half of them women and children); some 250,000 escaped to Russia; and about 200,000 were forcibly Islamized.*[57]

Under the leadership of Pope John Paul II, the Catholic Church, as part of her preparation for the Great Jubilee of 2000, formally apologized for the acts of violence and religious intolerance committed by some of her members during the long history of Christianity. No important Muslim leader has ever imitated this example of honesty and humility; even worse, much of contemporary Islam remains committed to the principles of *jihad*.

# The Nature of Islam Today

No one would deny that hundreds of millions of Muslims—perhaps the vast majority of the adherents of Islam—are good, honest, hard-working persons willing to live in peace with their non-Muslim neighbors. However, large numbers of Muhammad's followers in today's world genuinely believe Allah wants them to conquer, and even kill, infidels in his name—using all necessary means to do so, including religious persecution and terrorism.

This situation presents a very difficult challenge for the Church. In his book *Crossing the Threshold of Hope*, Pope John Paul II wrote,

> In countries were **fundamentalist movements** come to power, human rights and the principle of religious freedom are unfortunately interpreted in a very one-sided way—religious freedom comes to mean freedom to impose on all citizens the "true religion." In these countries the situation of Christians is sometimes terribly disturbing. Fundamentalist attitudes of this nature make reciprocal contacts very difficult. All the same, the Church remains always open to dialogue and cooperation.[58]

Mutual religious dialogue and respect cannot easily be achieved when one party is arguably committed to dominating, if not destroying, the other; moreover, as one political commentator notes, "it's not merely that there's a global *jihad* lurking within this religion, but that the religion itself is a political project—and, in fact, an imperial project—in a way that modern Christianity, Judaism, Hinduism, and Buddhism are not."[59] The political implications of Islam help explain why, even today, Muslims who convert to Christianity often risk their lives to do so.[60]

According to the apologetics apostolate *Catholic Answers*,

> The usual meaning of <u>Islam</u> in Arabic is not "peace" but "submission." And if the terrorists [of 9/11] were so far outside the mainstream, why did Muslims all over the world burst into joyful, spontaneous celebrations when the hijacked jetliners

*slammed into the World Trade Center and the Pentagon? Why are Islamic governments afraid to show "too much" public support for the war against terrorism? Further, why are all the governments that covertly support terrorism centered in the Muslim world? Though there are millions of Muslims who want peaceful relations with the West, millions who aspire to live in free societies like America, there nevertheless remains a deep and powerful strain of violence within Islam. . . .*[61]

Referring to Islam's ongoing persecution of disciples of Jesus, one commentator notes, "From Nigeria to Indonesia, Christians are under siege in virtually every single country in the Muslim world, the victims of countless acts of discrimination, depredation, brutality, and murder that are so widespread and systematic that it can rightfully be called the new Holocaust."[62]

The reference to the Jewish Holocaust may not be inappropriate—for even in moderate Muslim countries today, the viciously anti-Semitic books *The Protocols of the Elders of Zion* and Adolf Hitler's *Mein Kampf* are prominently displayed bestsellers.[63] Indeed, in the spring of 2001 an influential Egyptian newspaper editorialized, "Our thanks go to the late Hitler, who wrought, in advance, the vengeance of the Palestinians upon the most despicable villains on the face of the earth. However, we rebuke Hitler for the fact that the vengeance was insufficient."[64]

Radical Islam looks upon the West as decadent and deserving of destruction (a perception reinforced by the undeniable fact that there *is* much decadence to be found in Western societies), and perceives individual Christians as infidels. Indeed, as some commentators assert, Islam "is a religion of war. No religion could be better suited for a world of cultures in conflict. Unlike Christianity, Islam is not uncertain about the morality of war; it embraces war against the unbeliever wholly, enthusiastically, without reservation."[65]

Some claim that *jihad* is merely a "personal" struggle for spiritual growth—but this interpretation is derived from Sufi Muslims, a small mystical sect with no real influence. According to *The Concise Encyclopedia of Islam* (1989), *jihad* is "a Divine institution of warfare to extend Islam into the *dar al-Harb* . . . or to defend Islam from danger."[66] One commentator states,

*Jihad is not, as some Western apologists claim, simply a striving for individual perfection. Nor is jihad merely a series of unrelated clashes involving groups of Islamists, each with their own limited objectives. Rather, jihad is a radical, expansionist, totalitarian ideology that seeks to establish a global Islamic state ruled by Islamic law, or Sharia. The adherents of this ideology are willing and able to commit acts of violence to bring about their goals. . . .[67] Jihad as it's currently practiced doesn't involve outright warfare (for the West is still far superior militarily, in spite of its cultural decadence); instead, "There are three strategies Islam deploys against a dying West: first, demography; second, conversion; and third, the murky 'intertwining' of modern technology and ancient hatreds."[68]*

Quite often children in Muslim nations are raised in an atmosphere of hatred and repression.[69] For instance, the titles of the individual articles in one magazine examining the topic of "Palestinian Kids Raised for War" include "Children Taught to Hate, Kill Jews through 'Sesame Street'-type TV Shows," "'Mickey Mouse' Promotes Jihad," "Pentagon Sees 5 Million Child Terrorists in Iraq," "Al-Qaida Training Young Boys as Terrorists," and "Palestinian Official: Women Must Martyr Themselves."[70]

Most Islamic societies have little or no tolerance for the religious beliefs of Christians and other non-Muslims. For example, a State Department report on human rights in Saudi Arabia (2000) declared:

*Freedom of religion does not exist. Islam is the official religion, and all citizens must be Muslims. Neither the government nor society in general accepts the concepts of separation of religion and state, and such separation does not exist. Under Shari'a, conversion by a Muslim to another religion is considered apostasy. Public apostasy is a crime punishable by death if the accused does not recant. Islamic religious education is mandatory in public schools at all levels. All children receive religious instruction. . . . There is legal and systemic discrimination based on sex and religion.[71]*

This is a matter of serious concern because of the expansionist nature of Islam; every year, a greater proportion of the world's population lives under Islamic law.[72]

As Islam grows in size and influence throughout the world, the level of violence and religious persecution directed against non-Muslims also seems to rise: "With shocking regularity, human-rights groups report the death of Christians at the hands of Muslim militants in Africa, South Asia, and the Middle East,"[73] and as one author notes, "Wherever one looks along the perimeter of Islam, Muslims have problems living peacefully with their neighbors."[74] A description of Islamic violence in Algeria against Westerners and those perceived to be "corrupted" recounts how, in the 1990s, foreigners were killed (including seven Trappist monks seeking to reach out in peace to their Muslim neighbors), young women were gang-raped, school-girls not veiling their faces had their throats cut, and some 200 teachers were murdered and 500 schools destroyed.[75]

The situation facing the West is becoming increasingly serious, for

*After about 300 years on the strategic defensive, Islam has recently resumed the strategic offensive. It is now expanding outward in every direction: down both coasts of Africa, east through the South China Sea toward Australia, north into both eastern and western Europe, and west into the United States, where the fastest-growing religion is Islam. As has been through throughout its history, the expansion of Islam is not peaceful.* **More Christians are being martyred today than at the height of the Roman persecutions, and most of them are dying at the hands of Islam [emphasis added]. Christendom is again in peril.**[76]

# What Does the Future Hold?

Unlike the various antichrists examined so far, the threat posed to the Church (along with Christianity as a whole, and indeed, Western civilization itself) by radical Islam is ongoing, and likely to increase and intensify. Nevertheless, in spite of currently unfavorable or dangerous trends, there are reasons for confidence and hope.

Our Lady of Fatima had promised in 1917 that eventually "a period of peace" would be granted to the world, and because

Heaven never uses half-measures, this will surely include not only the disappearance of all threats from Communism (the primary concern throughout most of the twentieth century), but also those involving Islamic expansionism, terrorism, and other forms of violence. Also, "Fatima" was the name of Muhammad's favorite daughter, and the Virgin Mary's appearance at a town of that name was surely not coincidental. As one author notes, "Archbishop Fulton J. Sheen believed Mary wanted to be known as 'Our Lady of Fatima' as a sign and a promise that the Moslems, who accept the virgin birth of Christ, would eventually accept His divinity as well."[77]

Some theologians teach that Our Lady will play an important role in bringing about true peace (that is, the Triumph of her Immaculate Heart), and the esteem Muslims have for her will be a key element in this transformation. (For example, the Pilgrim Statue of Our Lady of Fatima has been received with great reverence among Muslims throughout the world.[78]) Several alleged prophecies foretell the conversion of Muslims to Catholicism; for example, an obscure Saxon prophecy states, "The Turk . . . shall forsake his Mohammed and choose unto him the name Christian, which is a sign the day of doom is at hand, when all the earth is subject unto God, or that all people acknowledge one only God."[79]

In the 17th century Ven. Mary of Agreda predicted that in the latter days "Mary will extend the reign of Christ over the heathens and Mohammedans and it will be a time of great joy when Mary, as Mistress and Queen of Hearts, is enthroned."[80] Using almost identical words, St. Louis de Montfort stated some three hundred years ago that Our Lady "will extend the Kingdom of Christ over the idolaters and Moslems, and there will come a glorious era in which Mary will be the ruler and Queen of human hearts."[81]

Exactly when and how this miraculous worldwide religious transformation will take place is still unknown, but there can be no real doubt that it will one day occur. Scripture teaches us that God "wills everyone to be saved and to come to knowledge of the truth" (1 Tim. 2:4)—and because Jesus Himself is "the way and the truth and the life" (Jn. 14:6), the Holy Spirit will surely make it possible for the misguided but sincere followers of Muhammad to come to salvation by acknowledging Jesus as their Savior and accepting the Gospel. Moreover, just as the fanatical Saul of Tarsus became the Church's greatest missionary, so it can be reasonably assumed that the conversion of large numbers of fervent and devout Muslims will lead to a glorious "explosion of evangelization" changing the face of the earth.

## NOTES TO CHAPTER 4

[1] Austin Flannery, O.P., ed. *Vatican Council II: The Conciliar and Post Conciliar Documents* (Costello Publishing Company, 1975).

[2] Thomas W. Petrisko, *The Fatima Prophecies* (St. Andrews Productions, 1998), p. 136.

[3] Michael H. Brown, *The Final Hour* (Faith Publishing Company, 1992), p. 215.

[4] Walid Shoebat and Joel Richardson, *God's War on Terror: Islam, Prophecy, and the Bible* (Top Executive Media, 2008), p. 133.

[5] *Ibid.*, pp. 133-134.

[6] *Ibid.*, end jacket.

[7] William E. Phipps, *Muhammed and Jesus* (Continuum, 1996), as quoted in James A. Beverly, *Understanding Islam* (Thomas Nelson Publishers, 2001), p. 16.

[8] Vincent P. Miceli, S.J., *The Antichrist* (Roman Catholic Books, 1981), p. 126.

[9] *Ibid.*, p. 109.

[10] Barnaby Rogerson, *The Prophet Muhammad* (Hidden Spring, 2003), p. 21.

[11] Keith D. Lewis, *The Catholic Church in History* (Crossroad, 2006), pp. 8-9.

[12] Rogerson, p. 204. The author adds, "Indeed, his immediate successors, men who had known him intimately, were at a complete loss as to what to do when there was a massive influx of non-Arab converts to Islam. Their quandary is ample testimony that there was no master plan to extend Islam beyond the Arabic-speaking peoples" (ibid.).

[13] Mike Aquilina, *The Resilient Church* (The Word Among Us Press, 2007), p. 45.

[14] Alvin J. Schmidt, *The Great Divide* (Regina Orthodox Press, 2004), p. 36.

[15] *Ibid.*, p. 12.

[16] Lewis, pp. 12-13.

[17] Serge Trifkovic, *The Sword of the Prophet* (Regina Orthodox Press, 2002), p. 45.

[18] *Ibid.*, p. 46.

[19] George Sale, "The Life of Mohammed," in *The Koran* (A. L. Burt, 1894), p. 41, as quoted in Schmidt, *The Great Divide*, pp. 13-14.

[20] Rogerson, p. 119.

## Defiance!

21 Schmidt, p. 16.

22 *Ibid.*, p. 34.

23 *Ibid.*, pp. 34-35. This fear wasn't entirely unreasonable, for Muhammad "was once given poisoned meat . . . by a Jewish woman whose husband, father, and brothers had been killed by him" (p. 35).

24 www.truthandgrace.com/mohammaddeathbed.htm

25 Rogerson, pp. 79ff.

26 Aquilina, pp. 46-47.

27 Hilaire Belloc, *The Great Heresies* (Sheed and Ward, 1938; TAN Books and Publishing, 1991), p. 42. Belloc further elaborates on this point:

> . . . *the very foundation of his [Muhammad's] teaching was that prime Catholic doctrine, the unity and omnipotence of God. The attributes of God he also took over in the main from Catholic doctrine: the personal nature, the all-goodness, the timelessness, the providence of God, His creative power as the origin of all things, and His sustenance of all things by His power alone. The world of good spirits and angels and of evil spirits in rebellion against God was part of the teaching, with a chief evil spirit, such as Christendom had recognized. Mohammed preached with insistence that prime Catholic doctrine, on the human side—the immortality of the soul and its responsibility for actions in this life, coupled with the consequent doctrine of punishment and reward after death* (p. 43).

28 Diane Moczar, *Islam at the Gates* (Sophia Institute Press, 2008), p. 6.

29 Surah Al-Nisa, no. 4, verse 175, as quoted in Rogerson, p. 142.

30 Rogerson, p. 142.

31 Trifkovic, pp. 25-26. This author also notes,

> *While the influence of orthodox Christianity upon the Qur'an has been slight, apocryphal and heretical Christian legends are the second most important original source of Qur'anic faith. Experts will also detect influences of Sabaism, of Zoroastrianism, and of native ancient and contemporary Arabian heathen beliefs and practices, either alluded to or included in the Qur'an, including the divine sanction for the practices of polygamy and slavery* (pp. 69-70).

32 *Ibid.*, p. 77.

33 *Ibid.*, p. 68.

34 H. W. Crocker III, *Triumph: The Power and the Glory of the Catholic Church* (Three Rivers Press, 2001), p. 132.

35 Moczar, p. 16.

36 Trifkovic, p. 106.

37 Schmidt, p. 64. Mr. Schmidt adds, "While it is theoretically true that the Koran states 'there is no compulsion in religion,' yet as [historian] Bat Ye'or has correctly observed, 'At no time in history has it been respected.' The *jihad* [holy war], or rather the alternative, forced on the Peoples of

the Book—namely, payment of tribute and submission to Islamic law or the massacre and enslavement of survivors—is, in its very terms, a contravention of the principle of religious freedom" (ibid.).

[38] Moczar, pp. 16-17.

[39] *Ibid.*, p. 16. As the author explains, "The slave was deprived of his liberty, but could rise to relatively high and responsible positions and sometimes even freedom, particularly if he were Muslim. The *dhimmi* on the other hand remained in his 'subdued' state until he converted or died" (ibid.).

[40] Trifkovic, p. 104.

[41] Schmidt, p. 61.

[42] Moczar, p. 17.

[43] *Ibid.*, p. 143. This important fact deserves elaboration: "A recent historian of the subject has calculated that between 1530 . . . and 1780, the Barbary Muslims enslaved at least a million, possibly as many as a million and a quarter, European Christians. The total equals or exceeds the number of black Africans shipped as slaves to the Americas, and that is leaving out the vast numbers of Christians enslaved throughout the former Byzantine Empire as well as the Asian territories taken over by the Ottomans. A single raid could often collect as many slaves from Europe as would be shipped from Africa to America during an entire year (ibid.)."

"One of the tragedies of the modern world is that, even today, slavery still exists in some remote areas: In 1983, the Arab-controlled government of Sudan instituted strict Islamic law in the entire country and subjected black Christians and other non-Muslims of the south in its decree. Then in 1992 a religious decree (fatwa) was ordered that gave justification to the military onslaught against non-Muslims. Since that time, the United Nations and human rights groups have *documented countless cases of slavery* [emphasis added]. People are taken as war booty to perform unpaid household labor and other tasks, or to be used for sexual gratification" – Trifkovic, pp. 177-178.

[44] *Ibid.*, p. 40.

[45] Michael Genin, *Forgotten Catholic Heroes* (Our Sunday Visitor, 2001), p. 12.

[46] Moczar, p. 21.

[47] Aquilina, pp. 68-69.

[48] *Ibid.*, p. 70.

[49] Anne W. Carroll, *Christ the King—Lord of History* (TAN Books and Publishers, 1994), p. 135.

[50] Schmidt, p. 219.

[51] *Ibid.*, p. 145, quoting W. Montgomery Watt, *The Majesty That Was Islam: The Islamic World, 661-1100* (Praeger, 1974), p. 247.

[52] Paul Fregosi, *Jihad in the West: Muslim Conquests from the 7th to the 21st Centuries* (Prometheus Books, 1998), p. 24, as quoted in Schmidt, p. 46.

[53] Trifkovic, p. 97.

[54] Schmidt, p. 148. Relying on the research of Paul Fregosi, the author states, "the Muslim jihads have effected and engulfed far more countries, and for much longer, than did the Crusades in the Middle East. The Crusades were only eight in number, compared to numerous, ongoing Islamic jihads before and after the Crusades. . . . Muslims invaded and occupied Spain for 800 years; Portugal, 600; Greece, 500; Bulgaria, 500; Rumania, 400; Serbia, 400; Sicily, 300; and Hungary, 150. In addition, the Muslims fought in Austria, Italy, Malta, Cyprus, Armenia, Poland, Georgia, Ukraine, and parts of Russia" (ibid.).

[55] *Ibid.,* pp. 52-53.

[56] "Endless Jihad," *A Catholic Answers Special Report* (Catholic Answers, 2003), p. 6.

[57] Schmidt, p. 55.

[58] John Paul II, *Crossing the Threshold of Hope* (Alfred A. Knopf, 1994), p. 94.

[59] Mark Steyn, *America Alone* (Regnery, 2006), p. 62. The author also notes that "there are moderate Muslims, but no moderate Islam. Millions of Muslims just want to get on with their lives, and there are—or were—remote corners of the world where, far from Mecca, Muslim practices reached accommodation with local customs. But all of the official schools of Islamic jurisprudence commend sharia [Islamic law] and a violent jihad. So a 'moderate Muslim' can find no formal authority to support his moderation" (p. 88).

[60] *Ibid.,* p. 89. Mr. Steyn relates the story of Abdul Rahman, "a man on trial for his life in post-Taliban Afghanistan because he had committed the crime of converting to Christianity. 'We will not allow God to be humiliated. This man must die,' said Abdul Raoulf of the nation's principal Muslim body, the Afghan Ulama Council. 'Cut off his head! We will call on the people to pull him into pieces so there's nothing left.' Needless to say, Imam Raoulf is one of Afghanistan's leading 'moderate' clerics." Intense diplomatic pressure from Western governments eventually led to Abdul Rahman being expelled from Afghanistan, instead of being executed.

[61] *Catholic Answers Special Report,* p. 3.

[62] Patrick Poole, as quoted in "Recent U.S. Report Reveals Christians Face Intense Persecution in Muslim Countries," *American Family Association Journal* (Nov. – Dec. 2007), p. 18.

[63] Steyn, p. 17.

[64] Trifkovic, p. 188. The quotation is taken from the April 18, 2001 issue of *Al-Akhbar,* which the author describes as "the second most influential Egyptian daily" newspaper.

[65] Paul M. Weyrich & William S. Lind, *Why Islam Is a Threat to America and the West* (Free Congress Foundation, 2002), p. 9.

[66] As quoted in Schmidt, p. 222.

[67] Robert Spencer, *What Americans Need to Know About Jihad* (David Horowitz Freedom Center, 2007), p. 5.

[68] Steyn, p. 138.

[69] Trifkovic, p. 167. According to the author, "Mass murderers are frequently found to have histories of sexual abuse as children, and Islamic terrorists are no exception. Unlike their lone Western counterparts, however, the abuse of which they are the victims is systemic, and inherent to their societies. They are victimized by virtue of growing up and living in a dysfunctional culture of sexual repression and misogyny, where 'love' is reduced to violent domination and its rejection reflects a deep-seated fear of individuality" (ibid.).

[70] *Whistleblower* magazine, March 2008.

[71] Trifkovic, pp. 138-139.

[72] Steyn, p. 202. The author notes that "Pakistan adopted Islamic law in 1977, Iran in 1979, Sudan in 1984. In the sixties, Nigeria lived under English Common Law; now, half it's in the grip of sharia, and the other half's feeling the squeeze. Today, there are more Muslim nations, more radicalized Muslims within those nations, more and more Muslims living within non-Muslim nations, and more and more Muslims represented in more and more influential transnational institutions" (ibid.).

[73] Kate O'Beirne, "Martyred: Muslim Murder and Mayhem Against Christians," *National Review* (Dec. 3, 2001), p. 38.

[74] Samuel P. Huntington, *The Clash of Civilizations and the Remaking of World Order*, as quoted in O'Beirne, (ibid.), p. 39. Mr. Huntington further notes that "Muslims make up about one-fifth of the world's population but in the 1990s they have been far more involved in intergroup violence than the people of any other civilization."

[75] Fergus M. Bordewich, "Radical Islam's Bloody Battlefield," *Reader's Digest* (Nov. 1997), pp. 170ff.

[76] Weyrich & Lind, p. 1.

[77] Brown, p. 171.

[78] Miceli, p. 266.

[79] Stephen A. Foglein, *The Age of "One Fold and One Shepherd" Is Coming* (Two Hearts Books & Publishers, 1981, 1994), p. 219.

[80] Edward Connor, *Prophecy for Today* (Apostolate of Christian Action, 1956, 1963), p. 45.

[81] *Ibid.*

# Chapter 5

# Dupes and Villains
# of the Reformation

*They will expel you from the synagogues; in fact, the hour*
*is coming when everyone who kills you will think he is*
*offering worship to God. They will do this because they*
*have not known either the Father nor Me.* (Jn. 16:2-3)

Niccolò Machiavelli's *The Prince*, published in 1532, five years
after his death, surely ranks as one of the most cynical books
ever written. His advice to political rulers is to ignore moral
and religious restrictions, and instead take all necessary measures
to assure national (and personal) security and success—no matter
how wicked or indefensible those measures might be. Because
there is no God, Machiavelli claimed, a successful ruler must ignore
the fantasies of eternal reward or punishment, and make cold-
hearted calculations as to his own best interests. That doesn't mean,
according to one author, "that Machiavelli ever advises being evil
merely for its own sake. He does something far more destructive:
evil is offered under the excusing pretext that it is beneficial."[1]

Machiavelli's cynicism is well expressed by his dying words:
"I desire to go to hell and not to Heaven. In the former I shall enjoy
the company of popes, kings, and princes, while in the latter are
only beggars, monks and apostles."[2] Based on his disdain for
religion, he may well have achieved his wish, for in reference to
being merciful, faithful, humane, honest, and religious, he wrote
that it is

> *not necessary for a prince to have all the above-mentioned*
> *qualities, but it is indeed necessary to **appear** [emphasis*
> *added] to have them. Nay, I dare say this, that by having*

*them and always observing them, they are harmful; and by appearing to have them they are useful.*[3]

As noted in Chapter 3, Machiavelli used Cesare Borgia as his model for *The Prince*, but he might also have referred to the example of other rulers using religion for their own purposes at the very time he was writing his guidebook for amoral politicians: large numbers of the princes and nobility of Germany, many of whom—along with other groups in society—supported Martin Luther's revolt against Church authority not out of religious conviction, but for their own political and economic advantage.

As one Catholic historian notes,

*Luther's support came from three groups. Many of the German peasants resented the power and wealth of the Church [even though much of this wealth was used to provide schools, hospitals, and alms-houses], which—because of their rapidly growing nationalism—they regarded as a foreign power. The middle classes (businessmen, merchants and manufacturers) were beginning to practice a form of capitalism. They regarded the Church as an enemy since it condemned some of their business practices. Most importantly, some of the noblemen thought that by rejecting the Church they could get more power and seize Church lands to increase their wealth.*[4]

Martin Luther and the other so-called Reformers may have been sincere in their desire for a renewal of the Church (which was admittedly in serious need of reform); however, they soon became pawns of influential figures with their own agenda, or were swept aside by powerful historical and societal forces unleashed by their ill-conceived revolt against the established order.

## Luther

According to the *New Catholic Encyclopedia*, "There is scarcely a single instance in which one individual has had such significance in a tremendous historical upheaval as Martin Luther assumes in the Reformation. To consider . . . that he was but an occasion and not a cause of the Reformation, is a view that no serious student of the period now accepts."[5]

The Dominican friar Tommaso Campanella, whose 1632

book *De Antichristo* had identified Muhammad as one of the Antichrist's precursors (see Chapter 4), placed Luther in this same category, quoting the opinion of a famous Catholic preacher of the day, Serafino Frimano, that the Reformer was undoubtedly the Antichrist's final herald—a judgment which may have been shared by the great Church theologian and Cardinal St. Robert Bellarmine.[6]

Many Protestants, of course (during the Reformation itself, and in the centuries which followed) regarded Luther as a saintly and heroic figure fighting against religious superstition and repression. Modern scholarship takes a more balanced approach, seeing Luther as neither as a saint or a villain, but as a religious figure genuinely concerned that the Church teach true doctrine. Even conceding this point, however, there is much evidence that Luther was a highly coarse and unbalanced individual, and it can be argued that his clumsy efforts to improve the state of Christianity in the 16th century actually made the situation far worse.

Luther was "often prone to drastic and bizarre mood swings,"[7] and according to one of his biographers, "three of Luther's contemporaries claimed that in his early or middle twenties, Luther had suddenly fallen to the floor in the choir during a reading of Mark 9:17 [the story of the boy possessed by an evil spirit, whom the apostles were unable to cast out], screaming for no apparent reason in a way that was foreign and frightening. Such torment followed Luther to the grave, as did his conviction that the Church was somehow to blame for his spiritual anguish."[8] He seems to have been obsessed with the devil,[9] while also suffering from severe emotional difficulties:

> *If anything at all can be said with certainty about Martin Luther, it is that he was deeply and chronically troubled by a combination of doubts and despair about his salvation and a sense of utter impotence in the face of temptations and sin. . . . Considering that Luther himself admits to an obsessive concern with his own sinfulness, as well as an inability to resist temptation, it seems reasonable to conclude that he suffered from scrupulosity, and even Lutheran scholars will admit to this.[10]*

One historian describes Luther as being "violent, incapable of restraint, poise or loyalty towards an adversary, and yet a lover of material order, of civil and religious discipline. Added to this, he had a vivid imagination haunted by strange visions and irresistible obsessions. . . ."[11] Luther was also known for his constant use of vulgarity, a weakness that shocked and dismayed even his friends and supporters.[12] Moreover, his confrontational temperament was ill-suited for the steady but careful program of reform Christianity truly needed. His ninety-five theses, posted on the cathedral door in Wittenberg (the typical means of proposing a public debate), were almost entirely defensible from a theological perspective,[13] but his gruff nature and mistrust of human reason and intellectual inquiry practically guaranteed misunderstandings and bitter controversies.

Luther's initially limited and largely reasonable aims soon spiraled out of control—to the point where, for the first time in Church history, he sought to excise or remove previously-established and accepted teachings about God from Christianity:

*Possessed now by the spirit of disorder and opposition to law, and jealous of the authority of the Church and the God-given supremacy of her visible head, he conceived the idea of a new religion, which he thought in his vanity he was capable of formulating. Forthwith, without the shadow of a pretense of direct and divine commission, he began to construct what he foolishly considered a church, and then assumed the right to inflict and impose his self-made work upon his fellow men. . . . In advancing this claim [supremacy of the individual conscience without Church interference], so destructive to the authority of the Church, he asserted a right never before recognized; a right, let it be understood, never known under any other form of revealed religion; a right never allowed even under Jewish theocracy; and a right hardly ever exercised among the more enlightened pagans. His program was one of the most daring in all human history.[14]*

A central target of this daring program was the Church's teaching on the Eucharist:

*The Protestant revolution instigated the rejection of many Catholic beliefs, traditions and practices. Yet, probably the abandonment of the Holy Sacrifice of the Mass was    the most serious of its effects. With no Mass, the Eucharist, the Living Presence of Jesus Christ that is meant to be a source of strength for all souls, was abandoned. According to some writers, this was a primary goal of Martin Luther's efforts. It was an insidious goal, for it sought to deliberately remove belief in Christ's True Presence in the Catholic Church and the world.[15]*

Because he undermined belief in teachings dating back to Christ Himself, and denied the authority of the Church on theological and moral matters, it's not surprising that Luther—lacking any religious foundation other than his own self-serving interpretation of Scripture—failed to maintain a consistent, logical position. For instance, in 1520, while hiding from Church authorities, he urged Christians to "vanquish heretics with books, not with burning"; a decade later, however, while implementing his own religious system, he uged civil rulers to execute without mercy all who preached false doctrine[16] (as defined by him, of course). This lack of intellectual and moral consistency also carried over to other teachings:

*He stubbornly referred to the pope as the "Antichrist" and rejected all but two of the seven sacraments. His former emphasis on faith developed into a dogmatic insistence on "faith alone, apart from works," a principle that contradicted both Scripture and tradition. (He inserted the word "alone" into Romans 3:28, about justification by faith, when he translated the New Testament.) Luther established himself with the same authority that he had denied the popes. He even went so far as to approve polygamy for a nobleman who had tired of his first wife.[17] A glaring example of Luther's theological inconsistency (or perhaps even dishonesty) involved his attempt to harmonize the Letter of James with his beliefs: "No matter how Luther translated it, the passage from James [2:14-26] clashed headlong with his rejection of 'works of righteousness.' Finally, he resolved the dilemma by dismissing the Letter of James as an 'epistle of straw' which 'contains nothing evangelical,' and relegated it to the back of his Bible among the apocryphal books,"[18] and when challenged on this and other arbitrary decisions shaping his translation of the Bible into German, he responded with anger and arrogance.*[19]

It's a truism of history that ideas have consequences—and even though many people were unaware of, or unconcerned with, the theological turmoil Luther was causing, everyone in 16th century Germany was affected by the social upheaval instigated by the Reformation—much to Luther's own surprise. In the words of Catholic historian Hilaire Belloc,

> *So far from leading, Luther fell behind in the furious mill race he had unwittingly let loose. He was frightened of it and unprepared for it. Authority took advantage of such hesitation in the man whose name was already used as a label for the new anarchy.*[20]

If Luther wasn't at first quite ready to take the Protestant principle of "each man his own pope" to its logical conclusion, there were many others who had no such qualms. Belloc continues,

> *Luther's own Sovereign, the Elector of Saxony, and a mass of small squires and cadets, seeing before them independence and the requisition for Church wealth, smelt opportunity for themselves and their fortunes in this still blind, almost universal protest and upheaval against established order as represented by the titles and claims to authority of the Emperor, and by the organization and endowment of the Church. Before the end of 1519 Luther had gone through a revolution within his own mind, and also as to his position. He had become a violent opponent of the whole Church system. He had allied himself for the moment with every form of discontent. He was the hero—and glad to be the hero—of a general insurgence.*[21]

The general rebellion against authority in German society (which Luther would later denounce in his tract *Against the Murdering, Thieving Hordes of Peasants*, while calling for the authorities to "smite, stab and slay all you can"[22]) was paralleled by a similar collapse of religious discipline. The Lutherans, as they became known, rejected the validity of all monastic vows, in some cases attacking convents and "liberating" the nuns residing there for marriage.[23] Luther himself married a former nun, Katarina von Bora, in 1526.

Violence and disorder soon spread beyond the boundaries of Germany; for instance, "A Lutheran mob descended on Rome in

1527, sacking the city, desecrating churches, raping the women, and torturing Catholic men, women, and children."[24] Wars of religion followed, as Emperor Charles V, a devout Catholic and highly qualified leader, tried to reestablish religious and political unity in his realm; however, his efforts were complicated by a treasonous alliance of Germanic Lutheran princes (the Schmalkdic League), and later a cynical alliance of Catholic France, with the Ottoman Turks.

Historian Paul Johnson called the Protestant Reformation "one of the great tragedies of human history, and the central tragedy of Christianity," echoing the sentiments of the some of the Reformers themselves. Philip Melancthon, Luther's close friend and colleague, lamented, "All the waters of the Elba [the Elbe River in Germany] would not provide enough tears to weep over the disasters of the Reform: the ill is without remedy," and Luther himself wrote shortly before his death,

*I must confess that my doctrines have produced many scandals. I cannot deny it, and often this frightens me, especially when my conscience reminds me that I destroyed the situation in which the Church found itself, all calm and tranquility, under the Papacy.*[25]

Though many consider Martin Luther a great religious leader and the hero of the Protestant Reformation, his legacy is an unhappy one.[26] St. Paul, writing from prison, had urged his converts to act with humility and patience, bearing with one another and preserving a spirit of unity and peace (Eph. 4:2-3). Luther and the other reformers, for all their good intentions, failed to do this, obviating Our Lord's prayer that all His followers might be one (Jn. 17:21). A final judgment, of course, must be left to God, but it's difficult to deny that by rending the unity of the Church, they did a grave disservice to the Body of Christ.

## Other Reformers

Ulrich Zwingli was a priest in Switzerland who had great difficulty observing his vow of celibacy.[27] He eagerly joined Luther's revolt against Church authority, married his mistress (who gave him a son four months later), and called for an ever-more radical rejection of Catholic teachings and practices. Zwingli somehow interpreted Luther's concept of the "priesthood of all believers" to mean that he himself was the most important of the reformers—an interpretation Luther angrily rejected. This question of the real leadership of the Reformation became moot, however, when Zwingli was killed leading troops in battle against a Catholic army in 1531.

The most important of the reformers, other than Luther himself, was undoubtedly John Calvin, a French intellectual who was invited to Geneva to "reform" the city along Protestant lines. Under his harsh and unforgiving leadership, the city became something of a religious police state (equal in severity and religious intolerance to some of the stricter Islamic societies):

> *The behavior, language and opinions of the citizens were subject to perpetual and ever-present inquisition. Penalties were exacted for purely religious or moral faults as well as for harmless games and even most innocent dances. From 1541 to 1546 alone fifty-eight death sentences were carried out and seventy-six people were banished.*[28]

Capital offenses included adultery, fornication, blasphemy, heresy, idolatry, and striking a parent, and in his *Institutes of the Christian Religion*, Calvin concluded that the Lord "commands all those who are disobedient to their parents to be put to death." As one historian notes, "The Catholic Church promised a sinner absolution through the sacrament of penance. The Calvinists looked to erase sin by erasing the sinner."[29]

A recent convert to Catholicism from the Reformed tradition (the religious denominations tracing their origin back to the reformer of Geneva) writes,

> *I recognized that my own founder, John Calvin, was a self-important, arrogant man who was brutal to his enemies, never accepted personal responsibility, and condemned anyone who disagreed with him. He called himself a prophet and ascribed divine authority to his own teaching. This contrasted rather starkly with what I was learning about Catholic theologians. Many of them were saints, meaning they had lived lives of heroic charity and self-denial. Even the greatest of them—men like Augustine and Thomas Aquinas—also recognized that they had*

*no personal authority to define the dogma of the Church.*[30]

The words of yet another convert serve as a fitting summary of the harm caused by all those who rejected Church authority: "They chose to deal with the problems in the 16th-century Church, not by following the way of prayer and humility and the Cross, but by following the path of rebellion."[31] Even though the Church amazed her adversaries by her rapid and unexpected resurgence (gaining millions of new members in Central and South America, and experiencing a time of vitality and renewal during the Counter-Reformation, ushered in by the Council of Trent), the effects of these tragic decisions by the early Protestants remain with us today.

## Protestant Errors and Excesses

The words of St. Gregory the Great, given almost 1000 years before the Protestant Reformation, might be applied to some of the religious and political leaders of the 16th century: ". . . let the haughty be told that, when they exalt themselves, they fall into the imitation of the apostate angel."[32]Jesus rebuked His followers for arguing among themselves over which of them was the most important (Mk. 9:35-37), but many religious leaders throughout the history of Christianity—Catholic, Orthodox, and Protestant alike—have found it difficult to take His lesson to heart, and the resulting anger, suspicion, and enmity benefit only the devil.

If pride was the defining sin of the religious leaders of the Reformation, greed was a foremost motivation of the political leaders—and the two groups sometimes worked closely together. As Hilaire Belloc explains,

*The first act of the Reformers, wherever they were successful, was to allow the rich to seize these funds* [i.e., the property of the Church]. *And the intensity of the fighting everywhere depended upon the determination of those who had looted the Church to keep their loot, and of those who tried to restore the Church to recover the Church wealth. . . . The French Crown, dreading the increase of power which this loot would give to the class immediately below it, resisted the movement, hence the French religious wars; while in England a child King and two women succeeding each other on the throne permitted the rich to get away with the Church spoils. Hence the absence of religious wars in England.*[33]

In Germany, as the Lutheran leader Melancthon admitted, the princes "do not care the least about religion, they are only anxious to get dominion in their hands, to be free from the control of the bishops; for a slight alteration in their theological garb they escaped from the [ecclesiastical] taxes and courts, and could appropriate pleasant parcels of ecclesiastical property." Melachthon summarized the situation by noting, "Under cover of the Gospel, the princes were only intent on the plunder of the churches."[34] Following the lead of Henry VIII in England, rulers in Scandinavia and Denmark also began converting to Lutheranism in order to seize Church wealth.

The Church was furthermore the victim of intense, even satanic, fury; Catholics frequently suffered persecution and violence where the Reformation gained the upper hand (though it must be noted that Protestants were also sometimes the victims of violent repression). In many places in Europe, "Calvinist and Huguenot [French Protestant] mobs were destroying Catholic churches, killing priests, and stealing Catholic property."[35] In the Dutch city of Gorcum, for example, nineteen religious and diocesan priests were taken captive by Calvinist forces, tortured, humiliated, and threatened with death unless they denied the Real Presence and the authority of the pope; when they refused to do so, they were hanged and their bodies desecrated.[36]

# Henry VIII

England was initially untouched by the Protestant Reformation, for King Henry VIII was opposed to Luther's errors; he even wrote a small book denouncing the Lutheran heresy—for which the pope gave him the title "Defender of the Faith" (a title which, ironically, English monarchs continue to claim for themselves to this day). However, the Church's unwillingness to annul Henry's marriage to Catherine of Aragon led him into revolt against the authority of the pope. Hilaire Belloc, writing in 1936, noted that Henry *is rightly regarded as the author of that great disaster, the English*

*Reformation. By this disaster the only one of the important districts of Europe which broke away from Christendom in the sixteenth century was turned against the general civilization of Europe. If England had not broken off, the Reformation would have failed and our civilization would have been today one Christian thing. It is impossible to exaggerate the importance of this historical catastrophe. It has had effects which have gone on spreading from that long distant date, more than 400 years ago, to our own time. . . .[37]*

Belloc also notes that "Henry had tried to keep England Catholic without the Pope, but he failed, and after his death in 1547 the break-up of religion in England began."[38] This process was assisted by the royal dissolution of English monasteries and the confiscation of their properties, urged by Henry's advisor Thomas Cromwell. Most of the loot went to nobles and great landowners, who thus had a vested interest in promoting the Reformation; moreover, the break-up of the monasteries—most of which were actively involved in caring for the poor and the dispossessed—was greatly detrimental to English society.[39]

Contrary to the popular image of Henry VIII as a strong, decisive leader, the king was impulsive and easily manipulated—though he was capable of turning on his self-serving advisors with sudden and unpredictable fury. As Belloc describes, he was known for

*extreme selfishness, which grew upon him with the years, as selfishness always does in selfish men, probably passed at last the boundary of sanity, and this showed itself especially in the horrible acts of cruelty in the last part of his career . . . in the orders he gave, a sort of hellish savagery and greed of suffering and gloat over the agonies of his victims—such as those of the unfortunate Friar Forest, whom he had roasted over a slow fire—and he mixed up horrors of this sort with the idea of grandeur. He seemed to think that they enhanced his stature in the eyes of his contemporaries and subjects. He came at last to rule by terror, and . . . his sudden changes and his violent laws and edicts showed a crazy lack of balance.[40]*

The story of Henry's desire for Anne Boleyn, the second of his six wives, and her eventual execution for treason, is well known; of greater significance, of course, are the consequences of the king's inability to control his desires. One Church historian writes, "What sinister power was it that made Protestants of a king and a nation who did not want to be Protestants at all, and brought hundreds of loyal Catholics to a cruel death? It was the demon of lust. All the world knows what happened to Anne Boleyn, for whose sake England separated from the Holy See, and to the other wives of Henry."[41]

The king chose to deny the religious authority of the pope in his realm; in his Act of Supremacy he declared himself to be head of the Church in England, and he required public acceptance of the Act by all prominent civil and religious figures. This helped make Henry's reign, as one scholar noted, a long nightmare of "truth forever on the scaffold, wrong forever on the throne."[42]

St. Thomas More, Henry's chancellor or prime minister, had noted that "A man may very well lose his head and yet come to no harm—yea, I say, to unspeakable good and everlasting happiness."[43] More had the opportunity to witness to his own words about the blessings of martyrdom, for in 1535 he was executed for treason: namely, for refusing to acknowledge Henry's authority over the Church. On the scaffold, he claimed to be "the king's good servant, but God's first," and he died confident in the final victory of the Church.[44] An English bishop, St. John Fisher, was also executed in defense of the Faith (but, sadly, most English bishops acquiesced in Henry's usurpation of the Church's prerogatives).

Henry always had a great fear of death, and his own demise, in 1547 when he was age 55, was not a happy one. He had become enormously obese, and during his final year was no longer capable of walking; "he spent his last eight days in bed, too weak even to lift a glass to his lips,"[45] and died amid the terrible stench of his bursting ulcers. Henry's final words are variously reported as being "All is lost. Monks, monks, monks!"[46] (perhaps an expression of guilt and regret over his dissolution of the English monasteries), or "So, now all is gone—empire, body, and soul!"[47]

It had been prophesied that "the dogs would lick his bones, as they did Ahab's" (cf. 1 Kgs. 21:19; 22:38), and this bizarre prophecy was fulfilled: when the king's body was being transported to Windsor for burial, during an overnight halt the coffin burst open, and in the morning the guards discovered dogs licking Henry's corpse.[48]

## Royal Parasites and Panderers

Like most monarchs, Henry, and in their turn his daughters Mary and Elizabeth, had certain royal servants and advisors whose first loyalty was to themselves, hangers-on willing to say or do whatever might be necessary for their own personal advantage. The bumbling, cynicism, and scheming of some of these figures contributed mightily to the tragic course of the Reformation in England.

For instance, Cardinal Thomas Wolsey, Catholic Archbishop of York, served as Henry's chancellor for fourteen years, during which he diligently placed his master's interests ahead of those of the Church, while making sure he himself was amply rewarded. As one author notes, Wolsey was "sycophantic and unprincipled. His 'loyalty' [was] merely a pretense to conceal his lust for gold and glory,"[49] and his lavish lifestyle gained him much notoriety. When Wolsey failed to obtain papal agreement to an annulment of Henry's first marriage, as he had foolishly promised, he fell from power. A year later he was arrested on false charges of treason, and died while being taken to London for trial, after lamenting, "If I had served God as diligently as I have done my king, He would not now have given me over to my grey hairs."[50]

Another powerful servant of Henry VIII who eventually fell from the king's grace was Thomas Cromwell, whom Hilaire Belloc describes as "not only the lay head of the country—a despotic minister with absolute power doing what he willed—but . . . also the spiritual head, for Henry delegated to him all his own spiritual power."[51] Concerned only with gaining further wealth and authority for himself, Cromwell flattered Henry, did everything possible to promote the schism with Rome, arrested prominent Catholics who remained loyal to the pope, interfered with the compliant bishops' administration of their dioceses, and was the driving force behind the confiscation of Church and monastic properties. Like his political counterparts in Germany, Cromwell "sided with the Protestants—not out of religious belief, for he had none, but because they were allies in centralizing power under the king"[52] (and thus indirectly himself).

When Cromwell finally overstepped himself (angering Henry by arranging his marriage to the unattractive Ann of Cleves for political reasons), the king turned against him and had him sentenced to death. The condemned man's desperate groveling was to no avail, but then Cromwell—widely known as an atheist— underwent a religious conversion. In the words of Belloc,

> Now that he was about to die, he declared himself, to the astonishment of everybody, a firm adherent of the national and traditional faith [Catholicism]. His sincerity has been doubted, but without sufficient grounds. . . . when he was face-to-face with death and had to deal with it, somehow he admitted Catholic truth and confessed his acceptance of it. The phenomenon is not uncommon and is quite explicable by all that we know of the human mind.[53]

Scripture tells us that "the king's wrath is [a] messenger of death" (Prv. 16:14), and in Cromwell's case this was literally true—but Henry's wrath may have been a blessing in disguise, prompting that repentance which saved him from a far worse divine judgment.

No deathbed conversion is recorded for one of the most sinister villains of the Reformation: Sir William Cecil (known as Lord Burghley), royal counselor first to the devoutly Catholic Queen Mary, then to her insincere Protestant half-sister Queen Elizabeth. During Mary's reign, he pretended to be a committed Catholic (even to the point of visibly carrying an enormous rosary); after her death, his behind-the-scenes maneuvering helped place Elizabeth on the throne, and then he made himself her secretary of state. Describing the new state of affairs, Belloc states:

> The truth about Elizabeth is this. She was the puppet or figure-head of the group of new millionaires established upon the loot of religion begun in her father's time. They had at their head the unique genius of William Cecil, who, in spite of dangerous opposition, accomplished what might have seemed the impossible task of digging up the Catholic Faith by the roots from English soil, stamping out the Mass, and shepherding the younger generation of a reluctant people into a new religious mood.[54]

Cecil accomplished his nefarious aims through an adroit mixture of cunning, deception, and ruthlessness. He tricked Philip II of Spain, a devout Catholic and would-be suitor of Elizabeth, into reassuring the pope that patience and inactivity by the Church would surely heal the schism; stirred up national feeling by identifying Protestantism with English independence and security; and established a very efficient spy network—somewhat akin to a modern-day secret police—which collected enough evidence of "rebellion" to justify an outright persecution of the Church, while hypocritically insisting that "no man suffered for religion, but only for treason." It's little wonder that Belloc called him "one of the greatest and certainly one of the vilest men that ever lived."[55]

## Elizabeth "the Great"

It's commonly noted that "history is written by the victors," and we see proof of this in the widespread belief, fostered by Protestant apologists during and after the Elizabethan era, that the short reign of "Bloody Mary" (1553-1558) was a time of terror and repression, while the much longer reign of "Good Queen Bess" (1558-1603) was an age of national unity, religious enlightenment, and a flowering of English civilization. The truth, of course, is rather different.

For example, many fewer persons were executed for religious reasons under Queen Mary than during the reigns of both her father Henry VIII and her half-sister Elizabeth I.[56] Also, Mary's decisions, even when misguided, were based on a sincere desire to restore and protect the well-being of Catholicism in England; for Elizabeth (and her royal advisors), however, religion was just a means to enhance her political power. This is most clearly seen in her cynical promise to a dying Mary that, if appointed as her successor, she would reign as a Catholic and safeguard the interests of the Church. (As the illegitimate daughter of Anne Boleyn, Elizabeth had no claim to the English throne, unlike Mary Stuart, known as "Mary Queen of Scots"—who would later be executed under Elizabeth. However, Cecil convinced Philip II, husband of the dying Queen Mary, that having Mary Stuart reigning in England would be gravely dangerous to Spain, and so Philip convinced his wife to choose Elizabeth instead—a disastrous decision he regretted to his dying day.)

Upon becoming queen, Elizabeth—at Cecil's urging—quickly went back on her word, reestablishing the Act of Supremacy and replacing Catholic bishops (restored under Mary) with Anglicans (that is, adherents of the Protestant Church of England). Before long, a widespread persecution of the Church ensued. Attending Catholic Mass was made illegal, and priests were subject to execution as traitors; persons caught at Mass, or who refused to attend Anglican services, could be fined or imprisoned.[57] Brutal methods, reminiscent of Henry VIII, were now combined with skillful public relations; as one historian notes,

> *Elizabeth's huge advantage over her father is that she made the Anglican Church popular. She did so by displacing the cult of the Virgin Mary with the cult of the Virgin Queen who was too devoted to her people to marry. Royal processions replaced religious ones. She became the embodiment of England.*[58]

The carefully-concealed truth about the "virgin" queen and her sexual escapades was quite disedifying;[59] far more significant, however, was the ruthless persecution of the Church conducted in her name. Some priests were hanged (still in their chasubles) for their opposition to Anglicanism; many others quietly went into hiding or exile.[60] A Jesuit priest who refused to acknowledge the queen's authority over the Church, John Nelson, was hanged, disemboweled, and quartered—a scene that became fairly routine, and involved clergy and laity alike. Indeed, over six hundred Catholic men and women died as martyrs in post-Reformation England.[61]

St. Margaret Clitherow, arrested for hiding priests in her home, was martyred by being crushed by heavy stones—a slow and agonizing death she endured cheerfully while praying for her persecutors.[62] Bl. Christopher Buxton, one of the seven Martyrs of Canterbury (executed in 1588), was an Englishman who studied in a foreign seminary, was ordained a priest in Rome, and who returned in secret to minister to the Catholics of England (a frequent occurrence under Elizabeth's persecution). When arrested with his companions, it was thought that he—as the youngest—might be persuaded to recant after seeing the gruesome execution of the others; however, he responded, "I will not purchase corruptible life at so dear a rate; and indeed, if I had a hundred lives, I would willingly lay down all in defense of my faith."[63]

Another martyr was the brilliant Jesuit priest Bl. Edmund Campion; after his arrest, he was taken to London and presented to

Elizabeth herself, who promised him great rewards if he renounced his faith and became an Anglican priest. When he refused, he was severely tortured, convicted of treason on false evidence, and condemned to death.[64] At his trial he unmasked the hypocrisy of his judges, stating, "In condemning us, you condemn all your own ancestors—all the ancient priests, bishops, and kings—all that was once the glory of England, the isle of saints, and the most devoted child of the See of Peter. For what have we taught, however you may qualify it with the odious name of treason, that they did not uniformly teach?"[65]

Bl. Robert Southwell, another Jesuit priest (and an accomplished poet) martyred in 1595, was fully aware of the consequences of bearing witness to the truth; as he wrote, "Christianity is a warfare, and Christians spiritual soldiers. In its beginning, our faith was planted in the poverty, infamy, persecution and death of Christ; in its progress, it was watered by the blood of God's saints; and it cannot come to full growth unless it be fostered with the showers of the martyrs."[66]

The Jesuit's words were prophetic, for English Catholicism endured, in spite of persecution by Elizabeth and her immediate successors, and officially sanctioned discrimination for several more centuries—and today the Catholic Church in Great Britain is more spiritually vibrant than Anglicanism, England's official religion (in spite of the latter's larger numbers and greater properties—many of them stolen from the Church in the 16th century).

The fate of the martyrs was far more blessed than that of Elizabeth herself, for as Belloc relates,

*And to what a death did the unhappy woman come! A death of madness and despair. The late Hugh Benson [an English priest and scholar] wrote a most powerful pamphlet contrasting that death with the holy, happy, and pious death of Mary. She crouched on the ground for hours, one may say for days, refusing to speak, with her finger in her mouth, after having suffered horrible delusions—thinking that she had an iron band pressing round her head and on one occasion seeing herself in a sort of vision as a little figure surrounded with flames.*[67]

In her final days, Elizabeth tried to force herself to remain awake (fearing she might die in her sleep), and she refused the spiritual ministrations of her Anglican clergy (contemptuously referring to them as "hedge priests"). Her last recorded words were "All my possessions for a moment of time!,"[68] though a longer version has her saying, "O my God! I have come to the end of it—the end, the end. To have only one life, and to have done with it! To have lived, and loved, and triumphed, and now to know it is over! One may defy everything but this."[69] Needless to say, these are hardly the words of someone expecting a merciful judgment.

# Philosophical Consequences of the Reformation

Protestantism's success in undermining the authority of the Church established a precedent that worldly men—including ambitious rulers and self-important philosophers—would exploit as fully as possible in the so-called Age of Enlightenment. St. Vincent Ferrer had observed that "Christ, the master of humility, manifests His truth only to the humble and hides Himself from the proud,"[70] and various intellectuals strove to outdo one another in demonstrating the veracity of these words.

René Descartes, for instance, claimed that because the only thing whose existence cannot be doubted is doubt itself, the self-awareness of the doubter is the foundation of all truth. (This reasoning is the origin of the famous summary of his thought, *Cogito, ergo sum*—"I think, therefore I am.") One modern commentator explains the significance of this revolutionary paradigm shift:

*Descartes' approach to religion is not only false, but creates the characteristically modern belief that God is whatever we "very clearly and very distinctly" imagine Him to be. And that means we fashion God after our own hearts, rather than our hearts and religion after God. Since God was caused by our thinking Him, then He must only be a thought and not a reality, a mere subjective projection of our own ego. . . . Rather than taking ourselves to be made in the image of God, with all the moral limitations that entails, we believe that we are self-creators with no limit but our own ever-increasing power.[71]*

Extreme subjectivism inevitably leads to a denial of God's existence, and atheism—a relatively recent historical phenomenon, largely limited to Western society[72]—has had disastrous effects for humanity, primarily because "in many respects all of modernity is an attempt to replace the biblical account of Eden with an entirely new story (just as it is an attempt to replace a heavenly kingdom with an earthly utopia)."[73] However, bitter experience—particularly in the 20th century, in which countless millions died to the policies of the officially atheist states of Nazi Germany, the Soviet Union, and Red China—has shown that "the old [Christian] 'myths' now . . . have a curious ring of truth. The safest place to put Heaven, as some wise Deity must have realized, is not on earth."[74] Indeed, the 19th century agnostic Ernest Renan acknowledged,

> Let us enjoy the liberty of the sons of God, but let us take care lest we become accomplices in the diminution of virtue which would menace society if Christianity were to grow weak. What should we do without it? . . . If rationalism wishes to govern the world without regard to the religious needs of the soul, the experience of the French Revolution is there to teach us the consequences of such a blunder.[75]

In other words, atheism is extremely unrealistic in its assumptions about human nature,[76] and—in addition to its potentially tragic personal consequences—a sure formula for moral disaster, and even widespread social collapse, if implemented or imposed on a large-scale basis.

Space limitations prevent a thorough examination of this subject, but a brief reference to the 18th century Scottish philosopher and atheist David Hume may be instructive. An extreme empiricist,[77] Hume insisted that nothing can be known without personal experience, and that everything else we believe to exist—including notions of self, substance, and God—results merely from our unreliable and unverifiable impressions. His life was filled with worldly success and distinction,[78] but when he died in 1776, his last recorded words suggested a terrible fate: "I am in flames!"[79] Ironically, a few years before his death Hume had predicted the imminent death of Christianity—but the first meeting of the Bible Society of Edinburgh was held in the very room where he died.[80]

The Protestant Reformation may have opened the door to the skepticism and atheism of the Enlightenment, but in the words of Ven. John Henry Newman, "Error may flourish for a time, but truth will prevail in the end. The only effect of error ultimately is to promote truth."[81] Sterile philosophies will one day be discredited and swept away, and religious rebellions and disunity will cease; the dire effects of the Protestant Reformation will be finally be erased, for in the words of St. Bridget of Sweden, "The time will come when there will be one flock and one shepherd, one Faith and one clear knowledge of God."[82]

## NOTES TO CHAPTER 5

1. Benjamin Wiker, *10 Books that Screwed Up the World* (MJF Books, 2008), p. 12.

2. http.users.belgacom.net.gc674645.grave.last.word.htm.

3. Wiker, pp. 9-10.

4. Anne W. Carroll, *Christ the King, Lord of History* (TAN Books and Publishers, 1994), p. 219.

5. *New Catholic Encyclopedia* (Catholic University of America, 1967), "Luther," Vol. VIII, p. 1091.

6. Vincent P. Miceli, S.J., *The Antichrist* (Roman Catholic Books, 1981), p. 126.

7. Michael H. Brown, *The Last Secret* (Queenship Publishing, 2007), p. 193.

8. Ibid., p. 194. The biographer referred to is Erik H. Erikson, author of *Young Man Luther* (Norton, 1958).

9. Christopher Nugent, *Masts of Satan* (Christian Classics, 1983, 1989), p. 90. This author writes, ". . . out of Luther comes, we are told, 'Protestantism's diabolical preoccupation.' We are even told that he 'filled Germany with devils.' This relates to such things as his existential if not physical struggles with the devil, a superfluity of Satan in sermon and tract, his encouragement of the Faust legend, and the prestige his support lent the witch-hunts. For Luther God was invisible and hidden—the *deus absconditus*—but the devil visible and ubiquitous. In fact, 'the whole world was possessed by Satan'" (*ibid.*).

10. Joel Peters, *Scripture Alone?* (TAN Books and Publishers, 1991), p. 62.

11. Msgr. Léon Cristiani, *Heresies and Heretics*, trans. Roderick Bright (Hawthorn Books, Vol. 136 of the Twentieth Century Encyclopedia of Catholicism, 1959), p. 80.

12. Msgr. Patrick F. O'Hare, LL.D., *The Facts About Luther* (Frederick Pustet Co., 1916; republished by TAN Books and Publishers, 1987), p. 345.

13. Hilaire Belloc, *How the Reformation Happened* (TAN Books and Publishers, 1928, 1992), p. 41.

14. O'Hare, pp. 134-135.

15. Thomas W. Petrisko, *Mother of the Secret* (Queenship Publishing, 1997), p.60.

16 Virgil Hurley, *Speaker's Source Book of New Illustrations* (Word Publishing 1995), p. 234.

17 Mike Aquilina, *The Resilient Church* (The Word Among Us Press, 2007), p. 88.

18 Keith D. Lewis, *The Catholic Church in History* (Crossroad, 2006), p. 86.

19 In regard to Catholic complaints about his addition of the word "alone" to Rom. 3:28 (dishonestly making it say that we are "justified by faith *alone*,"), Luther responded, "If your Papist makes such an unnecessary row about the word 'alone,' say right out to him: 'Dr. Martin Luther will have it so,' and say: 'Papists and asses are one and the same thing.' I will have it so, and I order it to be so, and my will is reason enough. I know very well that the word 'alone' is not in the Latin or the Greek text, and it was not necessary for the Papists to tell me that. It is true those letters are not in it, which letters the jackasses look at, as a cow stares at a new gate. . . . It shall remain in my New Testament, and if all the Popish donkeys were to get mad and beside themselves, they will not get it out" – quoted by John Stoddard, *Rebuilding a Lost Faith* (TAN Books and Publishers), pp. 136-137. Perhaps never before has the traditional saying that "Every translator is a traitor" rung so true. 20 Belloc, pp. 42-43.

21 *Ibid.*, pp. 44-45.

22 H. W. Crocker III, *Triumph: The Power and the Glory of the Catholic Church* (Three Rivers Press, 2001), p. 248.

23 Aquilina, p. 87.

24 *Ibid.*

25 Diane Moczar, *Ten Dates Every Catholic Should Know* (Sophia Institute Press, 2005), p. 99.

26 An unverifiable legend states that during an exorcism, an evil spirit was forced to reveal that Luther repented and was reconciled to the Church on his deathbed, thereby escaping damnation; because of his grave sin of destroying the unity of the Western Church, however, he was sentenced to 500 years in purgatory. If this admittedly doubtful legend is true, the father of Protestantism will only enter into Heaven in the year 2046.

27 Cristiani, p. 81.

28 *Ibid.*, p. 86.

29 Crocker, p. 254.

30 A. David Anders, Ph.D., "A Protestant Historian Discovers the Catholic Church," *The Coming Home Network Newsletter* (May 2010), p. 5.

31 Julie Swenson, "This I Seek: To Dwell in the House of the Lord," *Surprised by Truth*, ed. by Patrick Madrid (Basilica Press, 1994), p. 135.

32 Rosemary Ellen Guiley, *The Quotable Saint* (Checkmark Books, 2002), p. 133.

33 Hilaire Belloc, *The Great Heresies* (Sheed and Ward, 1938; TAN Books and Publishers, 1991), p. 121.

[34] William Durant, *The Reformation* (MJF Books, 1957), as quoted in Michael Genin, *Forgotten Catholic Heroes* (Our Sunday Visitor), 2001, pp. 92-93.

[35] Genin, p. 60.

[36] *Butler's Lives of the Saints,* "Ss. Nicholas Pieck and His Companions," Vol. III, p. 56, entry for July 9.

[37] Hilaire Belloc, *Characters of the Reformation* (Sheed and Ward, 1936; TAN Books and Publishers, 1992), p. 16.

[38] *Ibid.,* p. 17.

[39] *Ibid.,* p. 69. Belloc notes that "the 'dissolution' of the monasteries (and the guilds) led immediately to the creation of a large class of destitute persons who lived in misery, or who adopted begging and thievery as the means of livelihood. The rich became richer and the mass of the people became much poorer."

Moreover, in his book *How the Catholic Church Built Western Civilization* (Regnery, 2005), Prof. Thomas E. Woods Jr. states that archaeological explorations at Rievaulx Abbey in North Yorkshire (one of the monasteries closed by Henry's orders) found that the monks had built a furnace capable of extracting iron from ore, a necessary step in the large-scale production of cast iron. "Had it not been for a greedy king's suppression of the English monasteries, therefore, the monks appear to have been on the verge of ushering in the industrial era and its related explosion in wealth, population, and life expectancy figures. That development would instead have to wait two and a half more centuries" (pp. 37-38).

[40] *Ibid.,* p. 26. Belloc further notes that "There is his character as a whole in all its lack of proportion and, as he developed, its grotesqueness. None could be better suited to produce the ill effects which it did produce. If the evil powers had had to choose their instrument, assigning to it the right proportions of violence and weakness, incomprehension, passion and the rest, they could hardly have framed a tool more serviceable to their hands than that which did—without full intention—effect the main tragedy in the modern history of Europe" (p. 27).

[41] Fr. John Laux, *Church History*, as quoted in Prof. Courtenay Bartholomew, *Her Majesty Mary* (Queenship Publishing, 2002), p. 59.

[42] A. F. Pollard, *Henry VIII* (Harper and Row, 1966), p. 351, as quoted in Donald DeMarco, *The Heart of Virtue* (Ignatius Press, 1996), p. 139.

[43] Jill Haak Adels, *The Wisdom of the Saints* (Barnes & Noble, 1987), p. 76.

[44] Paul Thigpen, *Quotes from the Saints* (Servant Publications, 2001), p. 116. St. Thomas More wrote, "These modern men, who have sprouted up overnight as 'theologians' claiming to know everything . . . fail to agree among themselves about the great dogmas of the Christian faith. Each of them, whoever he may be, claiming that he has the truth, vanquishes the rest— only to be vanquished by the rest in turn. But they are all alike in this way: they all oppose the Catholic faith, and they are all conquered by it" (*ibid.*).

45  www.trivia-library.com/b/famous-people-cause-of-death-henry-viii.htm.

46  www.corsinet.com.braincandy.dying.html.

47  http.users.belgacom.net.gc674645.grave.lastword.htm.

48  www.trivia-library.com/b/famous-people-cause-of-death-henry-viii.htm.
An alleged visionary and prophet in Poland named Wladyslaw Biernacki,
who was a personal friend of Pope John Paul II, once claimed to have been
granted a vision of hell, and said, "I was curious to see if I could identify
any of the people in hell, out of the seething masses of devils that were
rushing around there; and although I didn't see everyone, I did recognize
a few. . . . I saw the English king, Henry VIII, and also an English queen (I
have since been told that this was possibly Queen Elizabeth I)" – quoted
from *Prophecies*, trans. by Henryk Szewczyk (Children of Mary, 1986), p. 47.

49  DeMarco, p. 141.

50  *Ibid.,* In his play *Henry VIII,* William Shakespeare slightly changes Wolsey's
words to read "Had I but served my God with half the zeal I served my
king, He would not in mine age left me naked to mine enemies."

51  Belloc, *Characters of the Reformation*, p. 54.

52  Crocker, p. 264. The author elaborates,

Cromwell's goal was the consolidate all power in the English state,
allowing no foreign interference—with meant the international Church—
and no domestic dissent. Cromwell's spy network was vast, his methods
ruthless, and an Englishman's traditional right to free speech was ended. . . .
Not understanding such a thing as principle, he took monks who refused to
recognize the king as their religious head and had them disemboweled as a
lesson to recusants. But it was easier, in the end, to simply hurl monks and
nuns—at least 15,000 of them—into the streets and tell them to get a real
job, while Cromwell had his henchmen seize their monasteries, nunneries,
hospitals, schools, churches, charitable houses, and land, dividing the booty
among his parvenu usurpers" (pp. 260-261).

53  Belloc, *Characters of the Reformation*, p. 58.

54  *Ibid.,* p. 103.

55  *Ibid.,* p. 125.

56  Carroll, p. 235.

57  *Ibid,* p. 237.

58  Crocker, p. 267.

59  Belloc, *Characters of the Reformation*, p. 103. The author writes, "Her
relations with men were continual, but they were not normal and they were
the more scandalous for that. Like others who have suffered the same tragic
disease of perversion in mind and body, it seemed to increase upon her with
age. Already within sight of the grave and approaching her seventieth year,
she was shamefully associated with one whom she had taken up as a lad, a

young fellow nearly thirty-three years her junior" (ibid.).

60 Eamon Duffy, *The Stripping of the Altars* (Yale University Press, 1992), p. 592.

61 Aquilina, pp. 90-91.

62 Carroll, p. 238.

63 Adels, p. 76.

64 Carroll, p. 239.

65 Adels, p. 112.

66 *Ibid.*, p. 79.

67 Belloc, *Characters of the Reformation*, p. 107.

68 Joseph F. Halloran, *Notable and Quotable* (1993), Vol. 1, #3, p. 25.

69 Robert J. Morgan, ed., *Nelson's Complete Book of Stories, Illustrations, & Quotes* (Thomas Nelson Publishers, 2000), p. 183.

70 Thigpen, pp. 110-111.

71 Wiker, pp. 28-29.

72 Paul C. Vitz, *Faith of the Fatherless* (Spence Publishing Company, 1999), p. xiii.

73 Wiker, p. 35.

74 *Ibid.*, p. 230.

75 Ted Flynn, *Idols in the House* (MaxKol Communications, 2002), p. 90.

76 Donald DeMarco & Benjamin Wiker, *Architects of the Culture of Death* (Ignatius, 2004), p. 53. As the authors note, "Atheism ties a person in knots. It rejects the pure goodness that is the true object of the will and replaces it with an illusory good. Being one's own god is not heroic. It is foolish and self-destructive. And it is so because it is essentially unrealistic. Genuine heroism takes place within the realm of the real. . . . no rebellion against the order of the Creator can ever be truly creative, but must end in destruction, so that 'every absolute experience of atheism, if it is conscientiously and rigorously followed, ends by provoking its psychical dissolution, in suicide" (*ibid.*).

77 Vincent P. Miceli, S.J., *The Gods of Atheism* (Roman Catholic Books, 1971), p. 312.

78 Samuel Enoch Stumpf, *Socrates to Sartre* (McGraw-Hill Book Company, 1966, 1975), p. 290.

79 http.users.belgacom.net.gc674645.grave.last.word.htm.

80 David F. Burgess, *Encyclopedia of Sermon Illustrations* (Concordia Publishing House, 1988), p. 114.

81 Thigpen, p. 239.

82 *Ibid.*, p. 240. Also, the 14th century seer Dolciano added, "Under a holy Pope there will be universal conversion" – Rev. R. Gerald Culleton, *The Prophets and Our Times* (TAN Books and Publishers, 1974), p. 155.

# Defiance!

Several hundred years later, the 18th century visionary Sr. Jane Le Royer described a vision granted her of the future: "Now all the true penitents will flow from all sides to the Church, which will receive them into her bosom. . . . All the false cults will be abolished; all the abuses of the [French] Revolution will be destroyed and the altars of the true God restored. The former practices will be put into force again, and our religion . . . will flourish more than ever" – Yves Dupont, *Catholic Prophecy* (TAN Books and Publishers, 1970, 1973), p. 56.

*Chapter 6*

# Illuminati, Freemasons, and the War on the Church

*Sin speaks to the wicked man in his heart; there is no dread of God before his eyes, for he beguiles himself with the thought that his guilt will not be found out or hated. The words of his mouth are empty and false; he has ceased to understand how to do good. He plans wickedness in his bed; he sets out on a way that is not good, with no repugnance for evil. (Ps. 36:2-5)*

The year 1776 is a hallowed one in American history: the United States marks its origin with the signing of the Declaration of Independence and the official beginning of the Revolutionary War. 1776 also has a much more sinister significance, however, for that year saw the creation of a secret society—the Illuminati, or Illuminism—dedicated to establishing a new world order. This *novus ordo seclorum* ("a new order of the ages," the inscription found on the U.S. $1 bill) would be radically opposed to the Christian world view, and the man most responsible for its creation would come from within the Catholic Church herself.

## Weishaupt

Adam Weishaupt was a professor of canon law at Ingolstadt University in Bavaria—the first Catholic layman to occupy this position. However, unknown to his superiors, his exposure to rationalistic thinking, and his quarrelsome nature, caused him to devote himself to finding the most efficient means of overthrowing the established order. Secretly rejecting his early training by the Jesuits, he instead immersed himself in the writings of those same French philosophers who would soon propel their own nation into revolution.[1] Like them, Weishaupt had a strong sense of intellectual superiority; in addition to pride, however, his path to revolution was also motivated by lust.

Weishaupt's brilliance and potential was noted by men with an agenda of their own. They called themselves the "Illumined (enlightened) Ones," and they carefully cultivated his friendship, while deepening his exposure to "modern" and "realistic" ideas (especially the assertion that human progress required the rejection of belief in God, and liberation from all conventional morality and the authority of the Church). Weishaupt came under their complete control when he engaged in an affair with his sister-in-law; upon learning she was pregnant, he begged his "friends" to help arrange for an abortion, lest the disgrace ruin him.[2] As one historian explains,

> Weishaupt found he had many "friends." But those who responded to his frantic appeal for help made him pay the full price. . . . He was then brought under the influence of the newly formed House of Rothschild. He was retained to revise and modernize the age-old Luciferian "Protocols." His pride was given further inflation when he was asked to, or it was suggested, that he organize the Illuminati to put the revised version of the continuing Luciferian conspiracy into effect.[3]

The appeals to Weishaupt's vanity were quite effective, and he gladly devoted himself to this project. His far-reaching scheme to create a new world order—one without any room for God, Christianity, the Church, patriotism, and even the family—involved secrecy, deception, and the recruitment of useful, influential figures, including lawyers (who were often skilled at persuasive public speaking), government officials, scientists, financiers, and educators. Weishaupt's plan was finished on May 1, 1776 (the reason why May Day became a revolutionary holiday).[4]

According to Weishaupt, universal love among all peoples and nations would "make the human race one good and happy family," removing the need for all currently existing, outdated loyalties. He "envisioned a dictatorship with himself and his Illuminati brethren at its head. But he also realized that he could accomplish nothing unless he could eliminate the bedrock of civilization, religion. Thus he taught that religion should be eliminated and replaced with the worship of reason. . . ."[5] In addition to calling for the communal education of children, Weishaupt insisted that his "utopia of rationalism" could only be achieved by abolishing all governments (especially monarchies), private property, the concepts of patriotism and nationalism, family life and the institution of marriage, and above all, religion.[6]

This grand scheme required a practical vehicle for implementation, and the already well-established institution of Freemasonry was ideal for the purposes of Weishaupt and his friends. "In 1777, Weishaupt was initiated into the Masonic Order, the Lodge Theodore of Good Councel [sic], in Munich, Germany. His purpose in joining was not to become part of this benevolent order, but to infiltrate it and then to control it altogether."[7]In his book *Make Yourself An Ark!*, Fr. Andrew O'Brien explains that

> *Weishaupt did this by observing lodge members and selecting promising candidates for his secret society. His selected few rose step by step in the Illuminati, and with each step a little more was revealed to them. If a candidate at any stage displayed shock or revulsion, he never advanced any further, which meant that only the most ruthless and irreligious rose to the highest levels, where they were shown the true Satanic purpose of the Illuminati. Weishaupt started with some two thousand paid followers, all highly talented men, and from the start the members were guaranteed the glory and rewards of personal success in the world.[8]*

Weishaupt's grand scheme experienced a serious setback in 1784, when a courier on his way to deliver a copy of his plans to the French political agitator Gabriel Mirabeau was killed by lightning, and the documents he was carrying were turned over to the Bavarian government. The ensuing official investigation resulted in the outlawing of the Illuminati and the publication of a warning to the governments of Europe titled *Original Writings of the Order and Sect of the Illuminati*. However, as one author states, "All the Bavarian government actually did was prune the Tree of Evil and make it grow stronger."[9]

Weishaupt, naturally, lost his position at the university; he went to Switzerland, where he reorganized the Illuminati—cunningly making it seem the order had been dissolved, when in fact he and his colleagues labored to make it more influential (and secretive) than ever. His own death in 1830 may have been intended to aid the deception, for one commentator states that "In an effort to convince the world that Illuminism was dead and no longer a threat, he reportedly made an impressive death bed repentance and rejoined the Catholic Church."[10] However, according to the on-line *Catholic Encyclopedia*,

> *After 1787 he renounced all active connection with secret societies, and again drew near to the Church, displaying remarkable zeal in the building of the Catholic church at Gotha. He died on 18 November 1830, "reconciled with the Catholic Church, which, as a youthful professor, he had doomed to death and destruction"—as the chronicle of the Catholic parish in Gotha relates.[11]*

Perhaps Weishaupt's reconciliation with the Church was a sham, part of the Illuminati's overall plan of deception. However, it may well have been authentic; it's also possible he deceived his fellow conspirators into believing he was only pretending to return to Catholicism, when in fact his conversion was genuine. In the case of a haughty, devious man facing death and the very real possibility of damnation, nothing can be ruled out; all we can say with certainty is that Weishaupt was—for good or ill—judged by the One Who says, "My eyes are upon all their ways; they are not hidden from Me, nor does their guilt escape My view" (Jer. 16:17).

## Illuminati

Does Illuminism still exist today? One of the reasons it's difficult to give a convincing answer, one way or another, is the inherently deceptive nature of a secret society. As Weishaupt wrote, "The great strength of our order lies in its concealment: let it never appear in any place in its own name, but always covered by another name and another occupation."[12] No one doubts the continued existence of Freemasonry, and the Masonic lodges were a primary target of the Illuminati. Fr. O'Brien notes that "The plan to control Freemasonry through Illuminati agents, and the success achieved, is plainly stated in Weishaupt's papers. He called Masonry 'our nursery garden,' and there was a general order for his people to enter it."[13] Moreover,

> *Cardinal Rodriguez, Archbishop of Santiago, Chile, wrote a book in 1925, exposing how the Illuminati, the Satanists, and the Luciferians had imposed a secret society upon a secret society. The Cardinal wrote that not even high thirty-third degree Masons know what goes on in the lodges of the Grand Orient, and in Albert Pike's New Reformed Palladian Rite.[14]*

One author describes Weishaupt's hidden, long-range, and ambitious scheme for implementing the goals of the Illuminati—a scheme that necessarily involved a war against the Church:

> *Weishaupt, after he was banished, remained the Devil's agent in human form. He directed the Luciferian conspiracy so that it developed into the Great French Revolution and others. . . . Weishaupt's Illuminati, and his Lodges of the [Masonic] Grand Orient, went underground. . . . When Weishaupt had destroyed France as a monarchy and a world power . . . he then moved to Italy. The plot cooked up by Weishaupt and [Italian revolutionary Giuseppe] Mazzini was for Italians and others posing as Roman Catholics to infiltrate into the Vatican and, as Weishaupt had previously stated, "bore from within until it remains nothing but an empty shell." What Mazzini was instructed to do in the Vatican by Weishaupt himself, he later instructed General Albert Pike to do at the top levels of Freemasonry. . . .[15]*

The revolutionary social agenda of Communism (including the abolition of private property, loyalty to family, and religion) embodies the specific aims of the Illuminati, and one aspect of this program—familiar to most contemporary Americans—makes use of the so-called "women's movement":

> *In order for the family unit to be destroyed (a necessary step to world domination through the destruction of Christian culture), it was critical for discontent to be sown broadly in order that women would rebel against supposed oppression and authority. This technique, as defined in great length by Weishaupt, was very similar to that which was to be used to fan the flames of revolution through racial and ethnic minorities throughout the world.* **Order out of chaos** *were the catchwords that ultimately became the motto of the Illuminati.[16]*

Chaos on a worldwide scale would be necessary to achieve the Illuminati's eventual goal of a one-world government—and this chaos, and the resultant bloodshed, would not occur randomly or by chance. One scholar notes that Albert Pike, a Confederate general and an avowed Satanist,

> *drafted a military blueprint for the achievement of world domination. It was, in essence, simply an updated version of the original plan of Spartacus [code name] Weishaupt. This particular plan is, however, extremely interesting when one realizes that it was written somewhere between 1859 and 1871. The reason that it is so interesting is that it details the necessity of three world wars; the first world war to communize Russia, the second to communize Europe—and the third world war, should it be necessary, would result in the communization of the world. Additionally, the revolutions of Spain, Mexico, Germany—the second revolution in France, and assorted other regional revolutions and wars that are now a part of history— were all described in detail in Pike's master plan—many decades before even the first events began to unfold.*[17]

Another scholar notes that the first global war, according to the master plan, was intended to overthrow the Czarist government of Russia, with the establishment of an Illuminati dictatorship (under the appearance of Communism) giving the society a secure base for further operations. The second war would allow a Communized Russia to capture Europe (or, as it turned out, the eastern half of that continent). Finally, "The third world war would be in the Middle East between the Moslems and the Jews, and would bring about the biblical Armageddon. Certainly by the end of this third world war, the battle-wearied nations would be ready to accept any proposal [e.g., a one-world government] as long as it promised peace, uniting the entire earth under the fatal banner of the Luciferian New World Order."[18]

Even a cursory knowledge of modern history and current events suggests this blueprint—whether or not there are actually Illuminati involved in implementing it—is well under way, but that does not mean it will succeed in the end. St. Paul reminds us that "the foolishness of God is wiser than human wisdom, and the weakness of God is stronger than human strength" (1 Cor. 1:25), and

Scripture attests that the Lord is able to use rebellious and arrogant worldly rulers as His unknowing instruments in the working out of His plan of salvation for His people (cf. Is. 10:5ff).

# Freemasonry

Freemasons (also known as Masons) trace their origin back to the builders of Solomon's Temple in Jerusalem, but in fact date back only to the Middle Ages, when stonemasons in England formed a religious fraternity. This group was abolished by King Edward VI during the Reformation, but was reestablished in 1717,[19] at the appropriately-named "Tavern of the Devil" in London. The Masons soon claimed that "Freemasonry alone possesses the true religion. All other religions, especially Catholicism, have taken what is true in their doctrines from Freemasonry. They possess only false or absurd theories" (from Freemasonry's 1723 handbook *Free and Accepted Masons*).

Beginning with Pope Clement XII in 1738, the Catholic Church—more than 200 times—condemned Masonry's teachings and forbade Catholics from joining the organization. (This prohibition remains in effect.[20]) The popes have frequently warned of Masonry's sinister nature. For instance, in 1829 Pope Pius VIII stated, "Their law is untruth; their God is the devil; and their cult is turpitude."[21] According to author Michael H. Brown, Pope Leo XIII, in his 1884 encyclical *Humanum Genus*, identified Masonry as

> as device of the devil. While they seemed on the surface like nothing more than a social club (in America many prominent men, including presidents, belonged), the Masons were out to quash Catholicism, railing against the Church and in their robes and arcane rituals practicing what was in effect a new form of witchcraft. . . . [Leo] saw Freemasonry as the coalescing of humanistic and materialistic factions for a full-scale assault on Christianity.[22]

Several years later, in *Dal'Alto Del'Apostolico*, Leo asserted, "It is needless now to put the Masonic sects on trial. They are already judged; their ends, their means, their doctrines, and the actions are all known with indisputable certainty. *Possessed by the spirit of Satan, whose instrument they are, they burn like him with a deadly and implacable hatred of Jesus Christ and His work* [emphasis added]; and they endeavor by every means to overthrow and fetter it."[23]

Within Masonry itself, the New and Reformed Palladian Rite was created in the 1870s by Pike and Mazzini (as described above) "with the stated goal of the destruction of Christianity and the establishment of a 'New Age' that in Pike's own written words would be 'maintained in the purity of the Luciferian doctrine.'"[24]

It wasn't only the Church which recognized Masonry's sinister and perverse nature; in the early 1830s the state legislatures of Massachusetts, Pennsylvania, and New York all investigated the secret society, and declared it to be "a moral evil—a distinct independent government within our own government, and beyond the control of the laws of the land by means of its secrecy, and the oaths and regulations which its subjects are bound to obey, under penalties of death."[25] Masonry in the United States was forced underground for a time, but eventually reemerged in the garb of a harmless, fraternal organization involved in many honorable social endeavors. However, "Masonry is fundamentally the same today as it was before the United States Government was organized, as Masons and their own documents show."[26]

Freemasonry, by its very nature, is both highly secretive and profoundly anti-Catholic,[27] and so it's little wonder that a number of alleged private revelations have warned against it. For instance, in 1820 the Augustinian nun Bl. Anna Katarina Emmerich was granted a vision of a subversive group working within the Church. She stated:

> *I saw how baleful would be the consequences of this false church. I saw it increase in size; heretics of every kind came into the city of Rome. The local clergy grew lukewarm, and I saw a great darkness. . . . Once more I saw that the Church of Peter was undermined by a plan evolved by the secret sect, while storms were damaging it. . . . I saw all sorts of people, things, and doctrines and opinions. There was something proud, presumptuous, and violent about it, and they seemed to be very successful. I did not see a single angel nor a single saint helping in the work. But far away in the background, I saw the seat of a cruel people armed with spears, and I saw a laughing figure which said: "Do build it as solid as you can;*

*we will pull it to the ground.*[28]

Masonry has conducted its war against the Church in various ways. In the 19th century, for instance, the Alta Vendita—a group of influential Italian Masons—openly stated that its goal was to destroy the Church by means of its Masonic lodges, an idea confirmed by the contemporary Church leader Bishop George Michael Wittman, who predicted, "Secret societies will wreak great ruin, and exercise a marvelous monetary power, and through that many will be blinded, and infected with the most horrible errors; however, all this shall avail naught."[29]

Fr. Andrew O'Brien writes, "Freemason Yves Marsaudon's book *Ecumenism As Seen By A Traditional Freemason* states: 'The goal is no longer the destruction of the Church but rather to make use of it by infiltrating it.' According to Bishop Graber that change of Masonic strategy can be dated to about the year 1908."[30] Thus, for just over a century, Masons have sought to obtain for themselves that influence Christianity, and especially Catholicism, exercise in today's world. Author Ted Flynn writes,

> *Freemasonry is perhaps the single greatest secular organized power on earth today and battles head to head with the things of God on a daily basis. It is a controlling power in the world, operating behind the scenes in banking and politics, and it has effectively infiltrated all religions. Masonry is a worldwide secret sect undermining the authority of the Catholic Church with a hidden agenda at the upper levels to destroy the papacy. The papacy remains a target because of the control and influence Rome exerts—something Freemasonry wants.*[31]

A major element in this war on the Church is ecclesiastical masonry—that is, the secret Masonic membership of many important Church leaders (akin to an act of religious treason). One author notes that the July 1976 edition of *Bulletin de L'Occident Chretien Nr. 12* "presented an extensive list of names, accompanied by dates of initiation and code names, that was discovered when a Masonic lodge outside of Rome was raided by police. The list names both cardinals and bishops, some with initiation dates going back a half-century."[32] Moreover, in numerous inner locutions allegedly received by the Italian priest Fr. Stefano Gobbi, Our Lady has supposedly spoken at great length about the dangers of ecclesiastical masonry, of how it subverts the Church and works against the spread of the Gospel, and of how, according to her Son's plan, she will be completely victorious in overcoming it.[33]

The Masons and other secret societies may have designs on the Church—but these cannot prevail in the face of Divine Providence.

## The Victory of Our Lady

St. Maximilian Kolbe, when studying in Rome in 1917, witnessed a Masonic parade featuring banners showing Satan defeating St. Michael the Archangel, and the Masons taunted the Church by carrying their insignia alongside the Vatican itself. As the saint later wrote, some "enraged hands dared to write such slogans as 'Satan will rule on Vatican Hill, and the pope will serve as his errand boy.'" This blasphemous scene later inspired the holy Franciscan to found the *Militia Immaculatae* "to bring help to so many unhappy persons [particularly Freemasons], to stabilize innocent hearts so that all can more easily go the Immaculate Virgin, through whom so many graces come down to us."[34]

1917, of course, was also the year of Our Lady's appearances to the three shepherd children Lucia, Francisco, and Jacinta outside the small Portuguese town of Fatima, and Freemasonry was quick to recognize and respond to this perceived threat. When steadily growing crowds came to be present at the apparitions occurring on the 13th of each month, a local government official—himself a Mason—tried to thwart Our Lady by kidnapping the three children early in August and imprisoning them in the local jail. He had them incarcerated with hardened criminals, expecting this would break the children's spirits, but their innocence inspired those sinful men to kneel down and pray with them; when the official next threatened to boil them alive unless they revealed the secrets Our Lady had given them, the children—fully expecting to die—refused to comply. Stymied, the man sent the visionaries home (and Our Lady thereupon appeared to them on August 17).

The Miracle of the Sun that occurred on October 13, 1917—the only recorded case in history of the date of a miracle being predicted in advance—was visible up to seven miles away, and was witnessed by some 70,000 people, including reporters whose honest account of what they saw was printed in their secular newspapers. Even so, within two weeks local Masons tried to discredit the event:

> Ten days later, men from the Masonic Lodge of Santarem, Portugal came at night to chop down the tree where the Blessed Mother appeared, and to take away a small table which served as an altar. Later those stolen objects were placed on exhibition, and the Lodge held a mock procession to ridicule Catholic practices. To the sound of blasphemous litanies, the procession passed through the principal streets of the city, returning to the Sa da Bandeira Square where it dispersed. The Brethren were surprised later to find they had chopped down the wrong tree.[35]

The events at Fatima, of course, were eventually declared by the Church to be worthy of belief, and the Fatima messages have strengthened the faith of countless millions of Catholics, while reminding them of the spiritual weapons entrusted to them (i.e., the Rosary, fasting and other sacrifices for peace in the world and the conversion of sinners, and Consecration to Our Lady's Immaculate Heart), and reassuring them through the Virgin's promise that "In the end, my Immaculate Heart will triumph . . . and a period of peace will be granted to the world."[36]

Freemasonry's inability to deny or discredit the events at Fatima epitomizes the far greater and irreversible failure awaiting the Illuminati, Masons, and other secret enemies of the Church, a failure which will involve the unmasking and thwarting of all their schemes, and result in the humiliation and despair (and, unless they repent, damnation) of all who foolishly choose to align themselves with Satan in combating the powerful and mysterious workings of Divine Providence.

It cannot be otherwise for those who oppose God's grace and place themselves in enmity to His Church, for the people of God are protected by "the woman clothed with the sun, with the moon under her feet, and on her head a crown of twelve stars" (Rev. 12:1)—and Our Lady's glorious role in the final victory over evil was foretold from the very beginning of human history (cf. Gen. 3:15). For the time being, Illuminism and Masonry represent a serious threat to the Church, but this threat will surely pass, as "they are like chaff which the wind drives away," for "the Lord watches over the way of the just, but the way of the wicked vanishes" (Ps. 1:4,6).

## NOTES TO CHAPTER 6

[1]  Ted Flynn, *Hope of the Wicked* (MaxKol Communications, 2000), p. 32

[2]  William Guy Carr, R.D., *Satan, Prince of This World* (Omni Publications, 1997), p. 77. The author elaborates, "Weishaupt's letters prove he was literally as proud as Lucifer. He wasn't penitent because he had sinned against God, betrayed his brother, and broken his vows of chastity. Oh no! His letters prove his panic was caused by his fear that exposure would cast him down from the pinnacle of learning to which he had been elevated at such an early age" (ibid.).

[3]  *Ibid.*

[4]  *Ibid.,* p. 79.

[5]  Flynn, p. 24.

[6]  *Ibid.*

[7]  A. Ralph Epperson, *The Unseen Hand* (Publius Press, 1985), p. 82.

[8]  Fr. Andrew O'Brien, *Make Yourself An Ark!*, Vol. One (The American Research Foundation, Inc., 1995), p. 3.

[9]  Carr, p. 94.

[10]  Flynn, p. 33.

[11]  http://www.newadvent.org/cathen/07661b.htm.

[12]  Epperson, p. 82.

[13]  O'Brien, p. 4.

[14]  *Ibid.,* p. 5.

[15]  Carr, pp. 111, 118.

[16]  Stephen Mahowald, *She Shall Crush Thy Head* (MMR Publishing, 1996), p. 121.

[17]  *Ibid.,* p. 110.

[18]  Flynn, p. 72.

[19]  Matthew Bunson, *Our Sunday Visitor's Encyclopedia of Catholic History* (Our Sunday Visitor Publishing, 1995), "Freemasonry," p. 341.

[20]  *Ibid.,* As the encyclopedia article explains, "In the 1983 Code of Canon Law, the penalty of excommunication for those Catholics who join the Masons is not included [as in the 1917 Code], although the prohibition remains in force. Bishops are not empowered to grant dispensations from the restrictions." More precisely, Canon 1374 states, "One who joins an association which plots against the Church is to be punished with a just penalty; one who promotes or moderates such an association, however, is

to be punished with an interdict."

Furthermore, according to Fr. Andrew O'Brien, "On November 26, 1983, the Sacred Congregation for the Doctrine of the Faith issued a document reminding the faithful that membership in Masonic associations remains forbidden, and that 'the faithful who enroll in Masonic associations are in a state of grave sin, and may not receive Holy Communion.' This was signed by Cardinal Ratzinger [the current Pope Benedict XVI], the Prefect, and approved by Pope John Paul II" -- *Make Yourself An Ark!*, Vol. Two (The American Research Foundation, 1995), p. 3.

21  Paul Fisher, *Their God is the Devil: Papal Encyclicals and Freemasonry* (American Research Foundation, 1991), p. iii.

22  Michael H. Brown, *The Final Hour* (Queenship Publishing, 2000), pp. 25-26. Masonry was also condemned by Benedict XIV, Pius VII, Leo XII, Gregory XVI, and Pius IX—who wrote five major papal documents against it. Paul Fisher notes that Pope Leo XIII, in his encyclical *Immortali Dei* (1885), wrote, ". . . it is unlawful to follow one line of conduct in private life and another in public; respecting privately the authority of the Church, but publicly rejecting it [as with the case of Catholic politicians 'personally opposed' to abortion, but who refuse to act upon that professed opposition]. This would amount to joining together good and evil, and to putting man in conflict with himself; whereas he ought always to be consistent, and never in the least point nor in any condition of life to swerve from Christian virtue" (p. 23). Moreover, in a later encyclical to Italian bishops named *Inimica Vis* (1892), Leo stated, "the spirit of all previous groups hostile to Catholic institutions has come to life again in that group called the Masonic sect, which, strong in manpower and resources, is the leader in a way against anything sacred" (p. 27).

Additionally, Leo XIII's 1884 encyclical *Humanum Genus* warns, "Freemasons, like the Manichees of old, strive, as far as possible, to conceal themselves, and to admit no witnesses but their own members. As a convenient manner of concealment, they assume the character of literary men and scholars associated for purposes of learning" – quoted in *Hope of the Wicked*, p. 146.

23  Fr. Andrew O'Brien, *Make Yourself An Ark!*, Vol. Two (The American Research Foundation, 1995), pp. 12-13.

24  Ted Flynn, *Idols in the House* (MaxKol Communications, 2002), p. 206. The author elaborates, "Pike professed that Lucifer is the God of Light and of good struggling for humanity against 'Adonay,' the god of darkness and evil [equated with the God of Judeo-Christian tradition]. To achieve their goal, Mazzini devised a strategy whose purpose was to embroil every nation in a conflict so bloody and chaotic that eventually these nations would surrender their national sovereignty to an international, world government directed by this Luciferian order" (ibid.).

25  Fisher, p. 18.

26  *Ibid.*, p. 4.

27  In his 1980 book *The Reappearance of the Christ and the Masters of Wisdom*, Benjamin Crème, New Age spokesman and publicist for the coming "world leader" known Lord Maitreya, wrote, "The Master Jesus [meaning Maitreya, or another servant of Satan] will take over the throne of St. Peter in Rome [and] the true apostolic succession will begin. This event is now imminent, following the declaration of the [false] Christ. . . . The new religion will be manifest, for instance, through organizations like Masonry. In Freemasonry is embedded the core or the secret heart of the occult mysteries" —as quoted by Fr. O'Brien, *Make Yourself An Ark!*, Vol. Two, p. 14.

28  As quoted in Flynn, *Idols in the House*, p. 212.

29  *Ibid.*, pp. 207-208.

30  O'Brien, Vol. Two, p. 2.

31  Flynn, *Hope of the Wicked*, p. 154.

32  Mahowald, p. 140.

33  *To the Priests: Our Lady's Beloved Sons* (The Marian Movement of Priests, 16th English edition, 1995), pp. 644ff.

34  Fisher, p. 40.

35  *Ibid.*, p. 39.

36  Mark Fellows, *Sister Lucia: Apostle of Mary's Immaculate Heart* (Immaculate Heart Publications, 2007), pp. 66-67.

*Chapter 7*

# The Rebellion of the Eldest Daughter of the Church

*Woe to those who call evil good, and good evil, who change darkness into light and light into darkness, who change bitter into sweet, and sweet into bitter! Woe to those who are wise in their own sight, and prudent in their own esteem! (Is. 5:20-21)*

Numbered among the vast multitude of saints are more than a few persons of royal blood: holy men, women, and young people who used their influence and authority for the glory of God and the well-being of His people. Included in this list are St. Stephen of Hungary, St. Margaret of Sweden, St. Elizabeth of Portugal, St. Joan of France (not to be confused with St. Joan of Arc), the empress St. Helena (the mother of Constantine), the prince St. Casimir, the princess St. Elizabeth of Hungary, St. Henry, St. Edward the Confessor, and St. Louis IX of France, whose thirty-five year reign in the 13th century was a time of blessing and prosperity for the French kingdom.

One day, while Louis was working in his study, Mass was being said in the palace chapel. At the moment of consecration, Jesus Himself appeared on the altar in the form of a beautiful Child, filling all those present with wonder and joy. A courtier immediately ran to the king, described the miracle occurring in testimony to the Real Presence, and begged him to come and see it for himself. However, Louis refused, saying, "I firmly believe already that Christ is truly present in the Holy Eucharist. He has said it, and that is sufficient; I do not wish to lose the merit of my faith by going to see this miracle."

The holy French king indeed possessed great faith, as did

many of his people—but unfortunately, that situation would change considerably over the coming centuries, especially during the so-called Age of Enlightenment. A major reason religion was increasingly displaced by science, and faith was more and more replaced by skepticism was, ironically, the Protestant revolt. As one historian explains,

> ... the triumph of the Reformation was, albeit inadvertently, to leave the skeptic with no need for religion at all. When a skeptic saw Protestants taking hammers to break down altars, smash crucifixes, obliterate statues of the Virgin Mary, stamp on the Eucharist, and shatter stained glass, he could ask: Why stop there? Why not tear down the whole thing? If man is saved by faith alone [the heresy Luther preached], why not leave every man's religion to his conscience rather than to institutional religion and all its attendant dangers of intolerance, censorship, and coercion? ... For post-Reformation rationalists, choosing agnosticism [an attitude of doubt or skepticism toward God's existence] became the logical conclusion of Luther's doctrine of every man his own priest.[1]

France in particular—the kingdom long known as the eldest daughter of the Church—was affected by an arrogant and excessive rationalism, skepticism, extreme anti-clericalism, and other misguided philosophies that, taken to their logical extreme, could only end up harming humanity (especially the innocent and defenseless). The corrupt and indifferent Louis XV (d. 1775) had famously said, "Apres moi, le deluge"[2] ("After me, the flood," meaning the collapse of social order in France). The scourge of revolution and war was not inevitable, but the behind-the-scenes maneuvering of secret societies, the incompetence of rulers like Louis XV, and the growing influence of some important French philosophers, made disaster almost impossible to avoid.

## Rousseau

The teachings of the political theorist and philosopher Jean Jacques Rousseau have been called a mixture of "genius and blunder,"[3] and he is considered an indispensable architect of the French Revolution—for he believed that "As civil society is based on injustice and law is merely a tool for the rich to keep their riches, then rebellion of the have-nots is always justified. They have nothing to lose but their chains" (an idea to be made famous by Marx and Engels in the 19th century).[4] Indeed, British historian Nesta Webster, author of *World Revolution*, observed that Rousseau's writings embodied all the principles of what would later be called communism."[5]

Rousseau, a friend of the philosopher David Hume, "created the euphoric atmosphere that fostered man's complete confidence in his own natural goodness and faith in the power of his reason,"[6] and a logical outgrowth of this naïve, overly-optimistic worldview was a rejection of all "artificial" limitations on human nature and desires—such as religious belief, morality, and every type of social laws and customs, including the possession of private property. As Rousseau wrote,

> *The first person who, having fenced off a plot of ground, took it into his head to say **this is mine** and found people simple enough to believe him, was the true founder of civil society. What crimes, what wars, what miseries and horrors would the human race have been spared by someone who, uprooting the stakes or filling in the ditch, had shouted to his fellow-men: Beware of listening to this impostor; you are lost if you forget that the fruits belong to all and the earth to no one![7]*

Needless to say, this analysis contradicts Scripture's recognition of the legitimacy of owning private property, as shown in the 7th and 10th Commandments (Ex. 20:15,17), and in Our Lord's parables of the talents (Mt. 24:14-30) and of the prodigal son (Lk. 15:11-32), among others.

Rejecting every external source of authority, Rousseau "sought human nature in the wholly private realm of intuition and conscience [and] looked inward for the fundamental source of moral obligation."[8] The radical "moral authenticity" he espoused not only served to undermine respect for Church and state (helping pave the way for the horrors of revolution); it also demonstrated the depths to which a person can sink in the pursuit of a disordered "freedom." Jesus said that we must judge a tree by its fruit (Mt. 7:20), and on this basis the French philosopher's record is abysmal:

*Despite Rousseau's grandiose praise of Roman virtue, he had a string of mistresses, some married, some not. He sired five children with one of them, Thérèse Levasseur, with whom he lived for more than twenty-five years and whom he treated as a mere maid (she delivered his torrid letters to other mistresses). Rousseau abandoned all five children to . . . a foundling home where the conditions were so deplorable that their deaths were all but certain.[9]*

In spite of his extreme self-centeredness and arrogance, Rousseau could claim in all seriousness, "I believe that there is not in the entire world a more humble man than I."[10] If the devil can appear as an angel of light (2 Cor. 11:14), it's not surprising that his deluded servants can, in their pride, claim for themselves a non-existent humility. Needless to say, this will do them no good in the end, for God—Who sees into the depths of every human heart—"opposes the proud but bestows favor on the humble" (1 Pt. 5:5).

# Voltaire

The highly influential French Illuminati Francois-Marie Arouet (who had adopted the name Voltaire after an irreparable falling-out with his father) was described by someone who knew him as "the most perfect incarnation of Satan that the world ever saw."[11]

Evidence of his intense, undying hatred for the Church is found in his correspondence. He once wrote, "The Christian religion is an infamous religion, an abominable hydra, which must be destroyed by a hundred invisible hands. Let us crush the wretch," and in a letter to the Prussian king Frederick II he eagerly predicted, "finally, when conditions are right, a reign [of Illuminism] will spread across the whole earth to wipe out all Christians, and then establish a universal brotherhood without marriage, family, property law or God."[12]

Voltaire dedicated his life to this unholy goal; one historian calls him

*the most complete incarnation of the irreligious spirit of the eighteenth century. . . . he was perhaps the most marvelous workman of destruction who has ever appeared. . . . in the war to death which he had declared against Christianity, he employed all the resources of a mind exceptionally constituted for intellectual struggles and all of the indefatigable activities of a satanic hatred against the Church. . . . he led the irreligious campaign with astounding obstinacy and—to use the expression of a great modern poet—he was the missionary of the devil among the men of his time.*[13]

A Deist (that is, a believer in an impersonal, remote God unconcerned with the struggles of humanity), Voltaire hated the Catholic Church and "called it *l'infame*, the infamous thing. He knew that the Jesuits constituted the strongest and most effective body within the Church in his time. 'Once we have destroyed the Jesuits,' he said, 'we shall have it all our own way with the infamous thing.'"[14]Through his influence as a noted author, Voltaire worked to discredit the Church and the Jesuits, especially by means of the plays he wrote; he also directed the Illuminati's publicity campaign against Catholicism.[15] In a letter to a fellow Illuminist, he insisted that the order must lie "not timidly, or for a while only, but like the very devil, boldly and always," while adding that "the opposite of what is said and promised can be done afterwards . . . that is of no consequence."[16]

Like many opponents of the Church, Voltaire was convinced of his own intellectual superiority; his "ambition and intellectual vanity are agreed upon by all his biographers. His passion was for fame; he was certainly not motivated by love for others."[17] Naturally, this arrogance blinded him to religious truth; he once admitted, "Even if a miracle should be wrought in the open marketplace before a thousand sober witnesses, I would rather mistrust my senses than admit a miracle."[18]

Nevertheless, Voltaire cynically acknowledged a certain usefulness for religion: namely, as a means of imposing morality upon persons of lower classes, all of them less enlightened than himself; as he remarked, "Don't tell the servants there is no God, or they will steal the silver."[19] Not feeling bound by conventional morality himself, Voltaire had many lovers—including his own niece, who served as his housekeeper and mistress (an arrangement his admirers managed to keep secret for two centuries after his death).[20]

Voltaire was convinced that the forces of reason and

enlightenment (represented by himself, naturally) would prevail over the tyranny and superstition of the Church. On February 25, 1758, he wrote to a friend, "In twenty years there will not remain a single altar to the God of the Christians"—but in fact, he was passing a terrible judgment on himself, for as one author describes,

> On February 25, 1778, twenty years later, day for  day, the arch-blasphemer was seized with the vomiting of blood that brought him to the grave. . . . The sick man falls into convulsions; with rolling eyes, pale and trembling, he throws himself into every position, devouring his own excrements, and tearing his flesh to pieces! That Hell which  he had so much ridiculed he now sees open before  him; he groans with terror, and his last sigh is that  of a reprobate.[21]

His final despairing words were "I am abandoned by God and man; I shall go to hell!,"[22] and the Christian woman who had been hired to assist him in his final agonies later said, "I was the nurse who attended Voltaire in his last illness, and for all the wealth in Europe I would never see another infidel die."[23]

Voltaire's confident prediction of the Church's demise was not only incorrect, but—in an ironic postscript to his life—forty years after his death, the Bible and other Christian literature were being printed in the very house in which he had once lived.[24]

## The Revolutionaries

One of Europe's greatest tragedies—the French Revolution—wasn't an historical accident or a mere human event; if it can be said its American counterpart was blessed by Heaven, the French Revolution definitely had a hellish imprint. According to author Michael H. Brown, it "was too instantaneous and pervasive, too well orchestrated, to be solely of human origin. Mystics provided astonishingly similar prophecies of a special period in which evil would run rampant—an evil that was born with modernism, got its wings during the French Revolution, and then burst upon the scene in a big way by the end of the 1800s."[25]

As noted earlier, Masonry—itself under the control of the Illuminati—sought to implement a carefully drawn-up, step-by-step scheme of world domination, and overthrowing the French monarchy and ending the Church's power in France was an essential first step. In this process, "It was the Illuminist influence that produced the [radical] Jacobin clubs that presided over the Reign of Terror. . . . The French Revolution marked the beginning of atheism in the history of Christian nations,"[26] and as such, was clearly a key element in Satan's ongoing assault on the Church.

In his 1970 book *The French Revolution*, Professor Douglas Johnson noted that

> *the eighteenth century had not been bad for France. The population was expanding, there had been no great plagues, and no wars had been fought on French soil. The French people loved their monarch, "no signs of disloyalty to it could be detected." We see in the French Revolution the first time where grievances were systematically created in order to exploit them. Most history texts tell us that the French Revolution of the late 1700s was a popular uprising sparked by a starving population, rioting in protest of a bankrupt government. We are also told that fewer than 50,000 lives were lost. The truth is, however, that the revolution was deliberately contrived by the machinations of the secret societies, rampant in France at that time, and the death toll was at least 300,000.*[27]

As stated by the 19th century Catholic historian Lord John Acton of England, "The appalling thing in the French Revolution is not the tumult but the design. Through all the fire and smoke, we perceive the evidence of calculating organization. The managers remain studiously concealed and masked; but there is no doubt about their presence from the first."[28]

Early in 1789, an artificial grain shortage—created by Illuminist manipulations of the grain market—served as a catalyst for popular protest against the government, but the stage had been carefully prepared well before then by men with secret and sinister motives. For example, the "spontaneous" attack on the Bastille wasn't intended to release the prisoners there, as commonly stated, but to capture weapons needed for the fighting to follow.[29]

Acton's contemporary Cardinal John Newman looked upon the godless French revolutionaries as precursors of the Antichrist,[30] and Michael H. Brown notes that

*In the way that Satan twists many things that start out noble, soon the liberals focused their wrath on the Church and began a horrifying persecution under the guise of rationalistic progress. Unlike the American Revolution, the French one was not against a foreign oppressor; it was against God. It was the extreme opposite of humility, the paragon of arrogance.*[31]

The war on the Church in France involved increasing restrictions upon the practice of Catholicism. As King Louis XVI lost power to the self-declared National Assembly, priests were required to abjure their allegiance to the pope by taking an oath to the new French constitution. Those who refused to do so—some 55% of the French clergy—were forced into hiding; many of them, at the risk of their lives, ministered in secret to faithful Catholics. (As a boy of thirteen, for instance, St. John Vianney made his First Communion, along with other children of the area, at a secret Mass held in a barn, while farmers worked nearby to forestall the suspicions of any potential spies.[32])

The revolutionary government tried to remake French culture by removing all Catholic influences. A new calendar was imposed on society, with all religious holidays and references to Christ removed; each week was made ten days long—for the specific purpose of abolishing Sunday.[33] Children were given "un-Christian" baptismal names, Marian shrines were desecrated, and church bells and liturgical vessels were confiscated and melted down, while churches were closed or destroyed."[34] The revolutionaries

*congratulated themselves as if they were Protestant reformers, "wiping out eighteen centuries of error" by abolishing the Catholic Church. Constitutionalist priests [those who swore allegiance to the new constitution, instead of to the Holy Father] were ordered to marry in order to propagate workers and soldiers for the state. Churches were stripped and religious art desecrated in the Protestant fashion. As Martin Luther altered the Lord's Prayer to condemn the pope, so now it was altered to praise the State and condemn enemies of the regime.*[35]

In the city of Lyon, a blasphemous memorial ceremony was held for a slain revolutionary leader, in which consecrated Hosts were desecrated, a donkey dressed in priestly vestments drank from a chalice, and a crucifix was burned. "Even yet more horrible profanities were in preparation when . . . the sky suddenly darkened and such a terrific storm burst over the heads of the infamous assembly that with one accord they dispersed and fled from the spot in terror."[36]

The famous cathedrals of Chartres, Reims, and Tours were turned into "temples of reason," as was the Cathedral of Notre Dame in Paris. In this greatest and most famous of all French churches, workmen had erected

> *a strange angular structure of wood and cardboard intended to represent a mountain. On top of it was a small imitation Greek temple dedicated to "philosophy." . . . one of the actresses played the goddess Reason. Clad in a flowing tricolor gown, she climbed the "mountain" and received the plaudits of the crowd from the imitation Greek temple at the top. . . .*[37]

As St. John Vianney later observed, "We can say that blasphemy is truly the language of hell."[38]

In 1793 the radical Jacobins executed the unfortunate Louis XVI, and set up the "Committee of Public Safety," which inaugurated the Reign of Terror the following year. Throughout these horrible months and years, the newly-invented guillotines were in constant use as the revolutionaries executed anyone suspected of opposition to the Revolution. "The Catholic Church was viewed as an enemy, so the clergy suffered especially; anyone who admitted being faithful to the Church was killed."[39]

During the Reign of Terror, "the full horror of government by Satanism was being played out, complete with human butchering and cannibalism. Not surprisingly, in November 1793, a campaign against religion was inaugurated by a massacre of priests all over France."[40] In Paris, 200 priests and several bishops were murdered; the Archbishop of Paris, however, apostasized to save his life—though he later repented.[41]

Throughout France, priests, nuns, and other faithful Catholics were hunted down and executed, along with real or imagined enemies of the regime. One historian writes, "It is impossible to read of this period without the impression that one is here confronted with forces more powerful than those controlled by men."[42] Another commentator noted, "Even reasonable men now succumbed to the contagion. A spirit was abroad which contemporary conservatives described at satanic."[43]

It's an historical truism that revolutions eventually consume their leaders, and within a one year period three of the most important leaders of the Terror did indeed die violent deaths: two in a spirit of tragic hatefulness, but one in a spirit of noble repentance.

Jean Paul Marat had long suffered from a terrible disease eating away at his skin; therefore, in an effort to alleviate the constant pain, he usually conducted business and received visitors while soaking in a large bathtub. Far worse than his disease, however, was the hatred eating away his soul: he sought to destroy all his political enemies without mercy. A brave young woman named Charlotte Corday, a supporter of Marat's opponents, decided to assassinate him in an effort to end the Reign of Terror; she gained access to Marat and pretended to inform him of the whereabouts of four wanted fugitives. Historian Warren Carroll describes what happened next:

> "'Excellent!' he said. . . . 'In a few day's time I shall have them all guillotined in Paris.' Rarely has a man died at a more appropriate moment. No sooner were the words out of his mouth than Charlotte Corday pulled the long knife . . . and drove it straight through his aorta. . . ."[44]

A similarly violent, but ultimately happier, fate awaited revolutionary leader Georges-Jacques Danton. Through his powerful oratory, he came to dominate the Committee of Public Safety, and was initially as radical and bloodthirsty as any of the Revolution's other leaders. However, his heart was not completely closed to the working of divine grace. Danton, a widower, fell in love with a woman who happened to be a devout Catholic, and they were married. Her influence, and that of some friends, helped moderate Danton's revolutionary views, and as he came to see the true nature of the Revolution, he began calling for an end to the Terror. However, Danton lost the ensuing power struggle with the most ruthless and dangerous revolutionary leader of all, Maximilien Robespierre, a disciple of Jean Jacques Rousseau.

Everyone in Paris was terrified of Robespierre, for he managed to become a virtual dictator, possessing the power of life and death over each French citizen. Danton tried to restrain his comrade's violent impulses; he hoped to intervene on behalf of some of the Revolution's victims, but only managed to turn Robespierre against him. On the last day of March, 1794, Danton was arrested; he apologetically told his fellow prisoners, "Gentlemen, I had hoped to get you all out of this place. Unfortunately, I'm now shut up in it with you." A few days later Danton was executed; however, "On his way to the guillotine in the tumbrel, Danton apparently made his confession and received absolution from a priest by the roadside."[45] His change of heart had come too late to end the violence of the Revolution, but not too late to save his own soul.

Robespierre was at the height of his power, but he would soon be overthrown—a downfall coinciding with the heroic deaths of sixteen Carmelite nuns from Compiègne, the last martyrs of the Reign of Terror. Over a century earlier, a Carmelite sister dreamt that the nuns of her convent were invited to "follow the Lamb," referring to Jesus, the Lamb who was slain (Rev. 5:6). This mystical revelation became part of the convent's heritage.

During the Revolution, "Believing that the mystic dream could very well refer to her community, the prioress [Mother Teresa of Saint Augustine] introduced a daily act of holocaust to be said by all the Sisters. . . . Gradually, they all came to grips with the reality that they could be guillotined."[46]Eventually the nuns were arrested, condemned to death, and taken to Paris for execution on July 17, 1794.

The Carmelites were led to the guillotine, one at a time, beginning with the youngest; when it was her turn, each nun knelt before the prioress and said, "Permission to die, Mother?," to which she answered, "Go, my daughter." All sixteen freely offered their lives for the intention of bringing an end to the Reign of Terror, and their sacrifice was accepted. "Ten days after the martyrdom of the Carmelites . . . Robespierre was guillotined, and after him, the notorious Public Prosecutor Fouquier-Tinville. The Reign of Terror was over thanks to the oblation of sixteen Carmelite nuns"[47] (all of whom were beatified by Pope Pius X in 1906).

Supremely confident in his own authority, and unable to imagine his political enemies might dare plot against him, Robespierre was caught off guard when other revolutionary factions rose against him. He and his allies were overthrown and arrested, and in the confusion which followed, his jaw was shattered by a bullet. Robespierre was carried into the very room from which he had decreed the death of so many people, and laid on a table, where he remained in agony for six hours. Many citizens of Paris, hearing of his downfall, came to mock or gape at him; one workman, after seeing his bleeding wound, said, "Yes, Robespierre, there is a God."[48] The next day the architect of the Reign of Terror was himself executed, and the worst phase of the French Revolution was over.

# Napoleon

The alleged 16th century seer and prophet Nostradamus is said to have predicted the coming of three antichrists before the end of the world, and the first of these was Napoleon Bonaparte, whom he identified with the anagram *Pau-Nay-Loron*, or *Napaulon Roy* (Napoleon the King).[49] That many 19th century commentators considered him an evil figure bringing death and destruction in his wake is beyond doubt, and for every admirer of the French emperor, there was an equally fervent detractor. The great French author Victor Hugo, for instance, called him "a living plague," a ruler "crowned in blood [who] made a sceptre of his sword, [and] used his tent as a throne"; Bonaparte, he said, "took the path of crime, and fell to disaster."[50]

Nevertheless, in spite of the wicked things he did, Napoleon's case is highly curious, or confusing: he restored the preeminent position of Catholicism in French society, spoke favorably of Jesus Christ, and was apparently reconciled to the Church at his death; however, he also insulted and mistreated Popes Pius VI and Pius VII so severely that they gained the sympathy and admiration of Protestant Europe, sought to use the Church for his own purposes, and by his remarks and behavior, caused some observers to question whether he truly believed in God. For instance, one important member of French society, Mme de Rêmusat, stated, "I do not know whether he was a Deist or an atheist, but in private conversation he constantly ridiculed everything concerned with religion."[51]

This assertion contrasts, however, with Napoleon's answer to a question put to him by his generals when he was at the height of his power: when had he been happiest? The French emperor responded, "The day of my First Communion was the happiest day of my life, for then I was brought nearest to my God."[52] Moreover, on another occasion, Napoleon testified to Christ's divinity, saying, "I know men and I tell you Jesus Christ was not a man."[53] Thus, Napoleon may have been the most ambivalent "antichrist" of history: an admirer of Jesus Christ who ignored many of His teachings, a loyal son of the Church who placed his political and dynastic ambitions above his religion, and a ruthless practitioner of *realpolitik* who defended Catholicism while scorning and mocking the authority of the popes.

According to historian John Jay Hughes, Napoleon was
> *an administrative genius and a pragmatist. As such he recognized the power of religion in human affairs. During his Egyptian campaign of 1798-1799 . . . Napoleon had posed as the protector of Islam and talked of conversion to that faith. Upon learning that this would require circumcision and lifelong abstinence from wine, he settled for a "certificate of competence in Mohammedan religious knowledge. "If I were to govern the Jews," Napoleon later declared, "I would rebuild the Temple of Solomon."*[54]

Once Napoleon came to power in France (overthrowing the ruling body known as the Directory and declaring himself First Consul), he made a Concordat, or official agreement, recognizing the religious position of the Church in French life and legalizing Catholic worship (previously outlawed during the Revolution). However, his purpose was purely a secular one: he wanted to restore order in the country, and knew that this could only be accomplished with the help of the Church.[55] Napoleon was careful to place severe limits on the authority and activities of the French bishops, concerned that the Church not become a source of opposition to his increasingly ambitious rule.

In that same year, 1799, Pope Pius VI—a fervent opponent of the Revolution—died in exile in France. It was widely feared that, with Rome under French control, he would in fact prove to be "the last pope," but the Holy Father had left instructions for holding a conclave under emergency conditions, and a Benedictine bishop was elected, taking the name Pius VII. (Because the French had confiscated the papal regalia, he had to be crowned with a papier-mâché tiara.)[56]

In 1804 Napoleon, temporarily victorious over his European enemies, conceived the idea of having the pope crown him as emperor. The formal invitation was so demeaning that Pius VII wanted to decline, but nevertheless journeyed to Paris late that year. Contrary to Napoleon's expectations, the French people welcomed him with great respect; as the Holy Father wrote, "We passed through France in the midst of a people on their knees." Napoleon himself insulted the pope with several calculated snubs: arranging to be off hunting when the Holy Father arrived, sneaking him into Paris at night (to prevent public expressions of acclaim), and assigning him a room in the Tuileries palace with a clear view of the square where thousands of Frenchmen (including hundreds of priests) had been guillotined less than a decade earlier. Moreover, in a change of plans at the coronation ceremony, Pius was not allowed to crown Napoleon; his role was merely to bless the crown, which the egotistical emperor then placed on his own head.[57]

As emperor, Napoleon's rule "became despotism—sometimes enlightened, often not. Instead of revolutionary terror, he relied on secret police. He asserted imperial authority over Church appointments, teaching, and other matters, and he imprisoned priests, bishops, and cardinals who annoyed him."[58] Napoleon even tried bullying the pope, but without success. He wanted Pius VII to move the papacy to Paris (where it would be under complete French domination), but the Holy Father dismissed the idea, saying, "How well you act comedy." An enraged emperor then took a drawing of St. Peter's in Rome and tore it to pieces, declaring, "This is what I shall do to the Church—I will crush her utterly." The pope calmly replied, "Now you act tragedy."[59]

On May 13, 1809, "Napoleon issued the decree by which the Pope was despoiled of the States of the Church [i.e., the Papal States in Italy]. From that time forward his fortune turned; four days later, for the first time in his triumphant career, he was defeated in battle, and Europe perceived that he was not invincible."[60] A few months later Napoleon ordered Pius VII arrested; when soldiers broke into the papal palace in Rome,

*the Pope sat calmly at a table, holding a crucifix. The soldiers
burst in but were awed by the dignity of the Pope. They removed
their hats, read their orders, genuflected, and kissed the Pope's
ring. He was put into a carriage and taken out of Rome. But
the soldiers did not know where to put the Pope because no
town wanted the responsibility of being the Pope's jail. He was
taken into France, then back to Italy, and finally imprisoned
near Genoa. All along the way, Pius VII, like Pius VI before
him, was cheered by the people. It was probably about then
that Napoleon said, in a flash of insight, "There are only two
powers on earth, the sword and the spirit. . . . In the long run
the sword is always beaten by the spirit.*[61]

Pius VII had previously signed a papal bull excommunicating
"all robbers of the Patrimony of Peter," and upon his arrest, copies
were quickly posted throughout Rome—leading the French general
commanding the troops occupying the city to complain to Napoleon
that "the Pope rules by moving his finger more effectively than
we with our bayonets." The emperor characteristically scoffed at
Pius' decree, saying, "Does he think the world has gone back a
thousand years? Does he suppose the arms will fall from the hands
of my soldiers?" However, during Napoleon's disastrous retreat
from Russia in the winter of 1812-1813, "the arms *did* drop from
the hands of Napoleon's soldiers, become either too weak or too
frozen any longer to clasp them."[62] In his *Grammar of Assent*, John
Henry Newman wrote that this was "No miracle, but a coincidence
so special, as rightly to be called a Divine judgment."[63]

From that point on, Napoleon fought a desperate, often
brilliant, but ultimately unsuccessful war to hold onto his empire.
He was unable to prevent his Prussian, Russian, Austrian, and
English enemies from invading France and seizing Paris itself. In
April 1814, the emperor, "who had ill learned the wisdom of the
old French proverb: *'Qui mange le Pape, meurt!'* (Who eats the Pope,
dies!), signed his abdication in the very Castle of Fontainebleau
where for so long he had held Christ's Vicar, Pope Pius VII, a
prisoner."[64] The Holy Father's return to Rome (which had been
predicted *to the exact date* two years earlier by Bl. Anna Maria
Taigi[65]) was a triumph:

*At the Porta del Popolo [Gate of the People], the papal*

*coachman took the horses out of the shafts so that the sons of the Roman nobility could draw the carriage up the Corso. . . . Pius VII was in his seventy-seventh year when he returned to Rome. . . . He was the only ruler in continental Europe who had withstood Napoleon. Deprived of his territories, without arms, isolated from his advisors, and relying only on spiritual weapons and his own inner strength, the gentle monk on the papal throne bent but never yielded to Napoleon's unceasing drive to dominate the Church.*[6]

The emperor himself was sent to Mediterranean island of Elba, from which he escaped the following year in a failed attempt to reclaim his throne. After his defeat at Waterloo in June, 1815, Napoleon was exiled to the remote island of St. Helena in the South Atlantic. From there, he requested the pope send him a chaplain, saying, "I was born in the Catholic religion. I wish to fulfill the duties it imposes, and receive the succor it administers." Even though the request was granted, Napoleon would sometimes amuse himself by pretending to believe that any religion was preferable to Catholicism. One of his former generals insisted, "I know your majesty does not believe one word of what you have just said." "Yes," the emperor admitted, "you are right. At any rate it helps to pass an hour."[67]

Reflecting on his fate and on the lessons to be learned therein, Napoleon addressed his colleagues in exile:

*You speak of empires and power. Well, Alexander the Great, Julius Caesar, Charlemagne and myself founded empires, but on what did we found them? Force. Christ founded His on love, and at this moment there are millions ready to die for Him. . . .*

*I see no army, no banner or battering-ram; yet a mysterious power is there, working in the interest of Christianity— men secretly sustained here and there by a common faith in the Unseen. I die before my time, and my body will be given to the earth as food for worms. Such is the fate of him called Napoleon the Great. But look to Christ, honored and loved in every land. Look to His Kingdom, rising over all other kingdoms. His life was not the life of a man; His death not that of a man but of God.*[68]

The emperor also noted that "The nations of the earth pass away, and thrones fall to the ground; the Church alone remains."[69]

Such comments suggest the experience of exile was good for Napoleon's soul, helping him grow in wisdom; he may also have grown in humility, as "For more than two years, Napoleon the Great, at St. Helena, taught the Catechism every day to the daughter of Gen. Bertrand, his faithful companion in captivity; and when she was old enough to make her First Communion, he procured a priest from France to continue the instructions and prepare her for that great act."[70]

In his will Napoleon declared, "I die in the Apostolic and Roman faith, in whose bosom I was born more than fifty years ago,"[71] and during his final weeks he ordered an altar to be constructed in his room, appropriately decorated for the reception of the Eucharist. When his aide, Count Bertrand, objected, Napoleon rebuked him, saying, "Surely, I am master in my own chamber."[72] As death approached, Bertrand—still not convinced his master's profession of faith was genuine—refused to let two Corsican priests approach Napoleon, but the younger one managed to sneak in the emperor's room and anoint him on May 2, 1821.[73] Three days later Napoleon died, with the name of his beloved (but often unfaithful) wife Josephine on his lips.

The French saying that "The more things change, the more they stay the same" was never better illustrated than by the restoration of the monarchy after Napoleon's abdication, with Louis XVIII, brother of the pious but ill-suited monarch Louis XVI, securely returned to the royal throne. The saying is perhaps even more appropriately applied to religion than to politics: Catholicism was, at least officially, restored to a central role in French life. The Church had survived the theories of hostile philosophers like Rousseau and Voltaire, violent persecutions by bloodthirsty revolutionaries, and cruel depredations at the hands of a power-mad emperor—and, in the process, converted some of those who fought against her. Catholicism's "eldest daughter" returned to the fold sadder but wiser. This was a great achievement by the Church in the early 19th century—but new challenges were about to unfold.

# NOTES TO CHAPTER 7

1. H. W. Crocker III, *Triumph: The Power and the Glory of the Catholic Church* (Three Rivers Press, 2001), p. 330.

2. Anne W. Carroll, *Christ the King, Lord of History* (TAN Books and Publishers, 1994), p. 313.

3. Benjamin Wiker, *10 Books that Screwed Up the World* (MJF Books, 2008), p. 44.

4. *Ibid.,* p. 51.

5. Ted Flynn, *Hope of the Wicked* (MaxKol Communications, 2000), p. 23.

6. Vincent P. Miceli, S.J., *The Gods of Atheism* (Roman Catholic Books, 1971), p. 311.

7. Jean Jacques Rousseau, *Discourse on the Origin and Foundation of Inequality among Men,* as quoted in Wiker, p. 49.

8. Ted and Maureen Flynn, *The Thunder of Justice* (MaxKol Communications, 1993), p. 220.

9. Wiker, pp. 52-53.

10. Joseph F. Halloran, *Quotable and Notable* (1993), Vol. 1, #5, p. 7.

11. Stephen Mahowald, *She Shall Crush Thy Head* (MMR Publishing, 1996), p. 102.

12. *Ibid.*

13. Godrey Kurth, *The Church at the Turning Points of History* (Naegele Printing Co., 1918; IHS Press, 2007), p. 102.

14. Warren H. Carroll, *The Guillotine and the Cross* (Christendom Press, 1991), pp. 27-28.

15. Flynn, *Hope of the Wicked*, p. 27.

16. William Guy Carr, R.D., *Satan, Prince of This World* (Omni Publications, 1997), p. 80.

17. Paul C. Vitz, *Faith of the Fatherless* (Spence Publishing Company, 1999), p. 141.

18. David F. Burgess, *Encyclopedia of Sermon Illustrations* (Concordia Publishing House, 1988), pp. 96-97.

19. Vitz, p. xiii.

20. *Ibid.,* p. 39.

21. Very Rev. Canon G. E. Howe, *Stories from the Catechist* (TAN Books and Publishing, 1922, 1989), p. 199.

22. Walter B. Knight, *Knight's Master Book of 4,000 Illustrations* (William B. Eerdmans Publishing Company, 1956), p. 159.

23. Burgess, p. 114.

24. Michael P. Green, ed., *1500 Illustrations for Biblical Preaching* (Baker Books, 1982), p. 27.

[25] Michael H. Brown, *The Day Will Come* (Servant Publications, 1996), p. 40.

[26] Fr. Andrew O'Brien, *Make Yourself An Ark!*, Vol. One (The American Research Foundation, 1995), p. 4.

[27] Flynn, *Hope of the Wicked*, p. 26.

[28] A. Ralph Epperson, *The Unseen Hand* (Publius Press, 1985), p. 86.

[29] *Ibid.*, p. 85. As the author notes, "This was confirmed by the fact that, when the mob reached the Bastille, so-called 'tortuous' prison of the 'oppressive' King Louis XVI, there were only seven prisoners incarcerated there: four forgers, two lunatics, and the Comte de Solages, incarcerated for 'monstrous crimes against humanity' at the request of his family. In fact, 'The damp, dark dungeons had fallen into complete disuse; since . . . 1776, no one had been imprisoned there" (*ibid.*, pp. 85-86).

[30] Vincent P. Miceli, S.J., *The Antichrist* (Roman Catholic Books, 1981), p. 109.

[31] Michael H. Brown, *The Last Secret* (Servant Publications, 1998), p. 234.

[32] Fr. Frederick L. Miller, *The Grace of Ars* (Ignatius Press, 2009), p. 20.

[33] Anne Carroll, p. 336.

[34] Brown, *The Last Secret*, p. 235.

[35] Crocker, p. 347.

[36] Rev. James Spencer Northcote (Peter F. Cunningham and Son, 1875), pp. 54-55, as quoted in Brown, *The Last Secret*, p. 236.

[37] Warren Carroll, pp. 138-139.

[38] Rosemary Ellen Guiley, *The Quotable Saint* (Checkmark Books, 2002), p. 19.

[39] Mike Aquilina, *The Resilient Church* (The Word Among Us Press, 2007), p. 113.

[40] Flynn, *Hope of the Wicked*, p. 29.

[41] Rev. Francis Spirago, *Anecdotes and Examples for the Catechism* (Roman Catholic Books, 1903), pp. 407-408. The author writes, "He actually went so far as to declare before the National Assembly that up to that time he had taught a false religion, and that henceforward he would profess the new religion of liberty and equality. He even trampled under foot his ecclesiastical insignia. But he soon received the reward of his treachery. He incurred the displeasure of Robespierre, who sentenced him to be guillotined. Then Bishop Gobel's eyes were opened; all at once he saw the full guilt of the crime he had committed against the Christian religion, and bitterly he repented of the scandal he had given to the people and to the clergy" (ibid.). The bishop managed to send his written confession secretly to a priest, asking him to come near his cell and whisper the words of absolution.

[42] Stanley Loomis, *Paris in the Terror* (1964), p. 328, as quoted by Warren Carroll, p. 166.

[43] R. R. Palmer, *Twelve Who Ruled: The Year of the Terror in the French Revolution*

(1941, 1969), p. 316, as quoted by Warren Carroll, p. 166.

44  Warren Carroll, p. 120.

45  Anne Carroll, p. 337.

46  Mark Regis, "The Carmelite Martyrs of Compiègne," *Garabandal Journal* (Jan. – Feb. 2005), p. 15.

47  *Ibid.,* p. 17.

48  Anne Carroll, p. 339.

49  John Hogue, *The Last Pope* (Element Books, 1998), p. 341. Nostradamus identified Adolf Hitler as the second antichrist (calling him *Hister*); he referred to the third antichrist with the mysterious name *Mabus.*

50  Desmond Seward, *Napoleon and Hitler: A Comparative Biography* (Viking, 1988), p. 303. The author includes a very informative passage which deserves to be quoted at length:
      In 1945, when Hitler's Germany was deservedly ending in horror, Professor Schramm asked his wife to type for him a chilling passage in Goethe's *Dichtung und Wahrheit.* "The most fearful manifestation of the demonic, however, is seen when it dominate an individual human being. In the course of my life, I have been able to observe several . . . they emanate a monstrous force and exercise incredible power over all creatures. . . . All moral powers combined are impotent against them. In vain do the more enlightened among men attempt to discredit them as deluded or deceptive—the masses will be drawn to them . . . they can be overcome only by the universe itself, against which they have taken up arms." The passage ends with the proverb *Nemo contra deum nisi deus ipse*—"No one can do something against God who is not God Himself." Naturally, Schramm applied Goethe's reflections to Adolf Hitler. Yet they had been written with Napoleon Bonaparte in mind (*ibid*).

51  *Ibid.,* p. 94.

52  Spirago, p. 303.

53  Seward, p. 94.

54  John Jay Hughes, *Pontiffs—Popes Who Shaped History* (Our Sunday Visitor, 1994), p. 168.

55  Sister Catherine, M.I.C.M., *Our Glorious Popes* (Loreto Publications, 1955), p. 217.

56  Richard P. McBrien, *Lives of the Popes* (Harper San Francisco, 1997), pp. 330-331.

57  Hughes, p. 173.

58  Crocker, p. 353.

59  Spirago, p. 141.

60  *Ibid.,* p. 142.

61  Anne Carroll, p. 352.

62  Sister Catherine, p. 218.

[63] Hughes, p. 181.

[64] Sister Catherine, p. 218.

[65] Joan Carroll Cruz, *Mysteries, Marvels, Miracles* (TAN Books and Publishers, 1997), p. 198.

[66] Hughes, p. 181.

[67] Crocker, pp. 354-355. Ironically, historians generally agree Napoleon was later poisoned by the general with whom he had this conversation.

[68] Burgess, p. 36.

[69] Howe, p. 66.

[70] *Ibid.,* p. 2.

[71] Seward, p. 297.

[72] Spirago, p. 136.

[73] Frank McLynn, *Napoleon: A Biography* (Arcade Publishing, 1997), p. 655.

Chapter 8

# Marx and His Disciples

*The thrones of the arrogant God overturns and establishes
the lowly in their stead. The roots of the proud God plucks
up, to plant the humble in their place: He breaks down their
stem to the level of the ground, then digs their roots from the
earth. The traces of the proud God sweeps away and effaces
the memory of them from the earth. (Sir. 10:14-17)*

In her apparition of July 13, 1917, Our Lady of Fatima warned
that if her requests for Communions of Reparation and the
Consecration of Russia to her Immaculate Heart were not
heeded, Russia would "spread her errors throughout the world,
causing wars and persecutions of the Church."[1] These errors, of
course, are atheism, materialism, and above all, Communism.

Our Lady's warning at Fatima echoed her message at La
Salette some seventy years earlier, in which she stated—in the
so-called "secret of La Salette"—that "the Church would be
severely attacked and monster"—meaning Communism—"would
be unleashed at the end of nineteenth or the beginning of the
twentieth century."[2] According to a message she allegedly gave
to Fr. Stefano Gobbi in 1983, the threat posed to the Church by the
associated evils of Communism and Masonry was foretold in the
Book of Revelation:

*The Woman clothed with the sun [12:1] is, with her cohorts,
openly waging war against the cohorts submissive to the Red
Dragon [12:3], at whose service is placed the Black Beast come
up from the sea [13:1]. The Red Dragon is Marxist atheism,
which has now conquered the whole world, and which has
induced humanity to build a new civilization of its own,
without God. In consequence, the world has become a cold and
barren desert, immersed in the ice of hatred and in the darkness*

144

*of sin and impurity. The Black Beast is also Masonry which has infiltrated the Church and attacks it, wounds it, and seeks by its subtle tactics to demolish it.*[3]

Communism represents one of Satan's most serious and ongoing assaults on the Church, and the man most directly responsible for it—Karl Marx—was in fact one of the devil's most devoted disciples.

# Marx

Karl Marx was identified by Pope John Paul II as one of three modern "Masters of Suspicion"; the Holy Father gave him that title "precisely because his thought represents the heart at war with itself. Indeed, there could be no greater war within the self than finite man trying to become God."[4] Also, Marx and his colleague Friedrich Engels have been called "history's most successful con-artist team. They took a valid insight [the reality of class struggle] that was hardly original and packaged it with an array of egregious errors, radical misunderstanding of history, human nature, social causes, ethnic groups, nationalism, labor management, and religion. Then they sold it to the world, and the world bought it and paid for it with its own blood."[5]

Marx and his parents were non-observant Jews, and so it was very easy for his father, an attorney, to "convert" to Lutheranism in order to improve his professional prospects in 19th century Germany. As a result of his father's cavalier attitude toward his ancestral faith, Marx came to view all religion as inauthentic and even oppressive—and eventually he saw his own mission, in part, as one of freeing humanity from its bondage to a non-existent God. Indeed, one of his friends wrote in 1841 that "Marx will surely chase God from His Heaven and even sue Him,"[6] and when Marx himself was asked his objective in life, he answered, "To dethrone God and destroy capitalism."[7]

As part of his rebellion against God, Marx claimed to be an atheist—for as he said, "Atheism is a *negation of God* and seeks to assert by this negation the *existence of man*."[8] Moreover, he was convinced that "religion and God had to be abolished as drugs that kept man enslaved in a destitute existence."[9] In fact, however, Marx's rebellion against the Creator required him to believe in

His existence—and he expressed his rejection of God in the most radical way possible:

> [Lutheran minister] Richard Wurmbrand demonstrated that many of the associates of Marx, such as Engels, Bakunin, Proudhon, Moses Hess, and many of those who put his program into practice, such as Lenin, Trotsky, Stalin, and Mao Tse Tung, were also Satanists. It is known that Stalin, Marx, and Engels were Illuminati recruits. So while Marx and his associates were anti-God, they were not atheists. They hated a God in whom they believed, and they sought the damnation of as many souls as possible.[10]

Marx himself admitted that the actual goal of Marxism wasn't to "form a new social order but to drag as many souls as possible to the depths of Hell," and to "replace Christianity with either naturalism or occultism."[11]

Strong evidence suggests that as a young man, Marx made some sort of pact with devil. In his poem *The Player*, he wrote:

> The hellish vapors rise and fill the brain. Till I go
> mad and my heart is utterly changed. See the sword?
> The prince of darkness sold it to me. For me he beats
> the time and gives the signs. Ever more boldly I play
> the dance of death.[12]

Marx was apparently initiated into Satanism as a disciple of Joanna Southcott, a Satanist priestess who claimed to be in contact with a demon named "Shiloh."[13] (It was at this time that he began allowing his hair and beard to become very long and unkempt—a practice characteristic of Southcott's followers.[14])

One would expect the personal life of an avowed Satanist to be severely disordered—and so it was with Karl Marx. He regarded everyone who disagreed with him to be an enemy of the proletariat (the working class, whom he claimed to champion); as his colleague Carl Schurz later wrote,

> I have never seen a man whose bearing was so provoking and intolerable. To no opinion which differed from his own did he accord the honor of even condescending consideration. Everyone who contradicted him he treated with abject contempt; every argument that he did not like he answered either with biting scorn at the unfathomable ignorance that had prompted

*it, or with opprobrious aspersions upon the motives of him who had advanced it. . . . he denounced everyone who dared to oppose his opinion.*[15]

Another colleague, Mikhail Bakunin—for a time one of Marx's closest friends—wrote of him, "One has to worship Marx in order to be loved by him. One has at least to fear him in order to be tolerated by him. Marx is essentially proud, up to dirt and madness."[16]

Marx's relations with his family were even more disedifying. He had little respect for his mother (once even threatening her with blackmail), and he had a strained relationship with his long-suffering wife—to the point that when she died, he didn't even bother attending her funeral.[17] When his housekeeper bore him a son (three months after his wife gave birth to their fourth child), Marx convinced his friend Engels to claim paternity of the infant, as it was "important for Marx to create an image of himself as an innocent member of the working class who was oppressed by the ruling class (even though, in fact, he was never really a member of the working class)."[18]

In spite of his growing influence and reputation, Marx was frequently depressed—a condition he claimed prevented him from working—and as a result, was often in debt and unable to support his family. Four of Marx's six children predeceased him (due in part to malnutrition), and the two who survived, like him, struggled with alcoholism. (In a letter to Engels begging for money, he wrote, "The children appear to have inherited their father's lust for drink. . . .") Marx's daughter Laura committed suicide with her husband, and his favorite daughter, Eleanor, "married the Satanist Edward Eveiling, who lectured on such subjects as 'The Wickedness of God.' They too made a suicide pact. She died; he backed out at the last minute."[19]

When his children were young, Marx used to tell them a series of ongoing and terrifying stories about someone selling his dearest possessions—and ultimately himself—to the devil. As one of Marx's biographers noted, "There can be very little doubt that those interminable stories were autobiographical. He had the Devil's view of the world, and the Devil's malignity. Sometimes he seemed to know that he was accomplishing works of evil."[20]

Rev. Richard Wurmbrand noted that "Marx died in despair,

as all Satanists do. On May 20, 1882 [less than a year before his death], he wrote to Engels: 'How pointless and empty is life, but how desirable!'"[21]Marx's deathbed was surrounded by candles burning in honor of the devil; when a nurse asked him if he had any last words, the founder of Communism shouted, "Go on, get out! Last words are for fools who haven't said enough."[22] Because he had alienated so many of those who knew him, only eleven persons attended his funeral in London. Marx was then buried in London's Highgate Cemetery, which afterwards became a center of British Satanism; to this day, black magic rituals are celebrated at his tomb.[23]

Tragically, Marx's writings (in collaboration with Engels) remained highly influential after his death. One author describes his horrific legacy:

> *Marx envisioned a misty and impossible goal and set it just beyond the reach of his devotees who were desperate enough (severely oppressed laborers) or foolish enough (intellectuals in the worst sense, like himself) to believe the fantasy as fact. . . . According to Marx, the fulfillment of the communist dream requires the disappearance of an entirely corrupt class. There is no moral blame attached to the revolutionaries who exterminate this class, and there is certainly no God to keep accounts. So it's no surprise that communism advanced by epic brutality.*[24]

The decline of Christian influence in 19th century Europe left a spiritual void; Marx and his colleagues seized the opportunity to offer a secular religion for the masses—one in which Marx saw himself as the messiah.[25] As the philosopher Karl Stern noted, Marxism produces "a most fiendish form of dehumanization, something like a preternatural spectacle in which the human form can no longer be discerned."[26] This, of course, has always been Satan's goal: to "defeat" God by removing every trace of the divine image from His children. Anyone seeking to understand the true nature of Marxism must acknowledge this truth.

## Marx's Colleagues

Friedrich Engels, who wrote the first draft of the *Communist Manifesto* (with Marx's input and editorial revisions), was a notorious womanizer; as he once wrote from Paris to his friend, "If I had an income of 5,000 fr[ancs], I would do nothing but work and amuse myself with women until I went to pieces."[27] This self-indulgent sentimentality doesn't indicate a mellow or pleasant personality, however; early in 1849, for instance, Engels published an article calling for the liquidation in Europe of entire races of people, especially Slavs. He wrote, "The next world war will cause entire reactionary peoples to disappear from the earth. And that, too, is progress."[28] Fortunately, the end of Engels' life seems to have been touched by divine grace; one author states, "Apparently on his death bed, Engels repented for his participation in writing the Communist Manifesto and asked Jesus Christ for forgiveness."[29]

The Russian anarchist Mikhail Bukanin was seemingly more committed to Satanism than Engels, for he once wrote:

> The Evil One is the satanic revolt against divine authority, revolt in which we see the germ of all human emancipations, the revolution. Satan is the eternal rebel, the first freethinker and the emancipator of worlds. He makes man ashamed of his bestial ignorance and obedience; he emancipates him, stamps upon his brow the seal of liberty and humanity, in urging him to disobey and eat of the fruit of knowledge.[30]

This, of course, is the devil's original temptation, as voiced to Eve by the serpent: "your eyes will be opened and you will be like gods" (Gen. 3:5). Bakunin, who, like the French social theorist Pierre Proudhon, gave his allegiance to Satan, asserted, "In this revolution we will have to awaken the Devil in people, to stir up the basest passions. Our mission is to destroy, not edify; the passion of destruction is a creative passion."[31] Bakunin's reference to ruin and devastation may have been tragically appropriate, for Scripture says, "And You, O God, will bring them down into the pit of destruction; men of blood and deceit shall not live out half their days" (Ps. 55:24).

# Communism vs. Catholicism

The material presented in this chapter so far should make it quite clear that Communism has never been exclusively or even primarily an economic and political theory or system. It is, ultimately, a Satanic religion, and as such, is irrevocably opposed to Catholicism. According to Fr. Vincent Miceli, S. J.,

> For whatever solutions the Catholic Church advances to various problems, communism proposes diametrically contrary remedies. The Catholic Church teaches that she can be recognized by her distinguishing marks; she is one, holy, catholic, and apostolic. The communist quasi-contra-church claims as her distinctive qualities that she is one, anti-theistic, universal and Marxist. Both organizations arouse heroic zeal in their finest faithful; both pursue messianic goals. . . . communist humanism, the upstart newcomer, apes the Catholic Church with the calculated intention of transposing the Church's sacred doctrines and practices into its own atheistic teachings and profane rules for conduct.[32]

Exactly twenty years after Our Lady of Fatima warned that Russia would spread her errors throughout the world, Pope Pius XI, in his 1937 encyclical *Divini Redemptoris*, listed three reasons for Communism's rapid growth: (1) too few people were able (or willing) to grasp the true nature of Communism; (2) a diabolical propaganda campaign—unlike anything the world had ever seen before—helped Communism win adherents and forestall potential opposition; and (3) a large part of the world press practiced a conspiracy of silence or disinformation.[33]

(As an example of the third point, which occurred even as Pius was preparing his encyclical, *New York Times* columnist Walter Duranty wrote glowing reports of the progress being made in the Soviet Union, while completely ignoring or even denying the massive, man-made famine taking place in Ukraine.[34])

Communism, centered in the Soviet Union, would indeed prove to be a grave threat to the Church, to Western civilization, and to human dignity itself. However, before the murderous and hateful theories of Marx and Engels could be implemented, a violent and bloody revolution would be needed in Russia—and to help set the stage, Satan used, and then discarded, a willing servant whose pretended holiness masked an almost unthinkable perversity.

# Rasputin

The Russian Orthodox monk Grigori Rasputin gained great influence at the imperial court (due to his seeming ability to control the bleeding of the hemophiliac heir to the throne), and his favor with the Czarina, Alexandra, wife of Czar Nicholas II, forestalled genuine efforts at reform even in the face of rising discontent. As one historian states,

*Understanding Rasputin is the key to understanding both the soul and the brutality of the Russia that came after him. He was a precursor of the millions of peasants who, with religious consciousness in their souls, would nevertheless tear down churches and who, with a dream of Love and Justice, would murder, rape and flood the country with blood, in the end destroying themselves.*[35]

Early in the 20th century, Rasputin, styling himself a *starets*, or holy man, traveled throughout Russia and gained a following through his hypnotic preaching—while also indulging his carnal desires. "To his immense willpower, great physical presence and strength, natural wit and peasant's cunning was added an almost miraculous intuition."[36] As described by Michael H. Brown, Rasputin "was a vile, foul-smelling man with long coal-black hair, long large fingers, and unforgettable blue-gray eyes. His was a shocking visage, but his hypnotic personality and his reputation as a healer endeared him to Russia's ruling elite. He weakened the czar and exerted unusual power over palace decision-making. . . ."[37] Another scholar notes that Rasputin "was known to be deeply involved in Spiritualism and displayed signs of possible demonic possession."[38]

The evil Russian monk shamelessly seduced many women, including some who were socially prominent; his speech was filled with shocking obscenities, and he was frequently drunk in public. So great was Rasputin's influence over Alexandra that he easily convinced her to banish religious authorities who tried to hold him accountable for his scandalous behavior and misdeeds.[39] Eventually his fate caught up with him, however; some members of the royal court decided that Russia could not be saved from disaster unless he was eliminated.

One of the would-be assassins, Prince Yusupov, later testified,

"All of a sudden his expression [during the assassination attempt] changed into one of fiendish hatred. . . . I felt that, confronted with those satanic eyes, I was beginning to lose my self-control. A strange feeling of numbness took possession of me. My head reeled."[40] Further evidence of Rasputin's demonic protection is seen in the extreme difficulty his murderers had in killing him. First, they gave the unsuspecting monk enough poisoned food and alcohol to kill four men, but to no apparent effect. Then he was shot (causing two wounds that should have been fatal under normal circumstances), clubbed, beaten, tied up, thrown against a bridge, and finally hurled into the Neva River in Moscow, where he should have frozen to death almost instantly. However, his

> *body still breathed, for there was water in its lungs; it moved, for the ropes binding its hands were partially untied. How at last did it die? No one knows. Perhaps an angel from Heaven finally intervened to conquer the devil which was apparently possessing the body. The next day, the body was recovered, entirely encased in ice, its lungs full of water, its right hand freed of the rope and reaching out.[41]*

Rasputin was dead, but he had served Satan's purpose—for by undermining the Russian imperial throne, he helped pave the way for one of the most ruthless men in history to seize power in Russia.

# Lenin

The exiled Communist revolutionary Vladimir Ilyich Lenin returned to Russia just three days after Our Lady's October 13, 1917 apparition at Fatima. This Illuminati agent, whose code name was supposedly "Spartacus," told a friend, "We are . . . the real revolutionaries! . . . Yes, we are going to destroy everything, and on the ruins we will build our temple."[42] According to Michael H. Brown,

> *Mimicking Jesus is a trait of an anti-christ and indeed, one day soon every government building in the Soviet Union would have a little table altar with Lenin's picture next to those of Engels and Marx. As a child Lenin displayed an alarming lack of ordinary humanity, screaming at playmates and finding comfort only in the paria of the opera Faust [in which the title*

*character sells his soul to the devil]. . . . and in fifth grade he tore off a cross he was wearing, sat on it, and threw it to the ground. . . .*[43]

The Ukrainian Catholic mystic Josyp Terelya—one of the great Catholic heroes of the 20th century—described Lenin's youth: *What was Lenin like as a child? He was tempestuous. He was a chronic liar. He broke toys. He screamed at the top of his lungs. He tortured animals. . . . He avoided contact with schoolmates and one director wrote to Kazan University that the young Lenin showed a chilling remoteness and an alarming lack of ordinary humanity. One evening his sister heard him muttering to himself and realized he was talking nonsense— delirious, like he was talking to another world, in an unknown language. The spell passed, and he grew to become the Soviet godhead, deceiving much of the world.*[44]

Furthermore, Rev. Wurmbrand notes that Leon Trotsky, Lenin's friend and fellow revolutionary, recorded that Lenin, "at the age of sixteen, tore the cross from his neck, spat on it, and trod it underfoot, a very common Satanic ceremony. . . . In the end Satan deceived him, as he does all his followers."[45]

By the age of sixteen, Lenin was an atheist; influenced by Marx's writings, he denied the reality of Heaven and insisted that—under the right leadership—Communists could create their utopia on earth. Indeed, in the worldview of Marx and Lenin, "history has nothing to do with the unfolding of God's providence and the working out of man's free will. History inevitably marches . . . toward the utopian paradise of communism,"[46] and those who resist this preordained outcome have only themselves to blame if their opposition is overcome by the most ruthless measures. Lenin— whose favorite book was Machiavelli's *The Prince*—once wrote, "Atheism is an integral part of Marxism. Marxism is materialism. We must combat religion,"[47] and as his comrade Grigori Zinoviev boasted, "We will vanquish God in His highest Heaven."[48]

Lenin also claimed, "There can be nothing more abominable than religion," and as historian Paul Johnson explains,

*The men he really feared and hated, and later persecuted, were the saints. The purer the religion, the more dangerous. A devoted cleric, he argued, is far more influential than an egotistical*

*and immoral one. The clergy most in need of suppression were not those committed to the defense of exploitation but those who expressed their solidarity with the proletariat and the peasants. It was as though he recognized in the true man of God the same zeal and spirit which animated himself, and wished to expropriate it and enlist it in his own cause. No man personifies better the replacement of the religious impulse by the will to power.*[49]

Paraphrasing Marx (who had called religion the "opiate of the people"), Lenin stated, "Religion is a kind of spiritual gin in which the slaves of capitalism drown their human shape and their claim to any decent human life."[50]

Lenin was a cold, unfeeling human being who had little love for his loyal wife Krupskaya. For instance, because he was once staying up all night writing, she asked him to awaken her if her dying mother needed her for anything. Lenin agreed, but the next morning Krupskaya found her mother dead; when she confronted her husband, he brusquely replied, "You told me to wake you if your mother needed you. She died. She didn't need you."[51] Years earlier, as a young man, "when he heard about mass starvation among the peasants, his stone-hearted reaction was purely Marxist: don't interfere, let them starve. Because starvation must be caused by capitalism, mass starvation was good. It showed that history was moving forward, through conflict, toward the final revolution of the proletariat."[52]

The October Revolution of 1917 (which actually occurred in November, according to the Gregorian calendar used in the West) brought Lenin and his allies into power, and ushered in a killing spree far exceeding the French Revolution's Reign of Terror. Thus, "we should not be fooled into thinking, as leftist hagiographers of Lenin would have it, that Stalin represented a deviation from the more lenient and humane Lenin. Lenin's brutality was less than his successor's only because he died at a fairly young age."[53]Under Lenin, Russian Communism claimed some six to eight million victims—many of them as part of the Soviet Union's persecution of Christianity:

*The religious instruction of children was prohibited. Religious literature was banned. Parochial schools, seminaries and monasteries were closed. Church lands and religious objects were confiscated. Bishops and priests were arrested and many were killed.*[54]

In spite of his ruthlessness, however, Lenin was unable to eradicate all religious belief; he also failed to remake the government bureaucracy—let alone Russian society itself—completely according to his will. After several years in power, he complained, "The state does not function as we desired. How does it function? The car does not obey. A man is at the wheel and seems to lead it, but the car does not drive in the desired direction. It moves as another force wishes."[55] This other "force," naturally, was Satanic in origin—and only when it was too late did Lenin realize that in attempting to implement his grand schemes of a Communist utopia, he was actually a pawn being used to further a different agenda. On his deathbed in 1924, Lenin said, "I committed a great error. My nightmare is to have the feeling that I'm lost in an ocean of blood from the innumerable victims. It is too late to return. To save our country, Russia, we would have needed men like Francis of Assisi. With ten men like him we would have saved Russia."[56]

Instead of acting upon this realization by repenting of his sins, Lenin tried to cling to his power, but a stroke left him partially incapacitated. Josef Stalin—about whose ruthlessness Lenin had earlier warned some of his faithful allies—apparently seized the opportunity to have Lenin poisoned, and "the maker of the Communist revolution died in agony and terror, his body racked by convulsions so violent that at times they flung it up into the air."[57] Moreover, Michael Brown notes that "When Lenin died in 1924, a horrible howl was heard from his room, as if the demons he'd served so well had come to take him."[58]

# Gramsci

Of all the obscure, little-known figures of the 20th century, Antonio Gramsci may have been the most dangerous—for he formulated the long-term Communist strategy that is still wreaking havoc on Western society to this day. A co-founder of the Italian Communist party, Gramsci rejected the Church and its teachings about God—but he recognized that Christianity was far too strongly embedded in Western culture to be overcome by a direct revolution or a military assault, so he created a blueprint for Communist victory that relied on great patience and subtlety.

Gramsci argued that Marxism could only prevail if it attempted to alter the Christian mindset of the average person, eventually turning it, by means of a "quiet and anonymous revolution," into an anti-Christian attitude; influential Communists and their sympathizers "needed to get individuals and groups in every class and station of life to think about life's problems without reference to the Christian transcendent, without reference to God and the laws of God."[59] This would be done by a "long march" through the West's cultural institutions—particularly education, the arts, the entertainment industry, the press, labor unions, and philanthropic and even some religious organizations; by subverting them and changing their missions, political power would finally fall into the laps of the revolutionaries without a shot being fired.[60] Soviet-style Communism, Gramsci knew, held no attraction for most Westerners, so a much-more gradual, non-violent socialistic approach would be necessary—and his strategy has borne great fruit over the last half-century.[61]

Gramsci was imprisoned by Mussolini's government, but his failing health led to an early release; he died in Rome in 1937 at the age of 46. There is some confusion regarding his possible reconciliation with the Church. One archbishop claimed that he "returned to the faith of his infancy" and "died taking the sacraments"; however, other accounts of his death deny this claim and make no mention of a deathbed conversion.[62] In either case, a scriptural warning continues to be very applicable to his tactics: "There is a shrewdness keen but dishonest, which by duplicity wins a judgment" (Sir.19:21). Like the serpent of Gen. 3, socialism—following Gramsci's formula—continues to tempt the unwary with promises of "progress," "equality," and "social justice," and remains all the more dangerous for its subtlety.

# Stalin

The behind-the-scenes manipulator who seized control of the Soviet Union after Lenin's death turned out to be one of the most ruthless murderers of history; scholars estimate that as many as 50 million people died as a result of Josef Stalin's hellish decrees.[63] As a later Soviet leader, Mikhail Gorbachev, stated, "The mark of Stalin's evil was that he turned morality on his head: what was bad became good, what was good, bad. This was a man who lost sight of the fact that human dignity and well-being lay at the heart of all progress."[64]

While a student at an Orthodox seminary, Stalin (whose actual name was Dzhugashvili) became interested in radical politics, and eventually a member of the Bolsheviks (as the Communists were first known). He played a minor role in the October Revolution, but after he came to full power in 1924, he had all the historical records and documents rewritten so as to portray him as the heroic driving force behind the event.[65]

Claiming to be the legitimate successor of Lenin, Stalin rejected Leon Trotsky's call for an immediate "world revolution," and instead concentrated on making the Soviet Union a leading industrial power, while mercilessly destroying any opposition (real or imagined) to his dictatorial rule. Forced collectivization of farms, deliberate famines resulting in mass starvation, a fierce persecution of Christianity, show trials in which victims publicly "confessed" their crimes, massive building projects using political prisoners as slave labor, the creation of a vast gulag (prison camp system) into which countless millions disappeared, and a monstrous personality cult in which Stalin was venerated as practically a god, were all hallmarks of his satanic rule of nearly thirty-years.

During the early stages of World War II, Stalin hoped to play off Nazi Germany against the Western democracies; when Hitler attacked the Soviet Union itself in the summer of 1941, Stalin, in his desperation, temporarily halted his persecution of Christianity, hoping to enlist all his previous victims into a "Great Patriotic War." Indeed, at the urging of President Roosevelt, he pretended to grant full religious freedom to the Russian Orthodox Church, so as to lessen the opposition of the American people to giving the

Communists military assistance during the war.[66]  As it became apparent the Germans would not win an easy victory, the dictator's cynical contempt for religion returned. When British Prime Minister Winston Churchill suggested the desirability of enlisting the support of the Holy Father, Stalin is said to have scoffed, "The Pope! How many divisions [military formations] does he have?" (When Churchill later recounted this to Pius XII, the Holy Father responded, "Tell my son Josef that he will meet my divisions in eternity."[67])

As the years passed, Stalin became increasingly cruel; he enjoyed hearing how some of his many victims begged for their lives before being shot, and he once remarked, "The greatest delight is to mark one's enemy, prepare everything, avenge oneself thoroughly, and then go to sleep."[68] He enjoyed comparing himself to some of the great despots of history; in particular, he was "fascinated by Genghis Khan, whose belief that 'the deaths of the vanquished are necessary for the tranquility of the victors,' he concurred with."[69]

Some of Stalin's closest associates began recognizing, or at least suspecting, the inhuman depths of evil in his soul.  For instance, Nikolai Bukharin, secretary general of the Communist International, wrote about Stalin, "He is not a man, but a devil."[70] (Stalin had him arrested and executed in 1938.)  Stalin's own daughter, Svetlana Alliluyeva, stated, "A terrible demon had taken possession of my father's soul;" she also mentioned that he considered love and forgiveness to be a worse thing than the greatest possible crime.[71]

Throughout his adult life, Stalin had a fierce hatred for Christianity.  In 1931, he said that the Soviet Union had two major enemies:  the Catholic Church and the moral foundation of America.[72]  To attack the latter, he grudgingly allowed his international agents of influence to follow Gramsci's blueprint (though sometimes he insisted on more direct measures[73]); in regard to the former, he attacked Catholicism whenever it came under his direct control.

For instance, during the fierce repression of the Ukrainian Catholic Church in the early 1930s, "Communists began ruthlessly killing millions of Catholics in what became, in sheer number, the greatest persecution of all time. . . . Thousands of priests and nuns were sent to Siberia."[74] As Stalin cynically remarked, "Kill the eunuch priests and you kill this Christ;"[75] years later, in 1996, a Russian official admitted that 200,000 priests were persecuted or killed under Stalin's orders.[76] After World War II, in which the Red Army conquered much of Eastern Europe, the Catholic Church in Poland and Lithuania, and the Orthodox Church in neighboring countries, also experienced harsh—even demonic—treatment.

In his extreme egotism, Stalin demanded to be venerated as a god. The great Russian author and political prisoner Aleksandr Solzhenitsyn noted that many—though by no means all—Russians idolized Stalin and gave him their "boundless and unquestioning faith."[77] Those who didn't honor the dictator out of conviction did so out of fear; even the slightest indication of possible opposition to his leadership could find led to someone being denounced to the secret police and sent off to a prison camp. Stalin was idolized to a preposterous degree; posters with slogans like "Thank you Comrade Stalin for a Happy Childhood" were seen everywhere, and on his seventieth birthday "an image of his face was projected against the sky over the Kremlin. It was as if Stalin was a god and Stalinism a new type of religion."[78] Indeed, the official Soviet newspaper *Pravda* ("Truth") wrote, "If you meet with difficulties in your work, or suddenly doubt your abilities, think of him—of Stalin—and you will find the confidence you need. If you feel tired in an hour when you should not, think of him—of Stalin—and your work will go well. If you are seeking a correct decision, think of him—of Stalin—and you will find that decision."[79]

As St. Alphonsus Liguori noted, "The ambitious are not satisfied by the attainment of certain honors: their ambition and pride continually increase; and their inquietude, their envy, and their fears are multiplied."[80] This was certainly true of Stalin; as he grew ever more powerful (having killed all his enemies), he also grew more paranoid. In the Kremlin, for instance, he had seven different bedrooms—waiting until the last minute to decide which one to use on any given night, so as to minimize possible assassination attempts during his sleep. (One night, when he was kept awake by the barking of a dog, he sent some soldiers to shoot not only the dog, but also its owner.)

Stalin also employed fifteen personal food tasters, to guard against being poisoned, and his personal bullet-proof car had windows that were three inches thick. Also, "Tunnels were dug between his office and other government buildings so he could make a quick getaway should anything go wrong, and in the gardens of his country residence telephones were installed every few yards or so, in case Stalin suffered a heart attack or was set upon by assassins. . . ."[81] Moreover, his tea had to be prepared from specially sealed packs, each to be used just once; a cook who was seen taking tea leaves from a pack with a broken seal was sent to prison for this "crime."[82]

Extreme security measures did not, of course, save a paranoid dictator from divine judgment. On March 2, 1953, Stalin suffered a severe stroke. Three days later, according to his daughter, "His face was discolored, his features becoming unrecognizable. . . . He literally choked to death as we watched. The death agony was terrible. . . . At the last minute he opened his eyes. It was a terrible look, either mad or angry and full of the fear of death."[83] Svetlana also said, "Father died terribly and difficult. God gives the righteous an easy death,"[84] and an onlooker noted that his last gesture was "to lift his left hand as if to curse, or to ward off something."[85] Stalin's death was the occasion of intense mourning for many, and intense joy for others;[86] one can only imagine it ushered in an eternity of unimaginable misery and horror to a man who caused more suffering and terror than almost anyone else in history.

# Mao

If, in hell's "Olympics of Mass Murder," Adolf Hitler claimed the bronze medal and Josef Stalin earned the silver, the gold medal for the most murder victims of all time would surely be awarded to Mao Tse-tung, Communist dictator of Red China. In his rise to absolute power, Mao had declared, "Half of China may well have to die," and some scholars estimate the death toll at 70 million.[87] Moreover, "If we judge the extent of a dictator's power by the number of people over whom he wields control, then surely Mao Tse-tung would be at the top of the list. For over twenty-five years Mao commanded in excess of a billion people and his rule extended across a geographical area of over nine million square kilometers."[88]

When Mao and his Communist comrades came to power, many thousands of landlords had their property seized and redistributed to the peasants; other members of privileged classes, along with opponents of the revolution, were denounced, arrested, and either executed or sent to special labor camps for "re-education." This latter fate was also applied to the nation as a whole, for Mao,

> Before any other major Communist leader . . . understood the importance of Antonio Gramsci's basic teaching: You have to transform the culture of the people. In Mao's translation, that came out: Cleanse the people's memory of the past. Teach the people: "Do not think. We will think for you. You will be happy."[89]

Because the traditional culture he sought to erase was still alive in the people's consciousness, in 1966 Mao, who preferred to be known as the "Chairman," began the disastrous ten-year "Cultural Revolution," in which he "sent millions of young men and women out to uproot all traces of China's ancient culture. Mao's holocaust of human lives and torture certainly exceeded the European holocaust under Adolf Hitler, and the Ukrainian holocaust under Josef Stalin."[90] The dictator's arbitrary decrees resulted in incalculable human suffering and social disruption. "In Mao's world, nothing was to be left up to the individual, let alone be left to chance. A good picture of him would be as a god, one whose every whim had to be obeyed."[91] Indeed, the "little red book"—a compilation of quotes from Mao's speeches and writings—served as Communist China's Bible, and the leaders and people tried to outdo each other in using the booklet as a source of inspiration and morality.

Mao's contempt for traditional morality was well known. For instance, in regard to prohibitions against killing, stealing, and other serious moral offenses, he stated, "I do not think these have to do with conscience. I think they are only out of self-interest for self-preservation," and he also claimed that all considerations must "be purely calculation for oneself, and absolutely not for obeying external ethical codes. . . ."[92]

Naturally, this cavalier attitude carried over into a shocking lack of concern for human suffering and death; Mao asserted, "We love sailing on a sea of upheavals. To go from life to death is to experience the greatest upheaval. Isn't it magnificent!" Needless to say, "he applied his attitude only to other people, not to himself. Throughout his own life he was obsessed with finding ways to thwart death, doing everything he could to perfect his security and enhance his medical care."[93]

Like many of history's antichrists, Mao recognized the Church as a formidable adversary. He was

*very interested in the Vatican, especially its ability to command allegiance beyond national boundaries, and his Italian visitors often found themselves being peppered with questions about the Pope's authority. The tenacity and effectiveness of the Catholics perturbed the regime. . . . A high-decibel smear campaign accused Catholic priests and nuns of heinous actions ranging from plain murder to cannibalism and medical experiments on babies. Hundreds of Chinese Catholics were executed, and many foreign priests suffered physical abuse. . . . Almost all foreign clergy were expelled . . . by about 1953.*[94]

Mao's hatred for the Church may have been more than just a severe human malignancy; author Thomas W. Petrisko notes that the Chinese leader "openly embraced the ways of Satan," and "exhibited some signs of possible demonic infiltration and even wrote poems expressing his pleasure of fighting 'with Heaven,'"[95] and according to Michael H. Brown, "He was a man of such erratic emotions that at times he had to be carried out of meetings, his eyes flitting in rage, spittle frothing around his mouth."[96] Appropriately, Mao was born in the year of the snake, and his banner featured a red dragon.

Chairman Mao's final years were not happy ones. He and his wife constantly quarreled, and eventually they ceased living together, and "his last phase was marked by acrimony, consciousness of failure and confusion," in which his mind "wandered between religious and secular belief. 'My body is riddled with diseases. I have an appointment with God.'"[97]

This awareness did not lead to any type of repentance, for his last days were dominated by a thirst for revenge, frustration, and self-pity; as his biographers Jung Chang and Jon Halliday note, "Well over 70 million people had perished—in peacetime—as a result of his misrule, yet Mao felt sorry only for himself."[98] His futile attempts to delay death and escape divine judgment bring to mind Isaiah's prophecy that on the appointed day, the Lord "will slay the dragon" and destroy the great serpent (Is. 27:1).

Mao and his successors failed to eradicate Christianity;[99] millions of Catholics and other Christians belong to the underground Church, and even the official, "patriotic" Catholic bishops (those under government control) have recently taken some steps toward acknowledging the authority of the Vatican (with Rome in turn expressing a willingness to consider acknowledging their legitimacy). Moreover, Heaven has expressed its care for Chinese Catholics in various ways, including an event similar to Fatima's "miracle of the sun." At a Marian shrine in northern China,

> the sun was seen to move and suddenly lose its overpowering brightness at Dong Lu in 1995. As elsewhere, it seemed to be eclipsed by an off-white Host and surrounded by halos. "Rays of various colors emanated from the sun," said a report by the Cardinal Kung Foundation in Connecticut. "With the passing of the minutes, the sun changed colors, first to yellow, then to red and blue, followed by other colors. Subsequently people saw different apparitions in the core of the sun: a holy Cross, the Holy Family, Holy Mary, and the Holy Eucharist. At times, the sun would approach the crowd and then retreat. People were heard crying out, "Holy Mother, have pity on us, your children," and "Holy Mother, please forgive my sins." The people were all seeing similar things because they shouted out similar observations ("Yellow!" Red! Blue!"). This lasted about twenty minutes until a sudden white ray came and the sky returned to normal.[100]

About 30,000 people witnessed this miracle, which occurred at the moment of the Consecration during an outdoor Mass—a Mass the authorities had unsuccessfully tried to prevent.

This miracle was a vivid reminder to the suffering Catholics of China that Our Lord and Our Lady had not forgotten them. The Chinese Communist government, having witnessed the central role the Church played in the collapse of Communism in Eastern Europe, has placed further restrictions upon the practice of Christianity, but these will of no avail in the end. Christians in China may appear powerless and outnumbered, and their opponents may seem very strong and secure—but this will ultimately prove to be an illusion, for "the Lord watches over the way of the just but the way of the wicked vanishes" (Ps. 1:6).

# The Failed "Gods" of Communism

Other disciples of Marx brought great misery to their countries. The Cambodian Communist Pol Pot, for instance, after seeing China's Cultural Revolution, decided to implement his own version; along with members of the previous government, "police, Christian clergymen, military officers, Muslim leaders, teachers and public servants were arrested and executed without trial."[101] Pol Pot tried to stamp out all individualism, and his Communist political party—the Khmer Rouge—had a slogan which said, "To keep you is no gain and to destroy you is no loss." In terms of the percentage of Cambodia's population killed under his rule (perhaps as high as 25%), Pol Pot may have been the worst mass murderer in history. During an interview with a foreign journalist following his forcible removal from power in 1979, he calmly asserted, "Do you think I am a violent person? No. So far as my conscience and my mission were concerned, there was no problem. . . . We were new and inexperienced and events kept occurring one after the other which we had to deal with. . . . For the love of the nation and the people it was the right thing to. . . ."[102]

Another Asian nation cursed with an equally deluded and despotic Communist dictator was North Korea, where the long misrule of the ruthless Kim Il-sung and his mentally-unbalanced son Kim Jong-Il resulted in the bloody Korean War, (which, because a formal peace treaty was never signed, is still technically in effect today), grinding poverty and misery, widespread famines and the threat of mass starvation, and perhaps the most xenophobic society in the modern world.

Christians in North Korea have suffered severely. Several hundred thousand were martyred, and many others were sentenced to long prison terms; in addition, all churches were destroyed.[103] Kim Il-sung was so ruthless that he "issued a directive that if someone was found guilty of crimes against the state then three generations of his or her family should be wiped out in order to cleanse his 'socialist paradise.'"[104] He also implemented a religious system or ideology known as *Juche* ("self-reliance"), which proclaimed him the "immortal God and eternal Father," and insisting that he was "superior to Christ in love, superior to Buddha in benevolence, superior to Confucius in virtue and superior to Mohammed in justice."[105]

When Kim Il-sung died in 1994, his son and designated successor, Kim Jong-il, was disturbed that the people mourned for only three days; fearing this indicated the weakness of the family's carefully-constructed personality cult, he ordered every organization to send some of its members to weep publicly in front of his father's statue.[106] The younger Kim has continued his father's repression of Christians; however, even though

> *Kim Il-sung and his regime either executed or abducted 89 percent of those discovered to be Christian . . . they could not wipe out the Gospel message from their nation. God's faithfulness to His children remains. The underground church is alive and well, and the Holy Spirit continues to minister and grow Christ's Body in the Hermit Kingdom.*[107]

The Church has suffered severely in other Communist lands such as Cuba and Vietnam, along with certain newly-independent countries that were part of the former Soviet Union. Even today, Christians are sometimes an oppressed and embattled minority, but Communism has never succeeded in overcoming the Gospel.

Even though "the godless plight and plague of Communism has exacted from the human race a chilling, exorbitant price in blood, lives, and terror,"[108] it's Communism—not the Church—which finds itself on the "ash heap of history." John Paul II, in speaking of Communism (and also of Nazism), noted that the evil of the 20th century "was an evil of gigantic proportions, an evil which availed itself of state structures in order to accomplish its wicked work, an evil built up into a system." Nevertheless, he added, "Redemption is ongoing. Where evil grows, there the hope for good also grows."[109]

In the 1930s Jesus had revealed to the Polish nun St. Faustina Kowalska, "I bear a special love for Poland, and if she will be obedient to My will, I will exalt her in might and holiness. From her will come forth the spark that will prepare the world for My final coming."[110] In addition to the spiritual power unleashed by the devotion to Divine Mercy, Poland also played a key role in the peaceful collapse of Communism in Eastern Europe through the labor union Solidarity (under its leader, the devout Catholic Lech Walesa), and particularly through the inspired geopolitical leadership of Pope John Paul II. Our Lady of Fatima had promised that Russia would ultimately be converted, and a period of peace be granted to the world.[111] Communism is not yet completely vanquished, but the lessons of history clearly vindicate the teaching of Scripture: "Put not your trust in princes, in man, in whom there is no salvation; when his spirit departs he returns to his earth; on that day his plans perish" (Ps. 146:3-4).

## NOTES TO CHAPTER 8

1  Mark Fellows, *Sister Lucia: Apostle of Mary's Immaculate Heart* (Immaculate Heart Publications, 2007), p. 66.

2  Ted and Maureen Flynn, *The Thunder of Justice* (MaxKol Communications, 1993), p. 22.

3  *To the Priests* (Marian Movement of Priests, 1974, 1995, 16th English edition), pp. 390-391.

4  Donald De Marco & Benjamin Wiker, *Architects of the Culture of Death* (Ignatius Press, 2004), p. 130. The other two "Masters of Suspicion" identified by the Holy Father are Friedrich Nietzsche and Sigmund Freud.

5  *Ibid.*, p. 129.

6  Rev. Richard Wurmbrand, *Marx & Satan* (Crossway Books, 1986), p. 24.

7  Fr. Andrew O'Brien, *Make Yourself An Ark!*, Vol. One (The American Research Foundation, Inc., 1995), p. 10.

8  De Marco & Wiker, p. 122.

9  Vincent P. Miceli, S. J., *The Antichrist* (Roman Catholic Books, 1981), p. 135.

10  O'Brien, p. 42.

11  Michael H. Brown, *The Final Hour* (Queenship Publishing, 2000), p. 29.

12  Ted Flynn, *Hope of the Wicked* (MaxKol Communications, 2000), p. 35.

13  Paul McGuire, *The Day the Dollar Died* (M House Publishers, 2009), p. 142.

14  Wurmbrand, p. 26.

15  Benjamin Wiker, *10 Books that Screwed Up the World* (MJF Books, 2008), p. 59.

16  Wurmbrand, p. 13.

[17]  *Ibid.*, p. 34.

[18]  De Marco & Wiker, p. 128.

[19]  Flynn, *Hope of the Wicked*, p. 36.

[20]  Robert Payne, *Marx* (Simon & Schuster, 1968), as quoted in Wurmbrand, p. 24.

[21]  Wurmbrand, p. 48.

[22]  http://users.belgacom.net.gc674645.grave.last word.htm.

[23]  Flynn, *Hope of the Wicked*, pp. 38-39.

[24]  Wiker, p. 70.

[25]  De Marco & Wiker, p. 125.

[26]  Karl Stern, *The Third Revolution* (Harcourt, Brace, 1954), pp. 131-132, as quoted in De Marco & Wiker, p. 132.

[27]  De Marco & Wiker, p. 129.

[28]  O'Brien, Vol. Two, p. 42. The article, which appeared in the *Neue Rheinisch Zeitung*, was referred to with approval by Josef Stalin in his book *The Foundations of Leninism* (ibid.).

[29]  McGuire, p. 140.

[30]  Flynn, *Hope of the Wicked*, p. 36.

[31]  Wurmbrand, p. 27.

[32]  Vincent P. Miceli, S. J., *The Gods of Atheism* (Roman Catholic Books, 1971), p. 123.

[33]  Ted and Maureen Flynn, *Thunder of Justice*, p. 221.

[34]  Thomas Sowell, *Conquests and Cultures* (Basic Books, 1998), p. 245. The author writes,

> . . . the Soviet Union benefited from the protective efforts of a large and prominent segment of Western intellectuals to ignore or deny its failures. The man-made famine in the Ukraine during the 1930s, for example, was ignored, down-played, or denied outright by such prominent Western intellectuals as George Bernard Shaw and the *New York Times'* Pulitzer-Prizewinning columnist Walter Duranty, even though the facts that finally came out during the last days of the Soviet Union under Gorbachev showed that even more people were killed in that famine than the millions estimated in Robert Conquest's chilling and monumental study, *Harvest of Sorrow*. As Alexandr Solzhenitsyn put it, "the whole atrocity of communism could never be accommodated by the Western journalistic mind" (*ibid.*).

[35]  Edvard Radzinsky, *From Wastrel Monk to Political Power—Rasputin: The Last Word* (Weidenfeld & Nicolson, 2000), as quoted in Miranda Twiss, *The Most Evil Men and Women in History* (Barnes & Noble, 2002), p. 119.

[36]  Miranda Twiss, *The Most Evil Men and Women in History* (Barnes & Noble, 2002), p. 120.

[37]  Brown, p. 35.

[38] Thomas W. Petrisko, *Call of the Ages* (Queenship Publishing, 1995), p. 117.

[39] Warren H. Carroll, *Red Banners, White Mantle* (Christendom Press, 1981), pp. 18-19.

[40] Brown, pp. 35-36.

[41] Anne W. Carroll, *Christ the King — Lord of History* (TAN Books & Publishers, 1994), p. 408.

[42] Brown, p. 43.

[43] *Ibid.,* p. 44.

[44] Josyp Terelya, *Witness* (Queenship Publishing, 2000), pp. 188-189.

[45] Wurmbrand, p. 49.

[46] Wiker, p. 119.

[47] Flynn, *Hope of the Wicked,* p. 36.

[48] Courtenay Bartholomew, *Her Majesty Mary* (Queenship Publishing, 2002), p. 255.

[49] Paul Johnson, *Modern Times: The World from the Twenties to the Eighties* (Harper & Row, 1983), p. 51.

[50] Malachi Martin, *The Keys of This Blood* (Simon and Schuster, 1990), p. 415.

[51] James S. Hewett, ed., *Illustrations Unlimited* (Tynedale House, 1988), p. 330.

[52] Wiker, p. 125.

[53] *Ibid.,* p. 116. As the author elaborates, "Stalin picked up precisely where Lenin left off and was successful in slaughtering his own countrymen in large part because of the intellectual and political system Lenin had established" (*ibid.*).

[54] Anne W. Carroll, p. 420.

[55] Wurmbrand, p. 49.

[56] Flynn, *Hope of the Wicked,* p. 40.

[57] Warren Carroll, p. 130. Furthermore, Malachi Martin wrote, "There has always been a suspicion that a slow-acting poison was the cause of Lenin's death in January of 1924, and that Stalin had Lenin's viscera removed and cremated—against the violently expressed wishes of his widow, Nadezhda Krupskaya—to avoid later forensic medical detection" – *The Keys of This Blood,* p. 231.

[58] Brown, p. 44. An interesting postscript involves a vision allegedly given to Josyp Terelya some sixty years after Lenin's death, in which he saw "three large books—one red, one black, one brown. They were Talmuds and they floated liked three large boats. On each of these Talmuds was a large head. . . . On the red book I saw the head of Marx and around the head of Marx there were eight corpses missing their heads. On the black Talmud I aw the head of Lenin and around him six black cadavers. They too were headless. On the brown Talmud I saw the head of Hitler and around him four brown, headless cadavers" – *Witness,* p. 279.

[59] Martin, p. 251.

[60] Joseph Farah, "Finding Our Way Home Before It's Too Late," *Whistleblower Magazine* (April 2010), pp. 25-26.

[61] Ted Flynn, *Idols in the House* (MaxKol Communications, 2002), pp. 11-13.

[62] http://www.answers.com/topic/antonio-gramsci

[63] Michael Vincent Boyer, *The Hollywood Culture War* (Xlibris Corporation, 2008), p. 241. According to Fr. Miceli, the death toll is even higher: "It is estimated that in all his purges, collectivization plans and persecutions of religions, Stalin murdered some sixty to ninety million people" – *The Antichrist*, p. 138.

[64] Twiss, p. 132.

[65] Shelley Klein, *The Most Evil Dictators in History* (Barnes & Noble, 2004), p. 45. The author notes that "this 'revision of history'—as it became known—was not only to become a favorite pastime of Stalin's, it became almost his trademark, for he doctored hundreds of official documents with the sole purpose of making himself look better. He also tampered with photographs, often having those he'd killed removed from the pictures. . ." (*ibid.*).

[66] "Stalin's Key Deception," Iain Coloquhoun, *The Fatima Crusader* (#94, Spring 2010), pp. 39ff. According to the article, Roosevelt sent an envoy to Pope Pius XII "urging him to issue a statement qualifying his predecessor's encyclical [*Divini Redemptoris*, in which Pius XI condemned Communism as "intrinsically evil"] urging Catholics not to assist the Communists. Roosevelt's argument was that Hitler posed an even greater threat to religion than Stalin; and that as Russia was under attack, it had a right to military aid. This appeal put the Pope in a dilemma. If he took sides in this war, he would be compromising his role as Christian pastor. Instead, he instructed his Secretary of State to authorize the US hierarchy to issue a statement of their own to the effect that Pius XI had been attacking Communism, not Russia, and had not intended his encyclical as a blueprint to political leaders in the event of a war" (p. 39).

The article also states that "It is significant that on the 15th of September 1943, the very day Dr. Garbett [Dr. Cyril Garbett, Archbishop of York, flying to Moscow with a message of support from the Anglican church] left for Moscow, Sister Lucy, the seer of Fatima, was urged by her bishop to write down the Third Secret. Thus the start of events that will pose dangers for the Catholic Church coincides with the moment that the leaders of the Church were providentially apprised of those dangers" (pp. 44-45).

[67] Martin, p. 132.

[68] Klein, p. 48. Rev. Wurmbrand records a slightly different version of this remark; according to him, "Stalin said that the greatest joy is to cultivate a person's friendship until he lays his head confidently on your bosom, then to implant a dagger in his back—a pleasure not to be surpassed" (*Marx & Satan*, p. 53).

[69] Twiss, p. 137.

[70] Wurmbrand, p. 53.

[71] *Ibid.,* p. 54.

[72] Flynn, *Idols in the House,* p. 14.

[73] For instance, Stalin was a big fan of Hollywood gangster movies, but he hated actor John Wayne for his vocal opposition to Communism, and actually ordered him assassinated—though this order was never carried out. Cf. Boyer, p. 261.

[74] Michael H. Brown, *The Last Secret* (Servant Publications, 1998), p. 273.

[75] Martin, p. 416.

[76] Sr. Margherita Marchione, *Yours Is A Precious Witness* (Paulist Press, 1997), p. 137. The author writes, "In the newspaper *La Nazione* (Florence, February 5, 1996), Vladimir Naumov, Secretary of the Commission for the rehabilitation of people persecuted for political reasons, declared that about 200,000 priests were persecuted or killed under Stalin" (*ibid.*).

[77] Aleksandr Solzhenitsyn, *The Gulag Archipelago*, Parts V & VI (Harper & Row, 1976), p. 22.

[78] Klein, p. 52.

[79] Johnson, p. 454.

[80] Rosemary Ellen Guiley, *The Quotable Saint* (Checkmark Books, 2002), p. 2.

[81] Klein, p. 53.

[82] Twiss, p. 141.

[83] Simon Sebag Montefiore, *Stalin: The Court of the Red Tsar* (Vintage Books, 2003), p. 649.

[84] http://users.belgacom.net.gc674645.grave.last.word.htm

[85] Johnson, p. 456.

[86] Solzhenitsyn, for instance, later wrote, "This was the moment my friends and I had looked forward to even in our student days. The moment for which every zek [political prisoner] in Gulag (except the orthodox Communists) had prayed! He's dead, the Asiatic dictator is dead! The villain has curled up and died! What unconcealed rejoicing there would be back home in the Special Camp! But where I was, Russian girls, schoolteachers, stood sobbing their hearts out. 'What is to become of us now?' They had lost a beloved parent. . . . I wanted to yell at them across the square: 'Nothing will become of you now! Your fathers will not be shot! You husbands-to-be will not be jailed! And you will never be stigmatized as relatives of prisoners!' I could have howled with joy there by the loudspeaker; I could even have danced a wild jig!" -- *The Gulag Archipelago*, p. 421.

[87] Jung Chang and Jon Halliday, *Mao: The Unknown Story* (Anchor Books, 2005), as quoted in Boyer, p. 269.

88 Klein, p. 67.

89 Martin, p. 405.

90 *Ibid.*, p. 406.

91 Klein, p. 77.

92 Chang and Halliday, p. 13.

93 *Ibid.*, p. 14.

94 *Ibid.*, p. 321.

95 Thomas W. Petrisko, *Call of the Ages* (Queenship Publishing, 1995), pp. 117-118.

96 Brown, *The Final Hour*, pp. 63-64.

97 Johnson, pp. 562-563.

98 Chung and Halliday, p. 613.

99 In her book *My Journey to the Land of More* (CHResources, 2010), Leona Choy, a Catholic convert and former Evangelical missionary to China, writes, "What marvelous things the Holy Spirit had been doing in China for the fifty-plus years since the Communists sent all the missionaries packing! The [Chinese] Christians received the good seed of the Word from the missionaries, and the Holy Spirit remained in China to water and nourish the fledgling Chinese church! Statistics bear out that there have been more converts to Christ in China during the past few scores of years than in the entire world from the time of the early church until now! And more martyrs for the faith in China during that period as well" (p. 13).

100 Michael H. Brown, *The Day Will Come* (Servant Publications, 1996), p. 293.

101 Klein, p. 144.

102 *Ibid.*, p. 150.

103 The Voice of the Martyrs, *North Korea* (Living Sacrifice Book Company, 2008), p. 78.

104 Klein, p. 103.

105 The Voice of the Martyrs, p. 93.

106 Bradley K. Martin, *Under the Loving Care of the Fatherly Leader: North Korea and the Kim Dynasty* (Thomas Dunne Books/St. Martin's Press, 2004), pp. 506-507.

107 The Voice of the Martyrs, p. 83.

108 Miceli, p. 138.

109 Pope John Paul II, *Memory and Identity: Conversations at the Dawn of a Millennium* (Rizzoli International Publications, 2005), p. 167.

110 Saint Maria Faustina Kowalska, *Diary* (Marian Press, 1987, 2008), #1732, p. 612.

111 Fellows, p. 67.

# Chapter 9

# Satan's Evangelists

*You belong to your father the devil and you willingly carry out
your father's desires. He was a murderer from the beginning
and does not stand in truth, because there is no truth in him.
When he tells a lie, he speaks in character, because he is a liar
and the father of lies.* (Jn. 8:44)

A young Italian named Bartolo Longo was born on February
11, 1841 (exactly seventeen years before Our Lady's first
apparition at Lourdes). He practiced his Catholic faith until
he began his studies at the University of Naples—and then his life
took a radical and nearly disastrous detour. Through the influence
of some of his new "friends," he joined a satanic sect, and soon—to
the horror of his family—decided to become a satanic priest.

Bartolo was prepared for his "ordination" by a long process
of study, fasting, and self-denial; then, in a blasphemous mockery
of the Church's solemn ordination rite, he was consecrated to the
devil by a satanic "bishop." There was a price to be paid, of course:
Bartolo was thereafter plagued by nightmares and various physical
ailments, but even so, he exercised his evil office by preaching and
presiding at satanic rites, and by publicly attacking the Church and
her teachings and practices at every opportunity.

Fortunately for Bartolo, his family never ceased begging God
for his conversion; their prayers, along with the holy and influential
friendship of a young man from his hometown, and above all,
the intercession of Mary, the Mother of God, helped this deluded
disciple of the devil come to realize the horrible mistake he had
made. With the help of a holy Dominican friar, Bartolo withdrew
from the satanic sect, and after he made his Confession and received
Holy Communion, the priest convinced him he should spend the

remainder of his life making reparation for the scandal he had caused.[1] By promoting devotion to the Rosary, arranging for the construction of a church in honor of Our Lady, caring for orphans, and performing many other works of charity, Bartolo Longo did this so well that in 1980, fifty-four years after his death, he was beatified by Pope John Paul II.

The story of Bl. Bartolo Longo is not only edifying, but almost unique. While there are recorded instances of persons heavily involved in the occult repenting of this sin and embracing the way of Christ—such as the scriptural accounts of the conversion of Simon Magus (Acts 8:9-24) and the magicians of Ephesus (Acts 19:19)—it's very rare for the same person, at different stages in his or her life, to be a committed disciple of Jesus and also of the devil. Indeed, those who've experienced the loving goodness of their Heavenly Father cannot easily understand *why* anyone would willingly give allegiance to the Prince of Darkness—and yet it happens, far more often than many would suspect.

Satan does in fact have his evangelists—enthusiastic followers who not only worship and serve him, but who actively seek to recruit (or, more accurately, ensnare) others into their malign and horrific lifestyle—a lifestyle that can only end (barring genuine repentance) in the tragedy of eternal damnation. Some of history's more notorious Satanists can indeed be labeled "antichrists," and their stories serve as a reminder that evil is not only self-destructive, but inherently based on lies and delusions.

# Helena Blavatsky & Her Accomplices

The Russian mystic Helena Blavatsky (commonly referred to by her disciples as Madame Blavatsky) has been called the "Mother of the New Age," with adherents as diverse as Adolf Hitler, Abner Doubleday (the inventor of baseball), Karl Marx, Thomas Edison, Nicholas Tesla, George Bernard Shaw, Elvis Presley, and Mahatma Gahndi.[2] (Indeed, when a young Gahndi was considering converting to Christianity, it was Blavatsky who misadvised him by insisting Hinduism was the superior religion, and that Gahndi should thus hold fast to his Hindu heritage.)

According to Michael H. Brown,

*... Blavatsky had been a trance medium who claimed to be in touch with hidden Tibetan "masters" and formed her beliefs into the occult religion of Theosophy, which incorporated spirit communication with concepts of reincarnation. She was the female counterpart of [Aleister] Crowley [see below] and her apparitions were of the goddess Isis, another pagan idol. Included in her mystical brooch was a swastika and hexagram. Blavatsky's seminal work was* The Secret Doctrine, *a book of "ageless wisdom."*[3]

Blavatsky's first book, *Isis Unveiled* (for which she received a Masonic degree[4]) was, she claimed, written in Tibet, where she had made contact with higher spiritual beings, to whom she later dedicated an altar in her home.[5] In 1875 she founded the Theosophical Society, supposedly, according to Fr. Andrew O'Brien, "with the aim of making occult knowledge available to all. . . . What she really sought was the establishment of Lucifer's one-world religion."[6]

In her later two-volume work *The Secret Doctrine*, Blavatsky claimed that—according to her "spirit guides"—humanity is composed of "root races," either inferior or superior in nature. One of the latter was the Atlanteans, whose continent of Atlantis was destroyed 15,000 years ago; the survivors became humanity's super race, the Aryans.[7] This imaginative and highly influential doctrine "had spread throughout Germany and Austria by 1914. Hitler used her book. The Aryan Swastika is the symbol of the seventh ray of initiation, and Hitler was a sixth ray initiate."[8] Indeed, Hitler kept a copy of *The Secret Doctrine* next to his bed, and considered it one of the most important and influential books in his life.[9]

According to Ted Flynn, Blavatsky "traveled all over the world lecturing and practicing the occult, but her greatest impact, by far, was through her writings. . . . This material was allegedly dictated to her through her 'masters' who were called by the various names of Koot Hoomi, Morya, and simply the 'Ascended Masters of Wisdom.'"[10] After she moved to New York City, her writings became more readily available, and more influential, than ever before; Theosophy, as she called her religion, eventually inspired a number of other New Age groups and cults.

Deliberately cultivating an image of mystery and self-importance, Blavatsky claimed to have supernatural abilities; on one occasion, when a visitor expressed his skepticism, she supposedly made red roses rain down from the room's ceiling.[11] Whether this demonically-assisted "miracle" actually happened may be open to question, but there's no doubt of her satanically-inspired hatred for the Church. Author Stephen Mahowald notes that

> Blavatsky took her instructions at the feet of the Grand Masters, who taught her that, "**Some say that in order to destroy Catholicism, it is necessary to start by the suppression of women. This is true in a way, but as we cannot suppress woman, let us corrupt her with the Church. . . . The goal is too beautiful not to tempt men like us.**"[12]

Moreover, Blavatsky herself, in *The Secret Doctrine*, praised the devil in these words:

> It (Satan) is that Angel who was proud enough to believe himself God; brave enough to buy his independence at the price of eternal suffering and torture; beautiful enough to have adored himself in full divine light; strong enough to reign still in darkness amidst agony, and to have made himself a throne out of this inextinguishable pyre . . . the prince of anarchy, served by a hierarchy of pure spirits.[13]

The above passage is actually somewhat honest and insightful in recognizing that Satan, and the hierarchy of evil spirits who serve under him, endure eternal agony and suffering as a result of their pride; however, Blavatsky foolishly presents their chosen fate as something *admirable*—and if it's one she's come to share through her vehement rejection of Christ, she now realizes the horrible extent of her folly.

In 1920, a disciple of Madame Blavatsky named Alice Ann Bailey founded the "Lucifer Publishing Company," though soon afterwards it was renamed to the more innocuous-sounding title "Lucis Trust."[14] The organization's goal was to promote the teachings of Blavatsky and other occult figures. Bailey herself claimed an "Ascended Master" was working through her for thirty years, preparing for an "elite spiritual hierarchy" and a "New Group of World Servers," whose identity would be confirmed by receiving a special mark[15] (cf. Rev. 13:16), and who would lead the world into a New Age kingdom.

In a highly revealing passage from her 1939 book *The Externalization of the Hierarchy*, Bailey writes,

> *The men who inspired the initiating French Revolution; the great conqueror Napoleon; Bismarck, the creator of the nation; Mussolini, the regenerator of his people; Hitler, who lifted a distressed people on his shoulders; Lenin, the idealist; Stalin and Franco and all expressions of the Shamballah force [the energy force of a mystical land in which dwell the so-called Ascended Masters of Wisdom], we call these people dictators, inspired leaders. . . . But all these leaders are in the last analysis, highly developed personalities. They are the agents of destiny, the creators of the new order and the initiators of a new civilization. They are the destroyers of what must be destroyed before humanity can go forward on the Lighted way.[16]*

Even allowing for the fact that in 1939 the fates of Hitler, Mussolini, and Stalin were still unknown, the sheer depth of self-delusion in this passage is breathtaking; to claim that the destructiveness of these murderous and unprincipled men, along with that of the already-deceased French revolutionaries, Napoleon, and Lenin, is somehow necessary and even laudable, reveals a freely-chosen love affair with error that's almost impervious to divine grace.

Moreover, Bailey's commitment to the "dark side" also had a very sinister and even genocidal aspect to it. In a later edition of her book (published in 1957), she wrote these chilling words:

> *The atomic bomb does not belong to the three nations who perfected it and who own the secrets at present—the United States of America, Great Britain and Canada.* [Note her omission of the Soviet Union.] ***It belongs to the United Nations for use (or let us rather hope, simply the threatened use when aggressive action on the part of any nation rears its ugly head.)*** *It does not essentially matter whether that aggression is the gesture of any particular nation or group of nations or whether it is generated by the political groups of any powerful religious organization, such **as the Church of Rome*** [emphasis added]*, who are as yet unable to leave politics alone and attend to the business for which all*

*religions are responsible—leading human beings to the God of Love.*[17]

The "God of Love" mentioned here, of course, has nothing to do with the Judeo-Christian God and His Son Jesus Christ (Who have no need to threaten sinners with atomic weapons); the figure for which Bailey and like-minded acolytes of evil yearn can be none other than the coming antichrist—one who will have no qualms about attacking the Church with every weapon at his disposal (no doubt with the fervent support and approval of the Church's enemies).

Yet another disciple of Madame Blavatsky, and her eventual successor as leader of the Theosophical Society, was an Englishwoman named Annie Besant. She was "a militant feminist and a member of the *Fabian Socialist Society* of England," and as such "was well-placed to spread theosophical thought in very influential circles."[18] In fact, Besant became so devoted to Theosophy that she abandoned her husband. While living in India, Besant

> *became entranced by a young Indian boy named Jiddu Krishnamurti. First, she adopted him as her son. Later, in 1925, Besant announced that Krishnamurti was the reincarnated "Christ" for the New Age. Besant's claim startled the worldwide followers of Theosophy, but most were willing to go along. However, the shy and unassuming Krishnamurti flopped badly during what was supposed to be a triumphal tour of the United States. . . . in 1931, a dejected Krishnamurti himself abruptly renounced his title of "Christ" and subsequently became an independent guru and "philosopher". . . .*[19]

Herself a thirty-third degree Mason,[20] Besant worked to undermine Christian belief; for instance, she claimed in her book *Esoteric Christianity* that Jesus Christ wasn't God, and that His body was actually inhabited by another spiritual being—whom she called the "Mighty One"; this allowed Jesus, she asserted, to evolve into one of the "Masters of Wisdom."[21]

St. Paul had warned the Church that "the time will come when people will not tolerate sound doctrine but, following their own desires and insatiable curiosity, will accumulate teachers and will stop listening to the truth and will be diverted to myths" (2 Tim. 4:3-4). That this infernal process would only intensify as history progressed, leading to a terrible fate for those assisting it, is further suggested by his words, "But wicked people and charlatans will go from bad to worse, deceivers and deceived" (2 Tim. 3:13). The apostle's warning seems to have been most fully validated by the life of a 20th century figure who in fact took great pride in being called the "wickedest man in the world."

# Aleister Crowley

Many eleven-year-old boys are fascinated by epic stories and tales of adventure; young Aleister Crowley, however, found himself entranced by descriptions of torture, and liked to imagine himself suffering at the hands of violent, immoral women. He also enjoyed reading the Book of Revelation—but not from a Christian perspective; instead, he identified with the Great Beast, the False Prophet, and the Scarlet Woman. Years later his own mother called him the Great Beast, and it's possible he imagined himself to be (or at least, wanted to be) the Antichrist.[22]

"Described variously as an explorer, teacher, writer, and philosopher, by 1900 [Crowley] was already being labeled as a guru, mystic, practitioner of black magic, occultist and chief promoter of Satanism in Europe and America. Aleister Crowley is the man who first coined and promoted [the term] 'The New Age' in 1904...."[23] He had joined various secret societies engaged in the worship of various ancient Egyptian gods, and in 1898—with the assistance of his wife Rose, herself an occultist—he decided to contact the devil on his own:

> At Rose's direction, Crowley summoned the ancient Egyptian god Horus on March 20. Crowley said a demonic voice spoke to him identifying itself as Aiwass, the High Priest of Horus. Crowley claimed that Aiwass announced the arrival of a New Aeon (New Age) and Crowley would be the chosen scribe to spread the New Age religion. For the next month, Crowley would dictate the words spoken to him by Aiwass and collect the "proclamations" into a text known as "The Book of the Law."[24]

During one of these sessions, Crowley surreptitiously glanced at Aiwass, and later described him as seeming to be "a tall, dark man in his thirties, well knit, active and strong, with the face of a savage king, and eyes veiled lest their gaze should destroy what they saw."[25]

Moving to Italy (until he was eventually expelled from there for his immoral activities), Crowley established what he called the Abbey of Thelema as an "anti-monastery," in where the only rule was pleasure and self-indulgence—including such things as drug use, orgies, bestiality, sorcery, occult rituals, and devotion to numerous pagan deities.[26] He also delighted in bestowing various strange names upon himself: Lord Boleskine, Brother Perdurabo ("I will endure"), Prince Chiao Khan, and Master Therion. The walls of the abbey were adorned with pornographic "masterpieces" painted by Crowley himself—but contrary to Crowley's expectations, he didn't have many customers, nor initially many disciples. "Perhaps this was partly because each new-comer, when there were any, was handed a razor with which he was instructed to slash his arms every time he used the word 'I.' Only the Great Beast, the Master Therion, was allowed to have an ego."[27]

Christianity was, for Crowley, a great curse upon humanity, and immorality served as an expression of his hatred for it; as he once wrote, "To me, every dirty act was simply a sacrament of sin, a passionately religious protest against Christianity, which was for me the symbol of all vileness, meanness, treachery, falsehood and oppression."[28]

Crowley had an intense and personal hatred for Christ, Whom he claimed had "plagued and affronted" him throughout his life. During one of his satanic ceremonies, during which he crucified a frog as a representation of Christ, he blasphemously stated: "Thine hour is come; as I blot Thee out from this earth, so surely shall the eclipse pass; and Light, Life, Love and Liberty be once more the law of Earth. Give Thou place to me, O Jesus; Thine aeon is passed; the Age of Horus is arise by the Magick of the Master, the Great Beast."[29]

All those who came into contact with Crowley were cursed by their association with him. His first wife, Rose, "entered an insane asylum in 1911; his second wife, Maria, entered an asylum in 1931, two years after her marriage to Crowley. In a locked room with only Crowley and his son present, Crowley performed a ritual in which his son died. On a London street in 1934, a nineteen-year-old girl rushed up to him and declared that she wanted to have his baby. Crowley took her to bed. She too later entered an asylum."[30] Five of his mistresses ended up committing suicide, and even the local butcher, "on one of whose bills Crowley had jotted some demonic-names, severed an artery while cutting up a joint and died."[31]

On one occasion a cat scratched Crowley, and in anger he decreed, "That cat must be sacrificed within three days." When it tried to escape, the Satanist traced a pentagram in the air with his wand and commanded, "You will not move till the hour of sacrifice," and the cat remained immobile, refusing all food, until judgment was executed. Also, "A Cambridge don testified to having seen him extinguish a candle from ten feet by 'willing' it to go out. At times also he seems to have been able to make himself invisible: not literally, of course, but by being able to compel those present not to see him."[32]

Crowley had inherited a fortune from his father, which he spent promoting the New Age through his self-published books on the occult (bankrupting himself in the process). He was a notorious anti-Semite (even as he conducted a sadistic homosexual relationship with a Jewish lover); he applauded the Soviet Union's repression of its Jewish population, and "even offered his services to the Soviet Communist authorities to help wipe out their Christian population as well. As Crowley wasted away during the 1940s, he believed himself to be the reincarnation of the 19th century magician Eliphas Levi, who happened to die the day Aleister Crowley was born. Crowley also believed that he was Pope Alexander VI, in a previous life. . . ."[33]

The man who liked to give himself bizarre titles seemed to have no real identity of his own; as one commentator notes, "Like all masters of mystification, his real commitment seems to have been only to himself. The strange consequence is a lack of identity, and for all his prating of self there seems to have been an intolerable emptiness at his center."[34] Suffering from a severe heroin addiction (in which he took up to eleven grams a day—perhaps *100 times* the normal dose), his final days were "given to black rages and doubts about the value of his life's work. His last words as he passed into a coma on December 1, 1947 were 'I am perplexed.'"[35] As one author notes, "He had practiced what he had preached, and his Satan worship was intense. Crowley created his own hell on earth and it made the lives of his followers—and eventually himself—intolerable."[36] Even so, a handful of his faithful disciples—in accord with their master's wishes—performed a satanic ceremony at his funeral, chanting a pagan litany in his honor.[37]

Crowley's influence, unfortunately, did not end with his death; his credo "Do what thou wilt shall be the whole of the law" proved to be very popular during the cultural upheavals of the 1960s. His image appeared on one of the album covers of the hit music group the Beatles, and John Lennon of the Beatles, along with Mick Jagger of the Rolling Stones, both expressed their admiration for him;[38] indeed, Jagger claimed Crowley as his inspiration for his theme song "Sympathy for the Devil."[39]

Other past and present entertainers and cultural figures influenced by Crowley's ideas include Jim Morrison, Paul McCartney, Jack Valenti, Timothy Leary, and Hugh Hefner. According to author Michael Vincent Boyer,

> The reason Crowley's New Age thinking became predominant in the entertainment industry throughout the last seventy years can largely be traced to his writings about spirit possession. This, combined with his open endorsement of drug abuse and sexual perversion, played well with the emerging secular Hollywood crowd that wanted nothing to do with "the establishment" or "rules." Crowley's deep-rooted hatred of Christianity, of which he wrote frequently, also sat well with a rootless industry of atheistic drifters. Hollywood's particular penchant today for Christian-bashing can be traced directly to Crowley.[40]

The founder of hip-hop music, Afrika Bambaataa, indirectly acknowledged Crowley's influence on his work,[41] and a much more direct link was admitted by L. Ron Hubbard, a science-fiction writer who founded of the highly influential cult of Scientology. Hubbard considered himself Crowley's successor, and in fact claimed that Scientology began on December 1, 1947—the date of Crowley's death.[42]

Hollywood and other cultural influences have helped make the occult appear mysterious and glamorous—but as Scripture warns, "Be not provoked with evildoers, nor envious of the wicked; for the evil man has no future, [and] the lamp of the wicked will be put out" (Prv. 24:19-20). Tragically, however, Satanism never seems to lack for willing recruits in contemporary American society.

## Satanism Today

In 1966, one of Crowley's disciples, a former carnival barker and "ghost hunter" for the San Francisco police department renamed himself Anton LaVey and established what he called the "Church of Satan."[43] On April 30 (a pagan feast known as Walpurgis Night), LaVey, who later portrayed the devil in the 1968 movie *Rosemary's Baby* (filmed inside the same building where John Lennon would be shot and killed in 1980), "stepped out of his hellish black house in San Francisco and, eyes of amber aglare, officially declared the 'Age of Satan.'"[44] Several years later LaVey published *The Satanic Bible*. Susan Atkins, one of LaVey's early followers and later a member of the Manson "family" (cult), stated that "Anton told me that as a Satanist he does believe in the God of the Bible but he refused to worship Him, and made a conscious decision to worship Satan instead."[45] However, LaVey "presented a seeker sensitive, user-friendly form of Satanism in the hope that it might appeal to the masses he was seeking to deceive."[46]

The masses never came, but LaVey did have a few high-profile recruits, most notably the actress Jayne Mansfield, who was later killed in a bizarre car accident. LaVey himself died in 1997; he had wanted to die on Halloween, but lingered until two days later. Showing no sign of repentance, he stated that his epitaph should read "I only regret the times that I was too nice."[47]

Another contemporary satanic cult is called the Temple of Set, founded by a U.S. Army officer, Col. Michael Aquino, who would lead "pilgrimages to [Nazi Heinrich] Himmler's SS castle in Germany in order to absorb occult influences."[48] Still more notorious, of course, is the convicted murderer Charles Manson, who in the 1960s provided sex and drugs to many Hollywood actors and actresses, rock stars, and promoters. Manson and his cult-like followers were involved in child pornography and other criminal activities,[49] and linked to a satanic church named "The Process." His followers were convinced he amazing powers of extra-sensory perception, and that he could restore life to dead animals. Manson and some of his disciples were convicted of the 1969 murder of actress Sharon Tate (wife of Roman Polanski, who directed *Rosemary's Baby*); to this day, he receives about 60,000 letters a year in prison from people asking to be accepted into his "family."[50]

St. Anthony of Padua had noted that "Those who love money and fickle honors, fall down before the devil and adore him,"[51] echoing the earlier observation by St. Anthony of Egypt:

*When sin is understood by the soul, it is hated by it like a foul-smelling beast. But when it is not understood, it is loved by him who does not understand it and, enslaving its lover, keeps him in captivity. And the poor miserable man does not see what can save him, and does not even think about it; but thinking that sin adorns him, he welcomes it gladly.[52]*

Because Satan is the "father of lies" (Jn. 8:44), it only stands to reason that those who give themselves over to evil become practically incapable of making clear moral judgments or of recognizing the extreme spiritual dangers surrounding them. As one author notes, "When worshipping Satan as a God, satanists believe that the God of the Old and New Testament, as well as Jesus Christ, are thoroughly evil—as are their commandments and condemnations. Anything forbidden by Christianity is taken up by the satanist. . . ."[53]

This hellish dynamic gives Satanism a strong (though misguided) sense of unity and purpose—making it a formidable enemy of the Church and, indeed, a type of "antichrist" in itself. Many times its influence is felt not only in popular culture, but also in national and even international politics and finance—particularly as part of the movement toward a one-world government. For instance, the previously-mentioned Lucis Trust

*receives substantial grants on an annual basis from such sources as the <u>Rockefeller Foundation,the Carnegie Trust, the Ford Foundation</u>—and a number of other interlocking tax-exempt trusts andfoundations—all of which support globalist interests. In turn, organizations that are sponsored in part or in total by*

*Lucis Trust include: The Findhorn Foundation, Greenpeace and Greenpeace International, International Wildlife Fund and International Wildlife Fund-U.K., UNICEF, UNESCO, Zero Option, Planned Parenthood, Amnesty International, and Planetary Citizens, etc. Lucis Trust even provided for building the Temple of Understanding, a testament to Pantheism — the only "chapel" in the United Nations Building.*[54]

Many people today know or care very little about global organizations and their agenda of a one-world government (an agenda ultimately intended to serve Satan and pave the way for a future antichrist), but quite a few have some awareness, or even experience, of the occult—though in all likelihood they're unaware of its link to the demonic. In his book on spiritual warfare, *Prayer of the Warrior*, Michael H. Brown gives this lengthy and thorough summary of such influences:

*Occultism has survived in the ages in hundreds of forms. We've all been touched by it. It comes through astrology, numerology, crystals, pyramid power, channeling, fortune telling, Taoism, Eastern meditation, superstitions, visualization, occultbooks, charms, amulets, pagan images, hypnosis, C'hi (or 'Ki), psychokinesis, psychic healing, automatic writing, false locutions, mantras, palm reading, witchcraft (both "black" and "white"), precognition, Santeria, Tarot cards, Atlantis, reincarnation, yoga, "inner space," self-actualization, "higher self," biofeedback, dianetics, global consciousness, color therapy, mind travel, New Age music, transpersonal psychology, water divination, tea-leaf readers, crystal balls, pendulums, rainbows, centaurs, unicorns, ying-yang, enneagram, UFOs, Mother Earth, occult symbols like the anhk, the horn of the "evil-eye," the five-pointed star, the all-seeing eye, or the swastika, and through any thing else that smacks of paganism, mediumship or parapsychology.*[55]

Another major avenue for occult influence in contemporary society is that or rock music. While not all rock musicians promote evil (with some, in fact, even having a Christian message), the industry as a whole is morally and culturally corrosive. One former insider claims, "Bent on public domination and rotted to the core, it is the ultimate social and moral rip off."[56]There are numerous documented cases of young people, under the influence of rock, punk, and heavy metal music, committing murder, rape, torture, suicide, animal sacrifice, perverted sex, necrophilia, and other dangerous or abhorrent behaviors.[57]

Occult influences in contemporary music have also exacted a heavy toll from musicians themselves. Shortly before his death from a drug overdose, Jimi Hendrix swore the devil was trying to possess him, and Jim Morrison—who claimed he was possessed by the spirit of an Indian—died at the age of 27, shortly after taking part in an occultic ritual. The guitarist for the rock group Grateful Dead, Jerry Garcia, admitted, "Maybe we're opening doors for some demons from the ninth dimension or something."[58] This disastrous influence was especially evident in the life of John Lennon, a student of Helena Blavatsky's *The Secret Doctrine*. With his wife Yoko Ono,

> *Lennon regularly consulted a network of psychics, Tarot-card readers, and spiritists. They attended séances at the apartment in the Dakota, and had mediums stop by to perform their magic in their very living room. . . . Lennon was killed . . . by a maniacal young gunman, Mark David Chapman, who claimed to be possessed by seven demons.[59]*

It's little wonder that, according to *The World Almanac and Book of Facts*, while the average lifespan for all Americans was 75.8 in 1997, the average age at death of rock stars was only 36.9 years.[60]

Still another diabolical trap is directed at young people today: satanically-themed video games, some of which specifically involve targeting God and the Catholic Church, while making a hero out of Satan and inviting the players to enter into pacts with the devil. The action in one game involves killing the archangels Michael, Gabriel, and Raphael, before going on to "destroy" God; the guide for another game blatantly admits, "The Judeo-Christian God is portrayed as the villain in the series. . . ." In another video game, the player "saves the world" by killing God, while in still another a demon describes the Church as "an eyesore" that deserves to be eradicated.[61]

# "I Saw Satan Falling"

In his book *Exorcism and the Church Militant*, Rev. Thomas J. Euteneuer writes,

> *Never in all of history have we seen evil promoted so effectively and the true good so roundly mocked and rejected as in this age of extreme technological prowess. Although evil has existed since the dawn of time and manifested itself to the world, the difference between the modern world and past generations is that Satan has a greater ability to use groups and institutions for increasing his wicked reach into human life and society. . . . The 21st century is a moral and spiritual battlefield of such immense proportions that no era of human history will ever have seen a war like it. Satan is using the cumulative force of this world's sinfulness to re-define life as we know it.*[62]

Any honest and perceptive observer will admit that the devil and his evil spirits, along with their dedicated human servants, seem to be working overtime—and with great success—in their efforts to further corrupt humanity and spread the gospel of greed, hatred, and violence. However, the unsettling and discouraging aspects of spiritual warfare—which every true disciple of Christ confronts on a daily basis—can lead us to overlook a very important truth: namely,

> *The battle against Satan **has already been won in heaven and purgatory** [emphasis added], and only in this earthly realm is the devil allowed to work. God, in His Mercy, certainly has not abandoned us to the forces of evil, though. There is one spiritual force on earth that can counter the hubris of Satan and his apostate angels and conquer them. That force is the "One, Holy, Catholic, and Apostolic Church". . . .*[63]

(Fr. Euteneuer goes on to express his belief that ever since the Second Vatican Council, the institutional Church has not been adequately engaged in this spiritual war, and needs to take it more seriously by training many more exorcists, and by more carefully and thoroughly instructing priests and laity of their duties, and spiritual authority, in this regard.)

One of the alleged visionaries at Medjugorje claimed that Our Lady had revealed that a climactic battle for souls is raging today—for God had granted the devil greater power than ever before (echoing the famous 1884 revelation granted to Pope Leo XIII, in which Satan boasted that, given enough time and power, he could destroy the Church—a request granted by Jesus, with the proviso that, if and when the devil failed, the Church would become stronger and holier than ever before).

According to the alleged visionary, when God allowed Satan greater power and influence than ever before in history, there were three things he did not know: first, the Lord would send the Virgin Mary to warn, encourage, and assist His children throughout this age of darkness; second, God would make available unprecedented graces to resist the devil to those who humbly and sincerely sought them; and third, the Heavenly Father would send certain chosen souls into the world who would remain faithful to Him no matter how severely the devil tempted or assaulted them, and their example would be a great source of inspiration and strength to others.[64]

When Our Lord's seventy-two disciples returned from a missionary journey exulting that even the demons were subject to them in His Name, Jesus said, "I have observed Satan fall like lightning from the sky" (Lk. 10:18), and a few days before His Passion, Christ said, "Now is the time of judgment on this world; now the ruler of this world will be driven out" (Jn. 12:31). Ever since Easter Sunday, the devil has in effect been living on borrowed time, desperately trying to delay his final and irrevocable condemnation to hell, an inevitable and disgraceful defeat in which all his followers will share (cf. Rev. 20:9-10).

On an individual scale, each member of the Church is offered the spiritual weapons and defenses needed to be successful in his or her own spiritual warfare (cf. Eph. 6:10-17; 1 Pt. 5:8-9). On a much larger scale, the entire Church—under the leadership of St. Peter and his successors—is promised victory over all the forces of hell (cf. Mt. 16:18), and there is nothing Satan and his doomed army of evil can do to prevent this.

In the words of the Roman poet Virgil, *Amor vincit omnia* ("love conquers all")—and there is no love more beautiful, or powerful, than that shared between Christ and His Bride, the Church (cf. Eph. 5:23ff; Rev. 21:2).

## NOTES TO CHAPTER 9

1    Joan Carroll Cruz, *Secular Saints* (TAN Books and Publishers, 1989), pp. 73ff.

2    Texe Marrs, *Texe Marrs Book of New Age Cults & Religions* (Living Truth Publishers, 1990), pp. 314ff.

3    Michael H. Brown, *Prayer of the Warrior* (Queenship Publishing, 2000), pp. 79-80.

4    Fr. Andrew O'Brien, *Make Yourself An Ark!*, Vol. One (The American Research Foundation, Inc., 1995), p. 58.

5    Marrs, p. 314.

6    O'Brien, p. 58.

7    Marrs, p. 318.

8    Fr. Andrew O'Brien, *Make Yourself An Ark!* , Vol. Two (The American Research Foundation, Inc., 1995), p. 40.

9    Ted Flynn, *Hope of the Wicked* (MaxKol Communications, 2000), p. 47.

10   *Ibid.*, p. 46.

11   Marrs, p. 314.

12   Stephen Mahowald, *She Shall Crush Thy Head* (MMR Publishing, 1996), p. 121.

13   *Ibid.*, p. 122.

14   Paul McGuire, *The Day the Dollar Died* (M House Publishers, 2009), p. 118.

15   *Ibid.*

16   Alice Ann Bailey, *The Externalization of the Hierarchy* (1939), pp. 133-135, as quoted in McGuire, p. 119.

17   *Ibid.*, 1957 edition, p. 548, as quoted by Constance Cumbey, *The Hidden Dangers of the New Age* (Huntington House, Inc., 1988), pp. 70-71.

18   Mahowald, p. 122.

19   Marrs, p. 317.  The author notes that after repudiating his ties with Theosophy, "From then on until his death in 1986, Krishnamurti traveled the world, writing and speaking to as many people who believed in him" (even addressing the United Nations).  Moreover, his work is carried on by the Krishnamurti Foundation of America, located in Ojai, California— *ibid.*, p. 233.

20   Flynn, p. 48.

21   Marrs, p. 41.

22   Anthony Masters, *The Devil's Dominion* (Putnam, 1978), p. 71.

23   Michael Vincent Boyer, *The Hollywood Culture War* (Xlibris Corporation, 2008), p. 355.

24   *Ibid.*, p. 357.

25   Masters, p. 76.

26 Boyer, p. 358.

27 Douglas Hunt, *Exploring the Occult* (Ballantine Books, 1964), p. 186.

28 Flynn, p. 51.

29 Michael H. Brown, *The Final Hour* (Queenship Publishing, 2000), p. 31.

30 Flynn, p. 51.

31 Hunt, p. 183.

32 *Ibid.,* pp. 186-187.

33 Boyer, p. 360.

34 Christopher Nugent, *Masks of Satan* (Christian Classics, 1983, 1989), p. 87.

35 Steve Turner, *Hungry for Heaven* (Intervarsity Press, 1995), pp. 97-98, as quoted in Boyer, p. 360.

36 Masters, p. 94.

37 Harry E. Wedeck, *The Triumph of Satan* (Citadel Press, 1970), p. 139.

38 Mahowald, p. 122. According to Michael Vincent Boyer, "'The whole Beatle idea was to do what you want . . . do what thou will. . . ,' declared John Lennon in an interview with *Playboy* magazine. It was an appropriate forum for Lennon to declare his open allegiance to Crowley. After all, Hugh Hefner's 'Playboy Philosophy' boiled down to the same guiding slogan. . . . The Beatles paid homage to a hodgepodge of their cultural heroes when they released their best-selling album *Sergeant Pepper*. . . . Prominent among the photos that graced the cover was a picture of Aleister Crowley. Paul McCartney would declare Crowley as one of the group's 'heroes'" – *The Hollywood Culture War*, p. 361.

39 O'Brien, Vol. Two, p. 28.

40 Boyer, p. 378.

41 *Ibid.,* p. 363.

42 *Ibid.,* p. 379. The author adds, "Hubbard's goals were the same as Aleister Crowley: to destroy Christianity and everything it stands for. Hubbard felt it was his duty to fulfill the New Age destiny. . . . This obsessive hatred for Christians is one of the reasons L. Ron Hubbard referred to himself as the one who 'came after' Crowley in order to finish what Crowley started, according to [his son] L. Ron Hubbard, Jr." (p. 381).

43 *Ibid.,* p. 425.

44 Brown, *Prayer of the Warrior*, p. 79.

45 http://www.goodfight.org/a-co-sataniccults.html.

46 *Ibid.*

47 http://www.panix.com/~scmiller/goodbye/nov97/lavey.html.

48 O'Brien, Vol. Two, p. 16.

49 http://www.whale.to/b/manson.html.

50  http://www1.csbju.edu/uspp/CrimPsych/CPSG-8b.htm.

51  Francis W. Johnston, *The Voice of the Saints* (TAN Books and Publishers, 1965), p. 11.

52  Ronda De Sola Chervin, *Quotable Saints* (Servant Publications, 1992), p. 202.

53  Masters, p. 109.

54  Mahowald, p. 123.

55  Brown, *Prayer of the Warrior*, p. 149.

56  Eric Barger, *From Rock to Rock* (Huntington House, 1990), p. 1.

57  Thomas W. Wedge, *The Satan Hunter* (Daring Books, 1988), pp. 91ff.

58  Brown, *Prayer of the Warrior*, pp. 78-79.

59  *Ibid.*, p. 80.

60  Boyer, p. 364.

61  Susan Brinkman, "Gaming for Satan," February 5, 2010, http://www.womenofgrace.com.

62  Rev. Thomas J. Euteneuer, *Exorcism and the Church Militant* (Human Life International, 2010), p. xxvii.

63  *Ibid.*, p. xxix.

64  Janice T. Connell, *The Visions of the Children* (St. Martin's Press, 1992), p. 40.

# Chapter 10

# Hitler, Nazi Germany, and the Occult

*The nether world below is all astir preparing for your coming;*
*it awakens the shades to greet you, all the leaders of the earth;*
*it has the kings of all nations rise from their thrones. All of*
*them speak out and say to you, 'You too have become weak*
*like us, you are the same as we. . . . You said in your heart: 'I*
*will scale the heavens; above the stars of God I will set up*
*my throne; I will take my seat on the Mount of Assembly, in*
*the recesses of the North. I will ascend above the tops of the*
*clouds; I will be like the Most High!' Yet down to the nether*
*world you go to the recesses of the pit!* (Is. 14:9-10,13-15)

If a poll were to be taken asking which historical figure so far has most resembled, in terms of his character and deeds, the coming antichrist, Adolf Hitler would undoubtedly win in a landslide. Even more than sixty years after his death, the world looks upon his life with a horrified incomprehension and fascination. The vast depth of his evil is widely recognized—but relatively few historians and scholars acknowledge the important role played in his life by the occult. Hitler was one of Satan's most pliable and cooperative servants, and this made him one of the Church's, and one of civilization's, most dangerous enemies.

It's said that Hitler privately enjoyed being called an antichrist, and though he was a baptized Catholic, his conscious rejection of the Gospel seems to have begun at an early age. For instance, "In school records at Linz, Hitler is charged with stealing and mocking a sacramental Host—one of the oldest blasphemies, and one associated with witchcraft."[1] When he received the Sacrament of Confirmation, he turned surly, finding the holy ritual repulsive.[2] The youthful Hitler was much more attracted to the Teutonic myths of ancient Germany; he particularly liked pretending to be Wotan, the god of death and destruction—one who constantly demanded human sacrifice. Ominously (and, as it turned out, quite fittingly), "One of Hitler's favorite paintings, by Von Stucke, was of Wotan, the mad huntsman. The face of Wotan in the painting bore a chilling resemblance to Hitler's own face."[3]

At the age of twenty, Hitler began reading the literature of the "Order of the New Templars." This group (founded in 1907 by a former Cistercian monk) sought to establish a new Germanic culture that would be based on occult religion; the goal would be to "purify" the Aryan race while developing and unleashing its previously dormant psychic powers,[4] a program which would later be adopted by Heinrich Himmler, head of the SS (Hitler's private bodyguard). Moreover,

> . . . in Vienna Hitler put himself in contact with magical traditions that reached back to people like Guido von List of the nineteenth century. Hitler became an addict of occult literature like Ostara, an anti-Semitic periodical. . . . Ostara featured old Germanic spells, number mysticism, and tales of Nordic women in the clutches of ape-like men as well as blood mysticism and Ayran religion. . . .[5]

In 1918 an occult organization known as the Thule Society was created. "Thule" was a legendary Nordic kingdom, a land of barren ice that was supposedly the origin of the Ayran race. Hitler later recruited many of his early followers from this secret society, and also borrowed from it the swastika (associated with the Norse god Thor) to serve as the emblem of the Nazi party.[6] As it happened,

> The Thule group had been seeking demonic guidance through séances, for there was at the time a general expectation among occultists that their occult messiah was soon to emerge. In one dramatic séance, demonic spirits materialized and announced that Adolf Hitler was the man for whom they were waiting. The same spirits announced that this man would lead Germany into a fiery catastrophe. The Thule group either chose to ignore the second part of the demonic prophecy, or was aware that it was a specific part of the mission which would eventually produce

*the true antichrist.*[7]

According to Michael H. Brown, "Hitler was steeped in black magic. When he became a politician his advisers included Erik Jan Hanussen, who was a seer and astrologer, and Karl Haushofer, who taught him Theology from Madame Blavatsky's *The Secret Doctrine*. Hitler was an occultist by his own description and like many who practice black magic, there were strong indications that he was possessed by demons...."[8] For instance, August Kubizek, one of his few friends as a young man, witnessed Hitler's face turn pale and sinister in appearance, and then heard him make angry and impassioned speeches with a voice not his own; as Kubizek explained, "It was as if another being spoke out of his body, and moved him as much as it did me. It was not at all a case of a speaker carried away by his own words. I rather felt as though he himself listened with astonishment and emotion to what burst forth from him with elementary force...."[9]

Another one of his comrades, who had known the future dictator in Vienna before World War I, later described Hitler's nighttime ordeals:

> "He! He! He's been here!" he gasped. His lips were blue. Sweat streamed down his face. Suddenly he began to reel off figures, and odd words and broken phrases entirely devoid of sense. It sounded horrible. He used strangely composed and entirely un-Germanic word formations. Then he stood quite still, only his lips moving. He was massaged and offered something to drink. Then he suddenly broke out: "There, there! In the corner! Who's that?"[10]

An equally sinister event occurred at the Hofburg Museum in Vienna, which exhibited (behind a glass case) the "spear of Longinus" (also known as the Holy Lance), the tapered spearhead used by the Roman centurion to pierce the side of the crucified Christ (cf. Jn. 19:34). Hitler would frequently stare at the exhibit for hours at a time, lifted out of himself in what might be called occultic mystical experiences. He later described what happened at one of these visits:

> The air became stifling so that I could barely breathe. The noisy scene of the Treasure House seemed to melt away before my eyes. I stood alone and trembling before the hovering

*form of the Superman—a Spirit [of evil] sublime and fearful, a countenance intrepid and cruel. In holy awe, I offered my soul as a vessel of his will.[11]*

Hitler also claimed, "A window in the future was opened to me through which I saw in a single flash of illumination a future event by which I knew beyond contradiction that the blood in my veins would one day become the vessel of the Folk-Spirit of my people."[12]

Most biographers ignore that supposed mystical event, but all agree that when the outbreak of World War I was announced, Hitler was beside himself with joy. Though an Austrian, he enlisted in the Germany Army, and in the fighting on the Western front received the Iron Cross (Germany's highest military award) for bravery. Corporal Hitler seemed to live a charmed life, as he narrowly escaped death many times. On one occasion he heard a mysterious voice warning him to move to a different location in his unit's trenches; as soon as he did so, an artillery shell burst above the spot he had just vacated, killing all those present.[13]

Events like this gave the future Fuehrer a growing belief in his sacred destiny, as did an experience immediately after the end of the war. At a military hospital where he was recovering from war injuries, Hitler went into a trance and heard voices telling him that he was the appointed messiah who would lead Germany from defeat to greatness.[14]

Hitler was quite willing to surrender himself to occult forces as a means of achieving his "destiny," as indicated in a poem he wrote:

*On rough nights, I go sometimes To the oak of Wotan in the still garden, To make a pact with dark forces. The moonlight makes runes [ancient symbols] appear. Those that were sunbathed during the day Become small before the magic formula.[15]*

As one author states, "The hand of Satan can be seen pulling the strings in the life of Adolf Hitler: in his personal life, in his political life, and in his military career, making him the visible manifestation of Satan's true intent, an accurate representation of his master's nature and character."[16] The direct and pervasive influence of the devil helps explain certain facts that might otherwise be inexplicable; for instance, *when in 1913 Hitler left Vienna behind for Munich he had no experience in politics or public speaking. He could scarcely bring himself to meet people. However, within seven years he was the charismatic and dynamic leader of National Socialism, and within twenty years the head of the German state. Mere accident? Perhaps. But then, perhaps not. His amazing transformation was, as it were, a species of metamorphosis. In this view Hitler effected some kind of union with Satan, becoming a "diabolical mystic," but this kind of perverse mysticism engenders more depression than joy.*[17]

Other phenomena suggesting a profound diabolical influence in Hitler's life (i.e., demonic possession, or perhaps even some sort of pact with the devil) include an almost unprecedented degree of hatred for various individuals and groups (including especially the Jews, but many others as well), an incredible series of almost miraculous escapes from numerous assassination attempts, and the overwhelming and almost hypnotic effect he had on others by means of his personal presence and oratory.

The famous psychiatrist Carl Jung stated that Hitler's "eyes have the look of a seer. His power is magic. He is like a man who listens intently to suggestions whispered to him from a mysterious voice and acts on them."[18] A young man present at one of Hitler's motorcades as part of a school outing applauded the Fuehrer as he rode by, and even made eye contact with him; it was as if the world stood still, and he knew he was willing to give his life for Hitler—an experience and feeling shared by all his classmates. Moreover, Sigrid Schultz, an American journalist who lived in Germany before World War II, reported that as Hitler reviewed a group of young SS members, "He would go from one to the other, grasping the hand of each man in both of his, staring into his eyes for seconds on end. When he moved on, the young man would stand there as if in a trance."[19]

Hitler's speeches had a strange power to unify and inspire his audiences, especially at mass rallies; one of his colleagues observed, "After about fifteen minutes, something occurs that can only be described by the ancient, primitive metaphor:  the spirit enters into him."[20]This malign spirit allowed Hitler to touch the hearts of listeners and convert them into fervent supporters; one early Nazi, after hearing him speak for the first time, later said:

> *I was a man of thirty-two, weary of disgust and disillusionment,*
> *a wanderer seeking a cause; a patriot without a channel for his*
> *patriotism, a yearner after the heroic with a hero. The intense*
> *will of the man, the passion of his sincerity, seemed to flow from*
> *him into me. I experienced an exaltation that could be likened*
> *to religious conversion.*[21]

Albert Speer, Hitler's architect (and later director of the German war economy), claimed after the war that he didn't foresee the eventual destruction of the Jewish people and Germany's disastrous defeat because "Hitler took possession of me." As he said, "Something swooped me off the ground, wrenched me from all my roots, and beamed a host of alien forces upon me."[22] Moreover, modern technology allowed Hitler to spread his evil influence on an unprecedented scale; as Speer noted, "Through technical devices like the radio and the loud-speaker, eighty million people were deprived of independent thought. It was thereby possible to subject them to the will of one man."[23]

Even foreign leaders sometimes experienced the effects of Hitler's psychological power; during an interview with the Fuehrer, Kurt von Schuschnigg, the Austrian chancellor, felt that "Hitler was possessed, for he always knew what von Schuschnigg was going to before he could say it."[24] It isn't surprising that traditional politicians and world leaders were usually outsmarted and outmaneuvered by Hitler in pre-war Europe, for he represented something far beyond their knowledge and experience. As one commentator notes,

> *Hitler took himself to be that rarest of things, the union of*
> *philosopher and king, political philosopher and practical political*
> *leader, program-maker and politician in one. . . . We might*
> *say that whatever hesitations to action one finds in Darwin,*
> *Schopenhauer, or even Nietzsche, Hitler casts aside with the*
> *ruthlessness of Machiavelli.*[25]

Furthermore, Hitler's aims went far beyond mere politics; one author states that ". . . we have it on Hitler's own word that Nazism cannot be understood as a mere political movement."[26] The Nazi dictator desired to reshape the soul of the nation and "inculcate a spiritualization of cruelty that, going beyond conventional notions of good and evil, allows for the ruthlessness to achieve the necessary solutions to poverty and Germany's other social problems."[27]

The "Jewish Problem" was always at the center of Hitler's thinking, for "He wanted to believe that the Jews were the cause of every evil—not only because he had a sinful hatred of the Jews but also because he needed some single simple thing that caused all evil, real or imagined, that he, like some omniscient deity, could remove."[28] On one occasion he said, "I shall have gallows erected, in Munich for example in the Marienplatz [the city's central square], as many as traffic permits. Then the Jews will be hanged, one after another, and they will stay hanging until they stink. . . . As soon as one is untied, the next will take his place, and that will go on until the last Jew in Munich is obliterated. Exactly the same thing will happen in the other cities until Germany is cleansed of the last Jew."[29]

Like a modern-day Pharaoh or Haman, Hitler came to desire the complete destruction of the Chosen People—even to the point of maintaining the Holocaust (that is, the systematic extermination of the Jews in Auschwitz and other death camps) as a national priority during a time of growing military reverses for the German armed forces. (Indeed, Germany devoted as many scarce resources to the militarily useless program of mass murder of the Jews as the United States did to the Manhattan Project—the creation of the atomic bomb.)

Believing himself to be the German messiah, Hitler often made little effort to hide his stubborn arrogance; as American journalist Sigrid Schultz reported, "In the first interview I had with Hitler, he staggered me by asserting at the top of his voice, 'My will shall be done!'"[30] The Fuehrer was also extremely narcissistic; he wanted his actions and speeches to be carefully recorded, and in less than twenty years, his official photographer took some *two-and-a-half million photographs* of him.[31] A massive personality cult honoring the Fuehrer was imposed on the German nation (with the vast majority of Germans accepting it willingly and even enthusiastically). Schoolchildren, for instance, were taught to sing,

*Adolf Hitler is our savior, our hero, He is the noblest being in the whole wide world. For Hitler we live, for Hitler we die.*

*Our Hitler is Lord, who rules a brave new world.*[32]

There was even a Nazi version of the "Our Father," rewritten in Hitler's honor, which schoolchildren were required to recite.[33]

(An interesting illustration of Hitler's irreconcilable differences with the Church is provided by an incident in the life of the famous German mystic and stigmatic Therese Neumann. The devout Catholic—who was afforded some measure of protection by an SS officer who was genuinely impressed with her—was on one occasion in an ecstatic state and unaware of her surroundings. A visitor surreptitiously placed in her hand a postcard bearing Hitler's image; the visionary immediately flung it away and exclaimed, "Smoke and fire of hell!"[34])

Throughout his life, Hitler had a deep suspicion of, if not an outright hatred toward, Christianity—but, as a politician and even later as Fuehrer of the German Reich, he was usually careful to follow Machiavelli's dictum that a leader should always appear respectful of religion. In his candid moments, however, he expressed his contempt for the Church, saying, "I will tear up Christianity root and branch and annihilate it. People set us down as enemies of the Spirit. We are. But in a much deeper sense than the conceited bourgeois dolts ever dreamed of."[35] The simple truth is that

> . . . *Hitler detested Catholicism and all forms of Christianity. Despite his pious mother's example, and although he is said to have taken Communion in the 1914-18 war, he had totally abandoned Catholic belief as well as practice if only, as he himself admitted, "after a hard struggle." While admiring Christ's gifts as a propagandist, he disliked intensely what he termed the "Jewish Christ-creed with its effeminate pity ethic." He particularly resented the Catholic Church's natural hostility to his racial theories. . . .*[36]

This opposition to Hitler's racial theories was expressed in an unmistakable way by the Church in 1937 when Pope Pius XI's encyclical *Mit Brennender Sorge* ("With Burning Anxiety") was smuggled into Nazi Germany and read from every Catholic pulpit on Palm Sunday. The encyclical

> catalogued the Nazis' violations of the concordat [the agreement Hitler signed with the Vatican in 1934 recognizing

the Church's rights in Germany], *pointedly affirmed Christianity's roots in Judaism, underlined the universality of the Catholic faith that treated all men of whatever nation and race as the children of God, and condemned the neo-paganism of the Nazis and their "mad prophet" Adolf Hitler.*[37]

Needless to say, the Nazis were furious over this public denunciation, and responded by intensifying their already severe repression of the Church;[38] however, because of Christianity's still considerable influence in German life, they were not able to react as ruthlessly as they desired.

According to the leader of the Hitler Youth movement, Baldur von Schirach, "The destruction of Christianity was explicitly recognized as a purpose of the National Socialist movement" from the start, but "considerations of expedience" made it necessary to delay the desired showdown until a later time.[39] Contrary to common belief, the Nazis were always very conscious of public opinion, and usually careful to avoid any measures that might prove controversial or unpopular with a majority of the German population (at least until their propaganda had a chance to manipulate popular feeling). That's why, for instance, a popular and outspoken Catholic leader like Bishop Clemens von Galen of Münster could denounce the Nazi's euthanasia program from the pulpit[40] without suffering any reprisals; instead of von Galen being arrested, as he fully expected, the regime temporarily suspended its efforts to kill the "useless" and "unproductive" members of society.

The outbreak of war forced the Nazi regime to turn its hateful gaze in other directions, though Hitler was recorded as saying, "If there were an uprising in Germany, I would respond immediately with the arrest and death of all the leaders of the Catholic Church and I would condemn all those [already] interned in concentration camps."[41] Hitler had a fierce hatred for Pope Pius XII (sometimes referring to him as the "Jewish Pope"), and even as the war turned against Germany, he toyed with the idea of occupying the Vatican and bringing the Pope to the Reich as a prisoner.[42]

Prior to World War II, the Polish priest St. Maximilian Kolbe had written, "Modern times are dominated by Satan and will be more so in the future. The conflict with hell cannot be engaged by men, not even the most clever."[43]  It was indeed only the grace of the Holy Spirit, and not any strength of his own, that gave St. Maximilan the courage and peace to overcome the hatred of Nazism with a supreme act of love: volunteering to take the place of another prisoner condemned to death at Auschwitz in 1941.

The heroic Polish priest was only one of many Catholics martyred by the Nazis; others included St. Edith Stein (a Jewish convert to Catholicism who became a Carmelite nun), Bl. Bernard Lichtenburg (a priest in Berlin who courageously preached against the Nazis' many crimes), Bl. Jacob Gapp (an Austrian-born priest executed for his opposition to Hitler's regime), Bl. Michael Kozal (a Polish bishop murdered by the Nazis at the Dachau concentration camp), Bl. Otto Neururer (a German priest put to death in Dachau), Bl. Rupert Mayer (a Jesuit priest executed at Sachsenhausen), Bl. Teresa Bracco (an Italian woman killed by a German soldier for defending her purity), Bl. Titus Brandsma (a Dutch Carmelite priest executed at Dachau), and Bl. Franz Jägerstatter (an Austrian peasant beheaded in 1943 after he refused to serve in the German army).

Hitler led the Third Reich into a war against three great military powers—first Great Britain, then the Soviet Union, and finally the United States; in spite of their immense resources in industry and manpower, as late as 1943 Germany might still have avoided total defeat, but Hitler doomed himself by stubbornly continuing his war against the Jewish people and the Church.

The spear of Longinus, or the Holy Lance—which had transfixed the future dictator as a young man—symbolizes the misuse of great spiritual power, and also traces the course of Hitler's rise and fall. When Germany absorbed Austria into the Third Reich in the *anschluss* of 1938, Hitler hurried to the Hofburg Museum in Vienna and confiscated the sacred relic. It was taken to Nazism's "holy city" of Nuremberg and remained there until the end of the war. On April 30, 1945 (the satanic "feast" of Walpurgis), American troops discovered the lance, and took possession of it at 2:10pm—shortly before Hitler committed suicide in his Berlin bunker.[44]  An ancient prophecy connected with the relic was fulfilled:  "And if thereafter the sword [another sacred relic never obtained by Hitler] or lance come into evil use, to him who holds them will they turn to his fall and death."[45]

The Nazis always had a fascination with the occult, even to the extent of conducting bizarre rituals and experiments (especially under the patronage of Heinrich Himmler), or undertaking far-flung archaeological expeditions in hopes of validating their racial theories. One of these expeditions brought the Great Altar of Pergamum back to Berlin. This massive stone altar, dedicated to the pagan god Zeus, is described in Revelation 2:13 as "Satan's throne." At the end of World War II, however, the Soviet conquerors removed it from a Berlin museum and took it away to Moscow[46] (a fitting symbol of Satan transferring his favor from one evil empire to another).

World War II wasn't only fought in a military sense; as Michael H. Brown explains, the war

> *also involved the black arts. Both Rudolf Hess* [the deputy fuehrer] *and Heinrich Himmler, two staunch leaders of Hitler's elite guard, the SS, were immersed in the occult. Hess had been a member of the Thule Society and Himmler claimed he was the reincarnation of King Heinrich I of Saxony, and that at night the "king" appeared to him and gave him orders. Himmler* [at one time a devout Catholic] *advocated the public execution of the pope and both he and Hess were were instrumental in the Holocaust. . . . This too had occult connotations. The use of poison was an ancient tactic of German sorcery, and the very word "Holocaust" comes from* holokaustein, *which is defined in witchcraft as "a burnt offering."*[47]

Himmler in particular sought after arcane knowledge and mystical power, to the point of sending explorers to Tibet to find a lost Teutonic tribe which had supposedly preserved ancient Nordic mysteries; he also made use of clairvoyants and astrologers, and on one occasion had a seer go into a trance on a couch in his own office in an attempt to gain special intelligence.[48]

The Nazis "had a metaphysical hatred of Christianity" and sought to replace it "with a new and more genuine gospel of 'Aryan supremacy.'"[49] Indeed, in 1942 "the Nazi hierarchy proposed the complete substitution of Christianity by neo-paganism. In all churches the Bible was to be replaced by *Mein Kampf* [Hitler's political manifesto], the cross by the swastika, and the Judaeo-

Christian God by Wotan and other deities. It was probably only the domestic imperatives of the war that prevented this from becoming a fact."[50]

Historians have written hundreds of books analyzing Hitler's conduct of the war and the reasons for Germany's defeat, covering the military, industrial, economic, technological, and diplomatic aspects of the conflict. Relatively few, however, have examined the spiritual nature of the struggle—and thus may have overlooked one of the decisive causes of the Allied victory.

In 1940, after Germany's surprisingly swift and successful invasion of France and the Low Countries, the British Army in France, along with some French troops, found itself trapped near the French port of Dunkirk. The victorious Germans were in a position to kill or capture the entire force—a disaster from which Great Britain would likely never have recovered. King George VI called for a National Day of Prayer on May 26, and then—over the next nine days—the owners and crews of hundreds of unarmed fishing boats and pleasure craft helped evacuate some 330,000 Allied soldiers to safety. The German Luftwaffe, or air force, harassed the retreat, but could not prevent it, while the German Army—which could have taken Dunkirk—stood down at Hitler's orders.

This "miracle of deliverance," as Prime Minister Winston Churchill called it, convinced the British King and Parliament of the value of prayer, and they implemented a simple idea:

*a daily minute when all of Britain's inhabitants should turn their thoughts to heaven. The proposed time would be a natural focal point in their war-torn nation: the BBC's nine o'clock news broadcast. So it was that on the night of November 10, 1940 . . .as Big Ben chimed nine commanding peals—a full minute—across the airwaves . . . BBC announcer Howard Marshall heralded this nightly "Big Ben minute" as a time for Britons everywhere to pause and seek unity of purpose as a free people. Pulpits and periodicals across the nation were swift to define the minute as a call to prayer. As one clergyman put it, "May the precious minute turn millions of hearts to seek strength in the Almighty God, Who is the Father of Mercies and the God of all consolation"* [2 Cor. 1:3].[51]

This "Silent Minute"—which most listeners used as a moment of prayer—had a powerful impact; from 1942 onwards, the BBC later claimed, many millions of people, not only in Great Britain, but also in occupied Europe, observed the nightly ritual. Moreover,

> *Soon after the end of hostilities in Europe in 1945, a British Intelligence officer, interrogating high Nazi officials, asked one of them why he thought Germany had lost the war. This was the reply: "During the war, you had a secret weapon for which we could find no counter-measure, and which we did not understand, but it was very powerful. It was associated with the striking of Big Ben each evening. I believe you called it the Silent Minute."*[52]

In 1942, the Catholic Church made an even greater spiritual contribution to the eventual Allied victory, for on October 31—at the height of World War II—Pope Pius XII consecrated the world to Our Lady's Immaculate Heart. It was later revealed to Sister Lucia, the surviving Fatima visionary, that this act by the Holy Father shortened the war by over a year.[53] Within a few days of the consecration, the tide of the war turned against Germany and its ally Japan; the November battles of Stalingrad in Russia, El Alamein in North Africa, and the campaign on and around Guadalcanal in the South Pacific, were all decisive Allied victories, and the Axis powers were never able to regain the initiative.

Adolf Hitler was truly one of the most evil men in history, and Nazi Germany was the closest approximation of hell yet to be seen on earth—but neither was able to overcome the Church. Catholics, along with many other Christians and non-Christians—and above all, the Jewish people—paid an unimaginably horrific price, but Hitler's Third Reich, which he boasted would last for a thousand years, came to absolute defeat, utter destruction, and unending disgrace.

Hitler surrendered himself to Satan, and paid the price for his arrogant folly. The words of Scripture are a fitting epitaph: "I saw a wicked man, fierce, and stalwart as a flourishing, age-old tree. Yet as I passed by, lo! he was no more; I sought him, but he could not be found" (Ps. 37:35-36).

# NOTES TO CHAPTER 10

1. Christopher Nugent, *Masks of Satan* (Christian Classics, 1983, 1989), p. 147.

2. Michael H. Brown, *The Final Hour* (Queenship Publishing, 2000), p. 45.

3. Bob Rosio, *Hitler & the New Age* (Huntington House, 1993), p. 124.

4. Fr. Andrew O'Brien, *Make Yourself An Ark!*, Vol. Two (The American Research Foundation, 1995), p. 40.

5. Nugent, p. 148.

6. *Ibid.*, p. 151.

7. Rosio, pp. 143-144.

8. Brown, p. 45.

9. *Ibid.*

10. Nugent, p. 150.

11. Brown, p. 46.

12. Trevor Ravenscroft, *The Spear of Destiny* (G. P. Putnam and Sons), p. 20, as quoted in Rosio, p. 135.

13. John Toland, *Adolf Hitler* (Doubleday & Company, 1976), p. 64.

14. Brown, pp. 45-46.

15. Rev. Richard Wurmbrand, *Marx & Satan* (Crossway Books, 1986), p. 22.

16. Rosio, p. 79.

17. Nugent, p. 149.

18. Rosio, p. 46. At first impressed with the Fuehrer, Carl Jung stated in 1937, "He is a medium. German policy is not made; it is revealed through Hitler. He is the mouthpiece of the gods of old. . . . He is the Sybil, the Delphic oracle" -- Marie Anne Jacques, "A Study of Psychology," Part 2, *"Michael" Journal* (May-June-July 2010), p. 11.

19. *Ibid.*, p. 47.

20. *Ibid.*, p. 170.

21. T. L. Jarman, *The Rise and Fall of Nazi Germany* (Signet, 1961), p. 97, as quoted in Donald DeMarco, *The Heart of Virtue* (Ignatius, 1996), p. 209.

22. Rosio, p. 160. That Speer wasn't simply making excuses for himself by blaming everything on Hitler is suggested by the fact that at the Nuremberg war crimes trials in 1946, he—unlike the other Nazi defendants—freely admitted his guilt and willingly accepted his sentence of twenty years in prison. While taken in by Hitler's "spell," Speer—virtually alone among the Nazi hierarchy—remained somewhat capable of objective thinking and independent action (as when he sabotaged the Fuehrer's "scorched earth" orders during the last weeks of the war).

23. Shelley Klein, *The Most Evil Dictators in History* (Barnes & Noble, 2004), p. 60.

24 Nugent, p. 150.

25 Benjamin Wiker, *10 Books that Screwed Up the World* (MJF Books, 2008), p. 152.

26 Nugent, p. 146.

27 Wiker., p. 158.

28 *Ibid.*, pp. 163-164.

29 Klein, p. 60.

30 Rosio, p. 108.

31 Nugent, p. 152.

32 Toland, p. 528.

33 Brown, p. 54. The blasphemous prayer said, "*Adolf Hitler, you are a great leader. Thy name makes the enemy tremble. Thy Reich comes, thy will alone is law upon the Earth. Let us hear daily thy voice and order us by thy leadership, for we will obey to the end even with our lives. We praise thee! Heil Hitler!*"

34 Albert Paul Schimberg, *The Story of Therese Neumann* (Roger A. McCaffrey Publishing, 1947), p. 18.

35 Rosio, p. 87.

36 Desmond Seward, *Napoleon and Hitler: A Comparative Biography* (Viking, 1988), pp. 114-115.

37 H. W. Crocker III, *Triumph: The Power and the Glory of the Catholic Church* (Three Rivers Press, 2001), p. 393.

38 In 1941, the German Catholic Church compiled a book of documents eventually translated and published as *The Persecution of the Catholic Church in the Third Reich* (later reprinted by Roger A. McCaffrey Publishing). The book thoroughly describes the numerous brutal, blatant, and sometimes ingenious methods used by the Nazis to obstruct, and eventually forbid, the Church's ministries and activities—including restrictions upon religious education, the abolition of Catholic organizations for youth and adults, the abrogation of legal protection for the Church, "immorality" trials against Catholic leaders, and public attacks on the Church's teachings and practices.

The volume's Publisher's Note quotes Msgr. F. D. Cohalan's review of this book for *Commonweal* magazine in 1941, in which he said:

It is precisely because National Socialism is fundamentally a religion that the bitter conflict between the Church and the Third Reich has developed. The Nazis claim the whole man, body and soul, and while professing high regard for religious liberty, attempt to restrict the Church to a very closely supervised administration of the Sacraments. The Church could never accept such a definition of her status and mission and hence must resist to the end. . . .

39 Ted Flynn, *Idols in the House* (MaxKol Communications, 2002), p. 55.

40  Ronald J. Rychlak, *Hitler, the War and the Pope* (Our Sunday Visitor, 2000), p. 116. In his courageous sermon, Bishop von Galen said,

> Do you or I have the right to live only as long as we are productive? . . . Then someone has only to order a secret decree that the measures tried out on the mentally ill be extended to other "nonproductive" people, that it can be used on those incurably ill with a lung disease, on those weakened by aging, on those disabled at work, on severely wounded soldiers. Then not a one of us is sure anymore of his life. . . . Woe to humanity, woe to our German people, when the sacred commandment "Thou shalt not kill" is not only violated, but when this violation is tolerated and carried out without punishment!

41  Sr. Margherita Marchione, *Yours Is A Precious Witness* (Paulist Press, 1997), p. 71.

42  *Ibid.*, p. 149.

43  Jill Haak Adels, *The Wisdom of the Saints* (Barnes & Noble, 1987), p. 143.

44  Brown, p. 60.

45  Col. Howard A. Buechhner, *Adolf Hitler and the Secrets of the Holy Lance* (Thunderbird Press, 1988), p. 129.

46  Brown, p. 60.

47  *Ibid.*, p. 59.

48  Nugent, pp. 160-161.

49  Klaus P. Fischer, *Nazi Germany: A New History* (Continuum, 1995), p. 359.

50  Nugent, p. 164.

51  Steve Badaracco, "Can You Spare A Minute?", *Celebrate Life* (American Life League, March-April 2010), p. 31.

52  *Ibid.*, p. 32.

53  Mark Fellows, *Sister Lucia: Apostle of Mary's Immaculate Heart* (Immaculate Heart Publications, 2007), p. 150.

# Chapter 11

# The Social Engineers

*Just as weeds are collected and burned with fire, so will it be
at the end of the age. The Son of Man will send His angels, and
they will collect out of His Kingdom all who cause others to sin
and all evildoers. They will throw them into the fiery furnace,
where there will be wailing and grinding of teeth.* (Mt. 13:40-42)

Catholicism has always insisted upon the reality of original sin, and as St. Paul taught, the disobedience of one man—Adam—made all humanity sinful (cf. Rom. 5:12,19). The doctrine of original sin not only means that each one of us needs Jesus Christ as our Savior if we are to live one day in Heaven; it also means that no matter how knowledgeable, prosperous, and scientifically and technologically advanced the human race may become, it will never be possible to build a perfect society on earth.

A refusal to recognize or admit this fact has resulted in much mischief, folly, and tragic and unnecessary suffering over the centuries; as the *Catechism of the Catholic Church* teaches, a denial of the reality that human beings have "a wounded nature inclined to evil gives rise to serious errors in the areas of education, politics, social action, and morals" (n. 407).

This is only to be expected when creatures rebel against their Creator. Because we are made in God's image and likeness (Gen. 1:27), trying to live without Him will inevitably result—despite our sincere intentions and best efforts—only in confusion, alienation, and disillusionment; even the most radical and ruthlessly enforced efforts to create a "Heaven on earth" are doomed to failure, often at a very high human cost.

Nevertheless, the temptation to achieve a "perfect" society, one created solely through our own efforts, without reference to God, never seems to disappear from human consciousness. Sometimes this project involves the "liberation" of humanity from outmoded religious superstitions and outdated morality, as supposedly represented by the Church; for other thinkers, true enlightenment and freedom can be found if only we take a rational and "scientific" approach to every aspect of life; still others insist that only a radical rejection of what we perceive as reality will finally allow us to claim a noble, if depressing, experience of "authenticity." In every case, however, the Church, and the spiritual and eternal life she offers in the Name of her Lord, is seen as an obstacle to be ignored or rejected, and often as an enemy to be scorned or attacked.

As Jesus said, "This is the verdict: that the light came into the world, but people preferred darkness to light. . ." (Jn. 3:19). The scientists, philosophers, sociologists, and social activists presented in this chapter were not "evil" in a manner similar to the political, military, and religious leaders examined earlier in this book, and most of them (so far as we know) were not directly involved in any form of violence or killing (other than, in one or two cases, the advocacy of abortion). Nevertheless, they can all be labeled "antichrists" because of their dangerous beliefs and their ongoing influence. We have a responsibility to beware of their mistaken teachings—for as Our Lord warns, "If a blind man leads a blind man, both will fall into a pit" (Mt. 15:14).

# Comte

The founder of sociology, Auguste Comte believed that the true development of human society required advancing from the primitive stages of theological and metaphysical belief (that is, accepting the reality of the supernatural, and of ideas themselves) to a positive, or scientific, view of existence: namely, everything we believe must first be tested and proved by hypothesis, experimentation, and observation. This enlightened approach, he asserted, would lead to a world in which individuals and nations would finally exist in mutual peace and prosperity.

Comte believed that a new society, suitable for humanity's growing self-awareness and abilities, was needed, and this would also mean a "new faith had to replace the decadent belief of tired

Christianity."[1] This new "faith," of course, had no room for God or religion, for both had supposedly failed. "Since the function of the mind now would be to *mirror* the truly real state of things, the contents of the new religion must be drawn from such an objectively real source, and this, says Comte, is *humanity* itself."[2]

Not only was there no room for God in Comte's thinking; his intent was to create a system of thought in which the very *idea* of God would never even occur to anyone. Indeed, he believed the trouble with atheism was that it was only a partial and "inadequate emancipation from the tyranny of God," vulnerable to theistic counterattacks.[3] Comte's plan

> *was to bring about the dethronement of this decrepit God Who ruled despotically over "the long minority of mankind" through the instrumentality of organized religions, particularly Catholicism, all of which were presently rotten to the core. The positivism of Comte was aimed at shocking atheists forward into becoming anti-theists.*[4]

In particular, Comte hated Jesus Christ, considering Him to be a false prophet Who founded a false religion, and thus "essentially a charlatan."[5] His new "religion of humanity," however, was more or less a secularized version of Catholicism, complete with its own hierarchy, calendar of saints, and sacraments.[6]

Comte's personality was as mixed-up as his ideas; he was known to be very self-centered, ungrateful, and egocentric, and after enduring years of misery, his wife left him. Some time later he met Madame Clotilde de Vaux, and immediately fell under her spell; though they remained only friends, Comte's infatuation taught him that "One cannot always think, but one can always love."[7] Unfortunately, this important insight wasn't taken to its logical conclusion; while he wanted all people to love humanity as he loved Clotilde, there was still no room in his heart for Love itself; to his dying day the "High Priest of the Religion of Humanity" refused to acknowledge God's existence. His final words were "What an irreparable loss"[8]—a judgment that may very well have been true in a sense he never intended.

# Darwin

The famous naturalist Charles Darwin had originally accepted the idea that the intricate order of nature obviously implied the existence of a Creator, but he later rejected this view and instead concluded the opposite: God (if He existed) would not have bothered creating so many slight variations within individual species. Therefore, another explanation for life and reality—namely, natural selection and evolution—was necessary.[9]

Darwin was certainly not the first scientist associated with the idea of evolution, but he presented it in what seemed to be an empirical and systematic way. However, there was another agenda being served:

> Darwin's work and research were funded through the same group of American _Illuminati_ who had funded Karl Marx. For, what the _Illuminati_ desperately needed was a **system of beliefs** which would both pander to their globalist vision and work to destroy their sworn and stated archenemy—the Roman Catholic Church.[10]

Because evolution was a highly controversial idea (commonly associated with atheists and radicals), and because he wanted to maintain an air of respectability in English society, Darwin carefully avoided any mention of human beings evolving in his famous _Origin of Species_, for he knew that if he did so, his theory would be rejected.[11] This, however, placed him

> in an interesting trap. His real views were radical, but his prestige depended upon the rejection of such radicalism. To deal with the dilemma, Darwin lived a double intellectual life, moving in aristocratic, anti-evolutionary circles even while, privately, he was working feverishly on the details of his account of evolution. He was convinced that the human mind was entirely material, that human beings had indeed evolved from some apelike ancestor, and that morality itself was one more evolutionary artifact. Very soon, the anxiety of this double life began to take its toll on his health, so much so that often Darwin was unable to do any work and instead lay like an invalid in bed.[12]

Darwin, who was not only a eugenicist, but also a racist and moral relativist,[13] believed that the idea of the "survival of the fittest" should be *applied* to human beings (a concept taken to its logical conclusion in Nazi Germany). He felt that "Society should not interfere with nature by artificially protecting the weak from destruction. Such charity is unnatural and hence unscientific. Instead, society should help natural selection with its work and wipe out the weak by even more efficient means. That is the science of eugenics."[14]

In a passage from *The Descent of Man* largely ignored by his admirers, Darwin made his views very clear:

> *There is reason to believe that vaccination has preserved thousands, who from a weak constitution would formerly have succumbed to small-pox. Thus the weak members of civilised societies propagate their kind. No one who has attended to the breeding of domestic animals will doubt that this must be highly injurious to the race of man. It is surprising how soon a want of care,* **or care wrongly directed** [emphasis added], *leads to the degeneration of a domestic race; but excepting in the case of man himself, hardly anyone is so ignorant as to allow his worst animals to breed.*[15]

The Christian response to this chillingly utilitarian "logic" is obvious: our value as human beings depends not on our physical and intellectual wholeness, nor on our "usefulness" to society. Rather, in the words of the *Catechism*, "The dignity of the human person is rooted in his creation in the image and likeness of God" (n. 1700). Moreover, "Endowed with a spiritual and immortal soul, the human person is the only creature on earth that God has willed for its own sake" (n. 1703). Not only are there secular heroes who labored under severe physical disadvantages (Beethoven, for instance, was born of a syphilitic father and a mother suffering from consumption, and himself became deaf later in life); there are also numerous saints who in spite of terrible illnesses, disabilities, or physical deformities, edified and inspired those around them (and who now shine with a special glory in their Heavenly Father's Kingdom).[16]

Darwin rejected the Church's defense of human dignity because he believed that human beings are naturally amoral, and that what we call "conscience" was itself the result of natural selection.[17]Naturally, the Nazis later found this concept to be very useful—along with much of Darwin's teaching—in their efforts to "purify" and preserve the Aryan race. Also, "Attempts to disengage Darwin from the eugenics movement date from a bit after World War II, when Hitler gave a bad name to survival of the fittest as applied to human beings. But it is impossible to distance Darwin from eugenics: it's a straight logical shot from his evolutionary arguments."[18]

Because Darwin's closest family members and friends were Christian, he refused to label himself an atheist, but insisted upon the less controversial term "agnostic." His health deteriorated throughout 1881, seemingly overburdened by the strain of downplaying or hiding his real beliefs. As one author observes,

> *It seems Darwin's doctrine of survival produced within the man a struggle that made him ever less fit. At the bottom of an old letter written by his wife and kept by Darwin all these years, a letter imploring him not to turn away from the saving doctrine of Christ for fear of the couple's eternal separation, Darwin tearfully scrawled during Easter of 1881, "When I am dead, know that many times, I have kissed and cryed [sic] over this." Charles Darwin died in the arms of his wife on April 19, 1882. Emma would not have her consolation.[19]*

Darwin hinted at his own doubts and regrets in a letter to his friend and colleague Charles Lyell, in which he said, "Often a cold shoulder has run through me, and I have asked myself whether I may have not devoted myself to a phantasy."[20]

His teaching on evolution, however, took on a life of its own. Not only was the concept embraced by the Nazis (with deputy Fuehrer Rudolf Hess insisting "National Socialism is nothing but applied biology"[21]), but many 20th century academics and authors eagerly adopted Darwinism as a justification for immoral behavior. For instance, Sir Julian Huxley (the grandson of Darwin's colleague Thomas Huxley, and a president of UNESCO), admitted, "I suppose the reason we leaped at the origin of species was because the idea of God interfered with our sexual mores," a point echoed by his brother Aldous Huxley, the famous author *Brave New* World, who added, "We objected to the morality because it interfered with our sexual freedom."[22]

By popularizing the ideas of natural selection and evolution, Darwin gave the denial of God an appearance of scientific respectability—and even though serious doubts have been raised about evolution over the years,[23] many people continue to assume that human life can be explained, or at least experienced, without reference to God, morality, and eternity. The errors propagated by Charles Darwin and his followers will never conquer the Church, but they have led many souls astray.

# Nietzsche

Adolf Hitler proclaimed Friedrich Nietzsche the official philosopher of Nazi Germany, and based on its use of his concept of the superman, "Even if Nietzsche would not have believed in Nazism, it is clear enough that Nazism believed in him."[24] As a youth, Nietzsche came to associate the weakness and illness of his father (who died when young Friedrich was four) with his father's profession as a Protestant minister. As one commentator notes,

*Nietzsche's major criticism of Christianity—of its morality, of the Jesus of Christian theology, and of the whole meaning of the Christian God—was that it suffers from an absence, even a rejection, of "life force." The God that Nietzsche chose was Dionysius—a strong pagan expression of the life force. It is therefore not hard to view Nietzsche's rejection of God and Christianity as a rejection of the weakness of his father.[25]*

At the age of thirteen, Nietzsche wrote an essay on ethics, in which he named God the father of evil. (In that same year, the self-centered young man also wrote the first of no less than nine autobiographies he would produce before the age of twenty-five.) He was a deep admirer of Richard Wagner—until the composer created *Parsifal*, an opera exalting Christianity. Enraged and feeling betrayed, "Nietzsche needed to find a new god and teacher. He found him in the form of Persian deity Zoroaster. And so, in 1883, he wrote his impassioned philosophical poem, his masterpiece, *Thus Spake Zarathustra*. It would be his Dionysian, anti-Christian retort to *Parsifal*."[26]

Nietzsche hated Christianity, believing it had destroyed truth, as understood and lived in classical times. "Although he made a sharp distinction between the message of Jesus and the creed of Christianity, Nietzsche rejected both with contempt."[27]  Indeed, he regarded Christianity as not only "a will to deny life," but "a secret instinct of destruction, a principle of calumny, a reductive agent—the beginning of the end—and, for that very reason, the Supreme Danger."[28]  The philosopher's quarrel was

> *not with the infidelity of Christians to their own premises*
> *but with the premises themselves; not just with Christians,*
> *but with Christ. His concern is not so much, as Zarathustra*
> *reports, that "God is dead," as why God should be dead, and*
> *Nietzsche the psychologist relishes explaining Him away as*
> *kind of wish-fulfillment of the weak.*[29]

We can almost hear Nietzsche's defiance as he exclaimed in *Thus Spake Zarathustra,* "Better to have no God, better to set up destiny on one's own account, better to be a fool, better to be God oneself!"

Looking with horror at the New Testament, Nietzsche complained that "the least qualified people . . . have their say in its pages in regard to the greatest problems of existence," and snidely remarked that "one does well to put on gloves" when reading the Christian Scriptures—whose only admirable figure, he claimed, was Pontius Pilate.[30]  Nietzsche felt Christianity contradicted Nature in requiring love of one's enemy, because Nature commands us to *hate* our enemies.[31]  This was part of the reason Nietzsche considered Christianity a type of slave morality (compared to what he called the master morality); in preaching God's love for the poor, the weak, and the lowly, Christian charity worked to "preserve all that was sick and that suffered—which means, in fact and in truth, to *worsen the European race.*"[32]

Rejecting Christian morality and transcendence, Nietzsche insisted that humanity must become its own lawgiver; in his book *The Antichrist,* he declared:

> *What is good? All that heightens in man the feeling of power,*
> *the desire for power, power itself. What is bad? All that comes*
> *from weakness. What is happiness? The feeling that our*
> *strength grows, that an obstacle is overcome. Not contentment,*
> *but more power; not universal peace, but war; not virtue, but*
> *forcefulness. . . . What is more harmful than any vice? Pity*

*for the condition of the ineffective and weak* — [as manifested by] *Christianity.*[33]

(It's easy to see from these words why Hitler was one of Nietzsche's admirers.)

Jesus had taught, "Blessed are the meek" (Mt. 5:5), and Nietzsche despised Him for this—but in addition to his hatred of weakness, there was another dynamic at work. According to Fr. Vincent Miceli,

> It was [French novelist] *André Gide* who shrewdly analyzed the sickness of Nietzsche's spirit. Nietzsche was insanely jealous of Jesus. Gide writes: "In the presence of the Gospel, Nietzsche's immediate and profound reaction was—it must be admitted—jealousy. It does not seem to that Nietzsche's work can be really understood without allowing for that feeling. Nietzsche was jealous of Christ, jealous to the point of madness." Nietzsche, then, suffered from a God-complex, from an obsession to be the Savior of mankind. And he fumed in envy and hatred that Jesus had pre-empted this role two thousand years before him.[34]

Nietzsche wrote *The Antichrist* to express his opposition to Christ, and "in his last work, *Ecce Homo* ["Behold the Man!"], sets himself up as the victorious rival of Him Whose teaching he proposed to supplant."[35] Indeed, by the time he wrote *Ecce Homo*, Nietzsche was boasting "Politics on a grand scale will date from me."[36] As one author notes, "in his euphoria Nietzsche was increasingly megalomaniacal, strident, and blasphemous. All caution was thrown to the winds: he was the Antichrist, 'a Man of Destiny,' and he would act like it, taunting Christ and cursing Christianity."[37]

In some of his letters, Nietzsche spoke of striking "a destructive blow against Christianity" and engaging in the "greatest decisive war in history"; he arrogantly boasted that "the old god is abolished, and . . . I myself will henceforth rule the world," and signed himself as "Nietzsche Caesar," "The Anti-Christian Friedrich Nietzsche," or simply "The Antichrist."[38]

In her *Magnificat*, the Virgin Mary rejoiced that God "has shown might with His arm, dispersed the arrogant of mind and heart" (Lk. 1:51). These words were certainly fulfilled in Nietzsche's case, for only four months after finishing his boastful *The Antichrist*, Nietzsche was afflicted with insanity. While staying in Turin, Italy on January 3, 1889, Nietzsche was

> guilty of the "final sin" of Zarathustra: "Pity!" Upon departing from his lodgings on the fateful morning, he was transfixed to see a cabman mercilessly beating a tormented horse. Nietzsche intervened, flung himself around the neck of the animal, and reportedly cried out something to the effect that he had never really meant to be hard. This act of pity was the point of his breakdown.[39]

The final decade of Nietzsche's life was one of madness and despair; at times he kept everyone in the house awake by repeating over and over, "I am dead because I am stupid; I am stupid because I am dead."[40]

Nietzsche's story is a tragic one, for he

> was one of the loneliest men who ever existed. In attempting to become his own god, he severed all lines of communication with everyone around him. There was no one left to help him to know who he was. He became a sacrificial victim to the god he mistakenly identified with Life.... In the end, he was incurably mad, blinded and paralyzed by syphilis, and in the care of two women, first his mother and then his sister. Ironically, he had ridiculed women.[41]

Nietzsche may have considered himself a superman who was "Beyond Good and Evil" (the title of one of his books), but in the end he was a pathetic figure, desperately in need of a Savior—a Savior, however, Whom he had contemptuously rejected.

# Freud

As the founder of psychoanalysis, Sigmund Freud's ideas had a profound influence on the twentieth century; however, many of them are now discredited—unfortunately, only after having done much harm. As historian Paul Johnston writes,

> Freud's attitude to scientific proof was very different from Einstein's and more akin to Marx's. Far from formulating his theories with a high degree of specific content which invited empirical testing and refutation, Freud made them

*all-embracing and difficult to test at all. And, like Marx's followers, when evidence did turn up which appeared to refute them, he modified the theories to accommodate it. . . . Freud betrayed signs, in fact, of the twentieth-century messianic ideologue at his worst—namely, a persistent tendency to regard those who diverged from him as themselves unstable and in need of treatment.*[42]

Various commentators have pointed out that psychoanalysis is fundamentally anti-Christian, for Freud regarded religion as an illusion; his utopian vision was of a world in which "the 'illusion' will be dispelled by the light of reason; science will replace religion in culture and in life; a new blissful age will begin when science reigns supreme."[43] Freud's *The Future of an Illusion* dismissed religion as a "foolish wish-fulfillment by infantile minds";[44] even worse,

*Freud's rooting of religion in incest and patricide was a direct attack not only on religion as a whole, but especially on Christianity—both on the Eucharist and perhaps on the idea of the Virgin Mary—with his implication that the most holy sacrament of the Christian Church was a vile recapitulation of patricidal cannibalism fueled by incest.*[45]

Freud, of course, assumed that God does not exist; the concept itself, he said, was merely a cosmic projection of a father-image, and religion was nothing more than a collective neurosis—one which psychoanalysis had the mission of dissolving.[46] However, Freud's view of religion is somewhat confusing or contradictory. He believed religion was useful—indeed, necessary—to keep the masses from acting on their aggressive (and sexual) impulses,[47] and he had no personal hostility toward religious believers, and at times even showed respect for religious customs.[48] In evaluating his theories, however, we must remember that

*Freud had very little psychoanalytic experience with patients who believed in God or were genuinely religious. None of his published cases deals with a patient who believed in God at the time of the psychoanalysis. That is,* **nowhere did Freud publish a psychoanalysis of the belief in God based on clinical evidence provided by a believing patient.**[49]

From a Christian perspective, Freud's stubborn refusal to admit even a possibility of spiritual or other-worldly forces at work in our world made it very easy not only for Satan to confuse him, but to use him as an unwitting pawn in hell's ongoing war against the Church. As Michael H. Brown explains,

> *Although the very female patient who inspired Freud's initial theory was in reality a case of demonic oppression (she complained about an evil spirit inside her!), the famous psychoanalyst scoffed at such notions and was contemptuous of religion. As far as he was concerned, she was delusional. Any miracles or "demonic" attacks were explained away as products of the subconscious, a childish reversion to "primitive" days when people believed in such "nonsense" as devils and angels. Freud sought to replace the idea of "good" and "evil" with his bizarre and to this day unproven psychosexual theories. It was all a grand deception, and while Freud was too blind to see it, unaware that he was being used, that's what it was: a supernatural scheme to hide the increasing presence of evil spirits. If Satan couldn't get people to worship at his séances and occult altars . . . the next best thing was to blind them to all forms of the supernatural so his demons could operate freely.[50]*

The case referred to here involved "Anna O" (a pseudonym), a talented and highly cultured woman whose disturbances included rapid mood shifts, hallucinations, an inexplicable ability to speak different (previously-unknown) languages, and two distinct and quite different personalities. One of Freud's colleagues, Josef Breuer, noted that

> *At moments when her mind was quite clear she would complain of the profound darkness in her head, of not being able to think, of becoming blind and deaf, **of having two selves, a real one and an evil one which forced her to behave badly [emphasis added], and so on.**[51]*

Breuer claimed to have "cured" her (using Freud's methods), but Anna continued to suffer these same abnormalities afterwards.[52] Freudian thought had no room for the demonic—though, ironically, Freud's most famous disciple, Carl Jung, developed his own theories with the help of a "spirit guide" calling itself Philemon.[53]

In his book *Sigmund Freud and the Jewish Mystical Tradition,* author David Bakan asserts that Freud saw himself as a new Moses, one destined to replace the old Law of religious fear and guilt with a new one of psychological liberty; he also demonstrates that

> at least metaphorically, Freud entered into a "Satanic pact" and that psychoanalysis was its result. . . . Bakan argues that it made logical sense for Freud to think of himself as the devil, since both he and the devil were the opposites of Moses. He cites a remark that Freud once made to colleagues: "Do you know that I am the Devil? All my life I have had to play the Devil, in order that others would be able to built the most beautiful cathedrals that I have produced." Bakan then adds, "The disease of the neurotic is guilt. This guilt is [for Freud], in itself, an evil and its removal is good. . . . If God is the guilt-producing image, then the Devil is the counterforce.[54]

Does Freud's reference to himself as the devil imply that—in terms of Judeo-Christian morality—he was an evil person? Jesus Himself taught that "by their fruits you will know them" (Mt. 7:20), and on the basis of his psychoanalytic legacy, and his own personal behavior, the judgment is highly negative:

> Critics have subjected Sigmund Freud to some withering broadsides. Freudian scholars willing to critique his theories and personal life find a rich source of inflammatory information. Accusations against Freud's impregnating his sister-in-law, then having her child aborted, and his murder [emphasis added] of a best friend provide merely the opening statement of a long indictment. Freud himself admitted, in letters to a friend, that some of the treatments he had given patients led to their deaths, through the use of cocaine and sexual, hypnotic drugs. . . . He viewed people as basically sexual beings—a fatal delusion since we are basically spiritual beings. He missed the essential factor in undisciplined sexuality: sexuality advances as the spiritual nature recedes.[55]

Nazi Germany's annexation of Austria in 1938 prompted Freud to flee to England. The following year, in great pain as death approached, the famous psychiatrist insisted his friend and physician, Dr. Max Schur, assisted by his daughter Anna, help him commit suicide through an overdose of morphine; his final recorded words were, "My dear Schur . . . you promised to help me when I could no longer carry on. It is only torture now, and it no longer has any sense."[56]

Hopelessness and agony were the fate not only of Freud, but in some sense are also the ultimate lot of all those who seek meaning in life without reference to God. According to Fr. Benedict Groeschel, "We should not be silent about the fact that Freudianism failed and that it is the Church that can explain man to himself," for "Freud and his theories are now an intellectual curiosity, but Jesus Christ remains the Light of the World—the same yesterday, today, and tomorrow" (cf. Heb. 13:8).[57]

# Sanger

Margaret Sanger, the founder of Planned Parenthood and avid promoter of birth control and abortion, was a baptized Catholic who, as a young woman, became involved in Helena Blavatsky's religion of Theosophy.[58] Not only did she forsake her childhood faith; she also abandoned any pretense at morality, giving herself over to adultery, treating her first husband with extreme cruelty, and generally neglecting her children by him. As one of her contemporaries, an author named Mabel Dodge, wrote,

> it was as if she had been more or less arbitrarily chosen **by the powers** to voice a new gospel of not only sex knowledge in regard to contraception, but sex knowledge about copulation and its intrinsic importance. She was the first person I ever knew who was openly an ardent propagandist for the joys of the flesh.[59]

Sanger edited a newspaper called *Woman Rebel* (whose motto was "No Gods, No Masters"), in which she urged women to "look the whole world in the face with a go-to-hell attitude," and in her book *My Fight for Birth Control*, she described herself as belonging to a "secret society of agnostics and atheists who were waiting for the coming revolution."[60] Though today's Planned Parenthood would prefer to ignore it (for obvious reasons), Sanger was an admirer of Adolf Hitler, and in her November 1939 issue of *Birth Control Review* (two months after he launched World War II by invading Poland), she praised the Nazi birth control program.[61]

Sanger's book *The Pivot of Civilization* has been called "one long rant against the existence—and worse, the breeding—of the 'feeble-minded' in general, and the 'moron,' 'imbecile,' and 'idiot' in particular, those 'who never should have been born at all.'"[62] The poor—rather than being seen as persons in need of society's help and protection—were viewed by Sanger as "human weeds," and instead of advocating charity as a response to poverty, she called for the segregation of "morons, misfits, and maladjusted" and for the sterilization of "genetically inferior races."[63] In 1932 *Plan for Peace*, Sanger identified her targets as including Blacks, Hispanics, American Indians, and Catholics.[64]

An ardent supporter of eugenics, Sanger

> *was one of the great leaders of the international eugenics movement, and the connections between the eugenic aspirations of pre-World War II Americans and Germans is a matter of hard facts. Even more revealing, Sanger didn't peddle birth control and also espouse eugenic views, as if these were two unrelated passions. Eugenics was at the very heart of her reasons for pushing birth control.[65]*

Particularly cynical was Sanger's desire to use religion to disguise and accomplish her ignoble agenda; in 1939 she stated that "the most successful educational approach to the Negro is through a religious appeal. We do not want word to go out that we want to exterminate the Negro population and the minister is the man who can straighten out that idea if it ever occurs to any of their rebellious members."[66]

Demonstrating St. Paul's teaching that "since they did not see fit to acknowledge God, God handed them over to their undiscerning mind to do what is improper" (Rm. 1:28), Sanger arrogantly declared the marriage bed to be "the most degenerating influence in the social order," and advocated a "voluntary association" between sexual partners.[67] Indeed,

> *For Sanger the release of sexuality from restriction became a kind of religious goal, a goal that heralded its own this-worldly view of paradise, one in which "men and women will not dissipate their energy" in the Christian belief in "the vague sentimental fantasies of extramundane existence," but will realize that here on earth, in a sexual Utopia of our own making, we shall find "our paradise, our everlasting abode, our*

*Heaven and our eternity.*[68]

Not surprisingly, Sanger's emphasis on sexual freedom wasn't balanced by a corresponding sense of responsibility. She loved her children only when it was convenient: freely hugging and kissing them, but finding herself seized by a mysterious "nervous malady" whenever they actually needed her for something; as her son Grant later stated, "Mother was seldom around. She just left us with anybody handy, and ran off we didn't know where."[69] This cavalier attitude was one she recommended to others; she once wrote to her sixteen-year-old granddaughter, "Kissing, petting and even intercourse are alright as long as they are sincere. I have never given a kiss in my life that wasn't sincere. As for intercourse, I'd say three times a day was about right."[70]

Scripture warns that "Lust indulged starves the soul, [but] fools hate to turn from evil" (Prv. 13:19). This truth is validated by a description of Sanger's last pathetic years:

> As she got older, her passion became only more inflamed, and she needed ever more assurance that she was indeed desirable. She purchased such assurance through money, having inherited five million dollars after the death of her [second] husband Noah Slee. Sanger would throw party after party to fill her empty days and use her wealth to attract younger men, who would pay her court. Becoming ever more depressed as age took its toll and her beauty waned, she turned to alcohol and (after an operation) to pain killers, often spending the day sleeping or incoherent. Finally, she had to be taken to a nursing home after she took to drunken wandering during the night.[71]

The Communist theoretician Antonio Gramsci (see Chapter 8) had insisted that Marxism could prevail only by destroying the morals and cultural institutions of Western societies. To paraphrase Lenin, Margaret Sanger, and her post-World War II counterpart Alfred Kinsey, unwittingly served the role of "useful moral idiots" as they and their followers undermined the Judeo-Christian sexual ethic which had helped make America great. The Church continues to proclaim God's truth regarding sexual morality—but far too many are unwilling to hear it.

# Kinsey

The 1948 publication of *Sexual Behavior in the American Male*, authored by Indiana University zoologist Alfred C. Kinsey, was one of the most decisive events in the remaking (or, more precisely, degradation) of American culture. Known as the "father of the sexual revolution," Kinsey, by claiming that sexual deviance was "normal," in effect gave permission for every imaginable sort of sexual activity and experimentation—and the resulting sexual revolution, though it didn't explode into the national consciousness until almost a decade after Kinsey's 1956 death, changed the face of American society, and continues to wreak its moral and spiritual devastation today.

Kinsey liked to promote the myth that he was an objective scientist of conservative personal habits, and that his research was nothing more than a disinterested—if rather controversial—presentation of a hitherto unrecognized cultural reality. The truth was rather different, for, as one author notes,

> *It would soon be revealed that Kinsey was not only an admirer of Aleister Crowley, but had pursued his writings with much vigor and would eventually travel to Crowley's old stomping grounds in Europe. Just as L. Ron Hubbard began Scientology on the date of Crowley's death in 1947, Kinsey picked this same year to begin his Institute [for Research in Sex, Gender and Reproduction at Indiana University] in hopes of picking up where Crowley left off, albeit in a more "scientific" endeavor.*[72]

This voyeurism in the name of science meant filming sexual activity involving his students, fellow faculty members, employees, and even his own wife; this also fueled Kinsey's own fascination with pornography—to the point that, "with new material added every day, the Kinsey Institute maintains the largest collection of porn in the *world*."[73]Furthermore, in conducting his statistically flawed "research," Kinsey and his team—in interviewing imprisoned felons—deliberately sought out sex offenders, so as to suggest a greater percentage of deviancy in American population as a whole than was actually the case.[74]

A far worse offense involved the methods Kinsey used to obtain "evidence" or "data" for his claim that children are inherently sexual beings:

> The problem with Kinsey was that almost all of his research was a sham and remains clouded in mystery to this day by the very institute founded in his name. The most shocking accusation was that most of the data on child sexuality was obtained by the largest alleged incident of mass child molestation in American history. . . . An American researcher named Dr. Judith Reisman . . . questioned pages 160 and 161 from Kinsey's 1948 book concerning children and infants as young as two months "enjoying" being sexually stimulated. How. . .did rape and molestation of children ever make the transition from criminal activity into research?[75]

According to Dr. Reisman, "Kinsey solicited and encouraged pedophiles, at home and abroad, to sexually violate from 317 to 2,035 infants and children for his alleged data on normal 'child sexuality.' Many of the crimes against children . . . committed for Kinsey's research are quantified in his own graphs and charts."[76] Kinsey outspokenly advocated adult-child sex, and

> According to his own personal correspondence, Kinsey was a homosexual with a marked preference for young boys. He was also an atheist and a confirmed bigot who refused to hire Jews, blacks, Christians, and anyone else who embraced traditional nmoral values. He oversaw the filming of live sex acts at Indiana University in his home, which were performed by members of his own staff and their families, all of whom were expected to participate whether they wanted to or not.[77]

One of Kinsey's co-workers, Wardell Pomeroy, later admitted that "One of the chief complaints was that he compiled too large a portion of homosexual histories;"[78] the reason for this, of course, wasn't just a flawed methodology, but a deliberate effort on his part to promote a particular ideology. The often-repeated but erroneous claim that 10% of the American population is homosexual dates from Kinsey's attempt to make homosexuality mainstream.

As one would expect, Kinsey not only rejected Christianity's teachings on sexual morality; he also came to despise religion itself; as one of his colleagues said, by the late 1940s Kinsey was "not only irreligious, he was anti-religious."[79] Jesus taught that those who do wicked things avoid the light of truth, so that their evil works might not be exposed (Jn. 3:20), and this helps explain Kinsey's aversion to Christianity, for his own "sexual perversities were so astounding that the only way to escape the unnaturalness of his activities was to declare them to be natural, to say that there was no sexual good or evil. In short, Kinsey's private life was a Hobbesian sexual state of nature."[80] For example, he regularly had sex with his male colleagues, and they frequently traded wives; he even had his own wife Clara perform deviant acts on film for his Institute.[81]

Kinsey was fascinated by nudist camps, taking his male graduate students there on field trips and walking around them stark naked; he often showered with them, probed the intimate details of their sex lives, and included erotic poems in his correspondence with them.[82] One of Kinsey's biographers, James H. Jones, wrote,

> *Professors did not engage in that sort of behavior with their graduate students, yet Kinsey seemed totally oblivious to sexual taboos . . .as though he was determined to flaunt them . . . . Kinsey had become a sexual rebel . . . manipulative and aggressive, a man who abused his professional authority and betrayed his trust as a teacher. Only a compulsive man would take such risks.[83]*

Also, Kinsey insisted in bringing in outside "subjects" to the Institute, supposedly for research, "but actually [as] an ongoing attempt to fulfill [his] insatiable masochistic and homosexual desires. . . ."[84]

How was Kinsey able to get away with all of this scandalous (and in some cases, illegal or at least extremely unethical) behavior? Using his research in a heavy-handed, manipulative way was the key. One author explains that

> *The collection of these [sexual case] histories was of critical importance to Kinsey's "research," and he went to great lengths to obtain them, which wasn't easy during the 1940s. He was increasingly prone to badgering and even bullying people to get them. This did not exclude university professors and administrators, whose histories contained details about*

*adulterous and homosexual activity unknown to anyone but Kinsey. "Kinsey's possession of such sex secrets amounted to a subtle form of coercion bordering on blackmail," Dr. Reisman writes. The clever use of this control device explains how Kinsey managed to maintain complete support from the university. His close friendship with Herman Wells, the president of the university and a bachelor who lived alone with his mother, also insured the continuation of his work.[85]*

Kinsey died in 1956—officially of a heart attack, but in reality as a result of his own sexual perversion. According to Dr. Reisman, this created a problem for the Institute and his disciples: "The sexual revolution faced a potentially serious setback were it widely known that the theoretical father of the movement had died from an advanced stage of sadosexual autoerotic (masturbatory) activity."[86] After all, Kinsey had always insisted there was no danger of contracting sexual diseases or otherwise causing oneself harm from any of the activities he promoted—and so his death had to be attributed to a different cause.

Author David Kupelian sums up Kinsey's disastrous legacy:

*. . . today virtually everything having to do with sex—from attitudes toward extramarital affairs and homosexuality to the nation's sex-education curricula, to the ways medicine, psychiatry, psychology, and even the criminal justice system define and deal with sexual pathology—is rooted firmly in the ludicrously fraudulent "data" of Kinsey and his cult of criminally deviant sex "researchers."[87]*

Kinsey's research helped give rise to the feminist movement, the radical "Gay Rights" movement, and even to the formation of the North American Man Boy Love Association (NAMBLA), which advocates the legalization of "intergenerational sex" (i.e., child molestation).[88] In spite of the ongoing harm he caused to American society, "The press had only praise for him when he died, sadly remarking on the death of a brave and dispassionate scientific pioneer."[89] Jesus, however, pronounced a very different judgment on Kinsey's legacy: "Whoever causes one of these little ones who believe in Me to sin, it would be better for him to have a great millstone hung around his neck and to be drowned in the depths of the sea" (Mt. 18:6).

# Sartre

The novelist and playwright Jean-Paul Sartre was one of the most famous atheists of the 20th century and, indeed, the "poster child" for a philosophy of meaninglessness and despair. As an adolescent upset over his widowed mother's remarriage, he decided, "You know what? God doesn't exist,"[90] and having drawn this conclusion, he spent the rest of his life trying to persuade others—unfortunately, with great success.

Sartre's philosophy was expressed primarily in his plays and novels, which "depict human beings as sickened by the fundamental, metaphysical experience of nausea, that realization of the primeval, intrinsic absurdity of all reality."[91] Sartre insists that each person is born into a world without meaning. Nevertheless, he can achieve a certain degree of intelligibility in his life by his freedom of choice. Freely choosing one way or another is an act of self-creation—but each person must live with the consequences of these decisions, and must make them without any outside guidance or support (human or divine). That's why Sartre refers to freedom as a burden; indeed, man is, in Sartre's phrase, "condemned to be free."[92]

The contrast between Sartre's philosophy and the Gospel becomes even more apparent when we realize that he denies not only the existence of God, but also the desirability of any type of unity or solidarity with other people. Each person must work out the meaning of his own existence, free of any outside influence; Sartre refers to this radical self-centeredness as "authenticity." When people begin to love each other, however, they become inauthentic, for they choose to act on behalf of each other, thereby preventing one another from facing up to reality, and thus destroying each one's personal autonomy. Indeed, Sartre believed that because love puts limits on each individual's quest for authentic freedom, every other human being is a threat to be kept at a distance (hence his well-known claim that "Hell is other people").[93]

The comforting but misguided idea of God, Sartre claimed, is the greatest threat to our freedom of all, because His existence—if real—would mean that He, not human beings, determines what it means to be truly human, and religious faith would "deceive us into thinking there is meaning for ourselves or in our world."[94] Relying upon this "illusion" is, for Sartre, the worst of all evils; instead, humans must bravely face the absurdity of life, no matter how painful that may be, for—as he concludes, "God does not exist . . . it is necessary to draw the consequence of His absence right to the end."[95]

Our Lord's teaching that "whoever finds his life will lose it, and whoever loses his life for My sake will find it" (Mt. 10:39) serves as a corrective and antidote to Sartre's depressing world-view. Sadly, his philosophical system proved to be rather trendy and influential. One commentator notes that "In the 1940s, scholars said he was great, journalists reported on his greatness, and teachers began telling students he was great. That did it. Until he died in 1980, no matter how stupid or callous his public statements, he wore the cloak of greatness."[96]

Following World War II, Sartre became an apologist for Communism, claiming that he found more political and personal freedom in the Soviet Union than anywhere else; years later, he admitted, "It's true that I thought well of it, but that's because I kept myself from thinking ill of it." When the terrorist Che Guevara was killed, the philosopher called him the most complete human being of the age, and when terrorists murdered eleven Israeli athletes at the 1972 Olympics, Sartre insisted it was wrong and irresponsible for journalists to describe the event in negative terms.[97]

Sartre's last words were "I failed!"[98]—an apt judgment on his self-proclaimed quest for truth and authenticity. His moral blindness illustrates the ability of human beings to close their minds to reality, and, even more importantly, to moral truth—a capability perhaps more widespread at the beginning of the 21st century than ever before. Many people today search for their own version of truth, claiming to be "spiritual" but not religious; others run after the allurements of a passing world, while seeking to make pleasure their path to "self-fulfillment"; still others—often despite many social and material advantages—succumb to various self-destructive addictions or pathologies symptomatic of wasted lives empty of all hope or higher purpose.

None of this was ever God's plan—but in order to be truly blessed by Him, it is necessary to be open to His truth and willing to obey His commands. That's why, when Jesus' disciples asked Him the meaning of one of His parables, He said, "Knowledge of the mysteries of the Kingdom of God has been granted to you; but to the rest, they are made known through parables so that 'they may look but not see, and hear but not understand'" (Lk. 8:9-10). More than a few people today have made themselves incapable of hearing and understanding the Gospel; they are like seed sown on the footpath, which "the devil comes and takes away the word from their hearts that they may not believe and be saved" (Lk. 8:12).

The 19th and 20th century social and intellectual leaders presented in this chapter are among the more influential and successful figures who have worked to undermine traditional religious faith and morality. Knowingly or unknowingly, they have served the Evil One very well in his scheme to remove God and religion from Western society, thereby setting the stage for the arrival on the "man of perdition." Before the final antichrist arrives, however, a "new world order" must be prepared as part of Satan's effort to ensnare all humanity in his rebellion against the Creator.

## NOTES TO CHAPTER 11

[1] Fr. Vincent Miceli, S.J., *The Gods of Atheism* (Roman Catholic Books, 1971), p. 143.

[2] Samuel Enoch Stumpf, *Socrates to Sartre* (McGraw-Hill, 1966, 1975), p. 347.

[3] Miceli, p. 156.

[4] *Ibid.,* p. 157.

[5] *Ibid.,* p. 163.

[6] Stumpf, p. 347. The author writes, "Instead of God, Comte substituted humanity, which he called *Grand-Étre*, the Supreme Being; he became his own High Priest, instituted a calendar of saints, mostly renowned scientists, created a catechism at the end of which Comte says, 'Humanity definitely occupies the place of God,' adding that 'she does not forget the services which the idea of God provisionally rendered'; the sacraments become 'social' and include *Presentation* (Baptism); *Initiation* at age fourteen; *Admission*, when at age twenty- one a person is authorized to serve humanity; *Destination* or choice of career at twenty-eight; *Marriage* for men at twenty-eight and for women at twenty-one; and *Retirement* at age sixty-three" (*ibid.*).

[7] Miceli, p. 159.

[8]  www.gkindia.com.

[9]  Donald De Marco & Benjamin Wiker, *Architects of the Culture of Death* (Ignatius Press, 2004), p. 72.

[10]  Stephen Mahowald, *She Shall Crush Thy Head* (MMR Publishing, 1996), p. 106.

[11]  Benjamin Wiker, *10 Books that Screwed Up the World* (MJF Books, 2008), p. 87.

[12]  De Marco & Wiker, p. 73.

[13]  *Ibid.*, p. 76.

[14]  Wiker, p. 88.

[15]  Charles Darwin, *The Descent of Man* (Princeton University Press, 1981), p. 168, as quoted in Wiker, pp. 88-89.

[16]  Rev. Joseph M. Esper, *More Saintly Solutions* (Sophia Institute Press, 2004), pp. 211ff. Examples include Bl. Margaret of Castello, who was hunchbacked and lame; Bl. Kateri Tekakwitha, whose face was disfigured by smallpox; St. Joan of France, who—like Bl. Margaret—was hunchbacked, and who—like Bl. Kateri—had a pockmarked face; St. Joseph Cafasso, who was slightly deformed due to a curvature of the spine; and St. Servulus, who was palsied as an infant, and thus never able to stand, sit upright, or feed himself.

[17]  De Marco & Wiker, pp. 77-78.

[18]  Wiker, p. 85. The author elaborates on this point in a passage which deserves to be quoted at length:

> . . . *eugenic thinking was not something tacked on to Darwin by thuggish brownshirts in 1930s Germany. Rather, it was and is a direct implication drawn from Darwin's account of evolution, one that Darwin himself drew quite vividly in his <u>Descent of Man.</u> Furthermore, in the latter half of the nineteenth and first half of the twentieth century eugenics was popular not just in Germany but all over Europe and America. It was understood to be a legitimate inference from Darwin, because Darwin himself made the deduction, and so it was written into biology textbooks—even in America.*
>
> *To be fair to Darwin, he did shrink back from suggesting direct extermination (as did Hunter's <u>A Civic Biology,</u> however reluctantly), but not because mercy was inherently good. After all, mercy was itself merely a by-product of blind evolutionary forces. According to Darwin, such charity was merely an "incidental result of the instinct of sympathy, which was originally acquired as part of the social instincts." To translate, Darwin believed that morality was neither natural nor God-given, but was itself the result of natural selection* (p. 91).

[19]  De Marco & Wiker, p. 85.

[20]  Marylou Barry, "Why Academics Embrace Darwinism," *Whistleblower Magazine* (February 2010), p. 40.

[21]  Wiker, p. 147.

22   Barry, p. 40. The author also quotes Nobel Prize winner Dr. George Wald, professor emeritus of biology at Harvard University, who admitted in an interview with *Scientific American* magazine, "I do not *want* [emphasis added] to believe in God. Therefore I choose to believe in that which I know is scientifically impossible, spontaneous generation arising to evolution." Also quoted is New York University philosophy professor Thomas Nagel, who says, "I want atheism to be true, and am made uneasy by the fact that some of the most intelligent and well-informed people I know are religious believers. It isn't just that I don't believe in God and, naturally, hope that I'm right in my belief. *It's that I hope there is not God!* [emphasis added]. I don't want there to be a God; I don't want the universe to be like that" *(ibid)*.

23   See, for instance, *Darwin's Black Box: The Biochemical Challenge to Evolution,* by Michael J. Behe (Touchstone Books, 1998); *Evolution: A Theory in Crisis,* by Michael Denton (Adler & Adler, 1985); *Darwin on Trial,* by Philip E. Johnston (Intervarsity Press, 1993); *Evolution?,* by J. W. G. Johnson (Perpetual Eucharistic Adoration, 1986); and *Icons of Evolution: Science or Myth?,* by Jonathan Wells (Regnery, 2000).

24   De Marco & Wiker, p. 52.

25   Paul C. Vitz, *Faith of the Fatherless* (Spence Publishing Company, 1999), p. 23.

26   De Marco & Wiker, p. 47.

27   Miceli, p. 53.

28   Friedrich Nietzsche, *The Birth of Tragedy* (Doubleday, 1956), p. 11, as quoted in De Marco & Wiker, p. 43.

29   Christopher Nugent, *Masks of Satan* (Christian Classics, 1983, 1989), p. 129.

30   *Ibid.,* p. 130.

31   Stumpf, p. 376.

32   Friedrich Nietzsche, *Beyond Good and Evil* (Vintage, 1966), section 62, as quoted in Wiker, p. 110.

33   Ted Flynn, *Idols in the House* (MaxKol Communications, 2002), p. 53.

34   Miceli, p. 84.

35   Fr. Vincent Miceli, S.J., *The Antichrist* (Roman Catholic Books, 1981), p. 134.

36   Nugent, p. 132.

37   *Ibid.,* pp. 137-138.

38   Wiker, p. 112.

39   Nugent, pp. 138-139.

40   Wiker, p. 113.

41   De Marco & Wiker, p. 50.

42   Paul Johnson, *Modern Times: The World from the Twenties to the Eighties* (Harper & Row, 1983), p. 6.

43 Rudolf Allers, *What's Wrong With Freud?* (Roman Catholic Books, 1941), p. 198.

44 Wiker, p. 165.

45 *Ibid.*, p. 167.

46 Miceli, *The Antichrist*, p. 135.

47 Vitz, p. xiii.

48 Fr. Benedict Groeschel, C.F.R., "All Things Are Passing, But God Never Changes," *The Priest* (August 2010), p. 32. The author notes that Freud "at times mysteriously seemed to support certain aspects of religion. His son recalls that Freud once took his two children along to the old boulevards of Vienna to collect wild-flowers to place in front of the statues of the Blessed Mother that were once found throughout that beautiful city. Freud is also quoted as saying that 'religion is the music of life'" (*ibid.*).

49 Vitz, pp. 8-9.

50 Michael H. Brown, *The Final Hour* (Queenship Publishing, 2000), p. 28.

51 Michael H. Brown, *Prayer of the Warrior* (Queenship Publishing, 2000), pp. 117-118.

52 *Ibid.*, p. 118. The author adds, "According to Freud himself, the case seized Dr. Breuer with a 'conventional horror' and ensnared the physician in an obsessive love-hate relationship. At one point, after hypnotizing Anna O, he fled the house in a cold sweat" (ibid.).

53 *Ibid.*, p. 148.

54 David Bakan, *Sigmund Freud and the Jewish Mystical Tradition* (D. Van Nostrand, 1958), p. 329, as quoted in De Marco & Wiker, p. 218.

55 Virgil Hurley, *Speaker's Source Book of New Illustrations* (Word Publishing, 1995), pp. 216-217.

56 www.eulogyspeech.net.famous.last.words.

57 Groeschel, p. 52.

58 Thomas W. Petrisko, *Call of the Ages* (Queenship Publishing, 1995), p. 117.

59 As quoted in Brown, *The Final Hour*, (Queenship Publishing, 2000), p. 32.

60 *Ibid.*, p. 33.

61 Fr. Andrew O'Brien, *Make Yourself An Ark!*, Vol. Two (The American Research Foundation, 1995), p. 43.

62 Wiker, p. 129.

63 http://www.ewtn.com/library/PROLIFE/PP04A.TXT.

64 Ted Flynn, *Hope of the Wicked* (MaxKol Communications, 2000), p. 5.

65 Wiker, p. 128.

66 http://www.ewtn.com/library/PROLIFE/PP04A.TXT.

67 *Ibid.*

68 De Marco & Wiker, pp. 296-297.

69 *Ibid.,* p. 292.

70 *Ibid.,* p. 294.

71 *Ibid.,* p. 301.

72 Michael Vincent Boyer, *The Hollywood Culture War* (Xlibris Corporation, 2008), p. 401.

73 *Ibid.,* p. 407.

74 De Marco & Wiker, p. 279. The authors note that Kinsey never kept a record of refusal rates (that is, the number of persons who, when asked for an interview, declined). Instead, he "eagerly took the histories of all who volunteered. . . . As social scientists have shown, it is precisely those who least represent the ideas, opinions, and activities of the society as a whole who are most likely to volunteer for an interview" (*ibid.*).

75 Boyer, p. 431. According to Benjamin Wiker, "Kinsey had no anxiety about using data collected by child molesters because he believed that the very notion of 'molesting'—a negative term—was a holdover from religious hang-ups. Science was the cure for such religio-moral obscurantism. A good Darwinian approach, a scientific approach, puts pre-adolescent sexuality in the proper context, as just one more way to 'express' ourselves" —*10 Books,* p. 208.

76 Dr. Judith Reisman, "Sex, Lies and Kinsey," *Whistleblower* magazine (July 2002), as quoted in David Kupelian, *The Marketing of Evil* (WND Books, 2005), p. 134.

77 Susan Brinkman, *The Kinsey Corruption* (Ascension Press, 2004), p. 24.

78 Boyer, p. 406.

79 De Marco & Wiker, p. 272.

80 Wiker, p. 204.

81 *Ibid.,* p. 205.

82 De Marco & Wiker, pp. 272-273.

83 James H. Jones, *Alfred C. Kinsey: A Public and Private Life* (Norton, 1997), as quoted in Brinkman, p. 9.

84 *Ibid.,* p. 275.

85 Brinkman, p. 32.

86 *Ibid.,* p. 64.

87 David Kupelian, *The Marketing of Evil* (WND Books, 2005), p. 142.

88 Boyer, p. 407.

89 De Marco & Wiker, p. 285.

90  R. Hayman, *Sartre: A Life* (Simon and Schuster, 1987), p. 31, as quoted in Vitz, p. 29.

91  Miceli, *The Gods of Atheism*, p. 217.

92  Anthony T. Padovano, *The Estranged God: Modern Man's Search for Belief* (Sheed and Ward, 1966), pp. 14-15.

93  *Ibid.,* p. 18.

94  *Ibid.,* p. 19.

95  Jean-Paul Sartre, *Existentialism*, trans. B. Frechtman (Philosophical Library, 1947), p. 25, as quoted in Padovano, p. 19.

96  Robert Fulford, "The Last Words of a Toxic Intellectual," *The National Post* (September 22, 2007); http://www.robertfulford.com/2007-09-22-sartre. html.

97  *Ibid.,* Mr. Fulford also states that Sartre's "writing often dwelt on despair; existential angst was his specialty. But he told [his assistant Benny] Levy [in the book *Hope Now: The 1980 Interviews*] this never reflected his feelings. 'I talked about it because other people were talking about it, because it was fashionable.' And what about anguish, a similar subject of his? 'I have never known anguish.' He wrote about it because other people were writing about it. 'It was fashionable. Everyone was reading Kierkegaard then'" (*ibid.*).

98  http://users.belgacom.net.gc674645.grave.last.word.htm.

# Chapter 12

# Architects of a New World Order

*They said to one another, 'Come, let us mold bricks and
harden them with fire.' They used bricks for stone, and
bitumen for mortar. Then they said, 'Come, let us build
ourselves a city and a tower with its top in the sky, and
so make a name for ourselves; otherwise we shall be
scattered all over the earth.* (Gen. 11:3-4)

In the introduction to his novel *The Screwtape Letters*, C. S. Lewis
observed,

*I live in the Managerial Age, in a world of "Admin." The
greatest evil is not now done in those sordid "dens of crime"
that Dickens loved to paint. It is not done even in concentration
camps and labour camps. In those we see its final result.
But it is conceived and ordered (moved, seconded, carried,
and minuted) in clean, carpeted, warmed, and well-lighted
offices, by quiet men with white collars and cut fingernails
and smooth-shaven cheeks who do not need to raise their voice.
Hence, naturally enough, my symbol for Hell is something like
the bureaucracy of a police state or the offices of a thoroughly
nasty business concern.[1]*

We no longer live in a world in which Christians are thrown
to wild beasts in arenas full of bloodthirsty spectators, or in which
defenseless monasteries and villages are ravaged and destroyed
by hordes of horse-mounted invaders, and while wars will likely
still be unleashed by power-mad dictators, the greater danger now
comes from groups of calm, "civilized" men capable of hiding their
contempt for religion and hatred of the Church behind a veneer
of forced politeness. International organizations, government
agencies, military units and security forces, political and financial
institutions, societal movements and cultural trends, scientific

research and technological applications, and even secret societies, all have a profound impact on today's world—and all are capable of being used, manipulated, and abused by Satan and his servants, including, ultimately, the antichrist.

# Secularism

It cannot be denied that Christendom is no longer truly Christian; nations and societies built on a Judeo-Christian foundation—including the United States of America—have largely abandoned, or at least severely degraded, their moral and religious heritage. Our secular world increasingly denies the reality and necessity of its Creator; in the words of John Paul II,

> . . . we cannot ignore the insistent return of the denial of Christ. Again and again we encounter the signs of an alternative civilization to that built on Christ as "cornerstone"—a civilization which, even if not explicitly atheist, is at least positivistic and agnostic, since it is built upon the principle of thinking and acting as if God did not exist. This approach can easily be recognized in the modern so-called scientific, or rather scientistic, mentality, and it can be recognized in literature, especially the mass media. To live as if God did not exist means to live outside the parameters of good and evil, outside the context of values derived from God. It is claimed that man himself can decide what is good or bad. And this program is widely promoted in all sorts of ways.[2]

The Holy Father noted that this "practical atheism" has very tangible, and highly undesirable, results: divorce, free love, contraception, abortion, euthanasia, and (in the form of genetic experimentation) the manipulation of life. There's a widespread assumption that anything promising certain benefits to humanity should be attempted if scientifically possible, regardless of any moral or religious objections. This 21st century mindset is backed up by enormous financial and political resources, and, as the Pope observed, "Faced with all this, one may legitimately ask whether this is not another form of totalitarianism, subtly concealed under the appearances of democracy."[3]

According to Pope John Paul II—the only Pope to live under

the twin scourges of Nazism and Communism—"In the twentieth century great efforts were made to stop people believing, to make them reject Christ. Toward the end of the millennium, those destructive forces were weakened, yet they left a trail of devastation behind them." The Holy Father was referring not only to the many millions of deaths, and the vast physical destruction, caused by World War II, but also the spiritual harm caused by decades of Communist rule in much of Europe, resulting in "a devastation of consciences, with ruinous consequences in the moral sphere, affecting personal and social morality and the mores of family life."[4]

Even as Soviet-style Communism was collapsing in the decade before the new millennium, its long-range plan of subverting Western society, formulated so many years earlier by Antonio Gramsci, continued to unfold—and, indeed, seemed to develop a momentum of its own. A world which honored—or at least, pretended to honor—Christian values was transformed in a relatively short time into a highly secular society, in which personal identification with the Church and a strong religious commitment was, at best, tolerated as merely one of many possible worldviews and lifestyles, none of which was entitled to claim superiority over any other. As Cardinal Josef Ratzinger asserted in his homily at the Mass initiating the conclave of 2005 (in which he would be elected as successor to Pope John Paul II), "We are building a dictatorship of relativism that does not recognize anything as definitive and whose ultimate goal consists solely of one's ego and desires."[5]

Pope Benedict XVI (as he would soon be known) was in effect describing a central principal of secular humanism, which rejects the idea of moral absolutes, and insists that human beings are not subject to divine law (assuming God exists). Accordingly, morality is understood solely in terms of situation ethics, which, in effect, means people are free to do whatever they can rationalize as good or necessary according to their circumstances and personal preferences. Under this perspective, writes one commentator, "life is experienced as a series of 'breakthroughs' against an oppressive moral order,"[6] and organized religion is considered irrelevant at best, or, more likely, as a set of arbitrary and unnecessary restrictions on human freedom that must be overthrown.

# Contemporary American Society

As St. Josemaria Escrivá noted, "The world thrives on lies even twenty centuries after the Truth came among men."[7] This aptly describes a society unwilling to confront the reality of what happens in an abortion, instead attempting to disguise or massage the truth by calling it a "termination of a pregnancy" or a "procedure," while framing the entire discussion in terms of "freedom of choice." Other moral issues such as euthanasia are serviced by euphemisms claiming "death with dignity" and the need to preserve the "quality of life," while gullible voters are convinced to support morally-objectionable procedures such as embryonic stem cell research for their supposed benefits to society.

At the same time, America has seen prominent politicians organize cover-ups and commit perjury in an effort to hide the violation of their oaths of office; business executives attempt to deny or excuse widespread corporate corruption; news media engage not only in selective reporting, but outright distortions and "advocacy journalism" in a blatantly partisan manner; scientific agencies manipulate statistics to create the appearance of certain "crises," while adopting an air of objectivity and superiority; religious leaders grievously abuse the trust of their congregations; and various entertainers, sports figures, and other celebrities and public figures overstate their achievements, lie about their problems, or otherwise rearrange the truth for their own benefit.

It's little wonder that the number of Americans expressing trust in government, news media, organized religion, and other cultural institutions verge on an all-time low—but even so, people continue to allow themselves to be deceived; the devil has a field day with those who will not subject themselves to the authority of divine truth. As Scripture warns, "Anyone who is so 'progressive' as not to remain in the teaching of Christ does not have God" (3 Jn. 9). Indeed, those who worship the idea of human progress, regardless of the cost involved and the moral restrictions to be violated, are in a very real sense possessed by the spirit of the antichrist.

The steady moral decline of American society over the past fifty years is no accident; as author David Kupelian notes,

*within the space of our lifetimes, much of what    Americans once almost universally abhorred has been packaged, perfumed, gift-wrapped, and sold to us as though it had great value. By skillfully playing on our deeply felt national values of fairness, generosity, and tolerance, these marketers have persuaded us to embrace as enlightened and noble that which all previous generations since America's founding regarded as grossly self-destructive—in a word, evil.[8]*

The counter-culture of the 1960s was a important part of the effort to undermine America's religious foundations—an essential step in the moral "disarmament" of the United States, thereby eroding American power and freedom and thus removing a major obstacle to an eventual one-world government. One author asserts:

*The goal was to change the mass consciousness of millions of people [in the United States and] around the world. It was a frontal assault on Judeo-Christian beliefs, Christianity, the God of the Bible, family, and Christian moral beliefs. The agenda was to destroy those beliefs by replacing them with mystical and occult beliefs which encouraged sexual immorality. The reality is that the counter culture was a planned event, just like many of the things happening in our world today, such as the environmental movement* [which, some have argued, actually promotes contrived "crises" as an excuse for further government control over individuals' freedoms and lifestyles]. *Fabian Socialists, like Aldous Huxley and numerous "change agents," were actively at work promoting New Age and the use of mind-altering drugs.[9]*

The "guru" of the drug culture was Dr. Timothy Leary, a failed psychology professor at Harvard, who bragged, "I've been an admirer of Aleister Crowley. I think I'm carrying on much of the work he started over a hundred years ago. . . . He was in favor of finding yourself. . . . I'm sorry he isn't around to appreciate the glories he started." Leary's "sole purpose in life would be to wage a full-scale drug legalization campaign,"[10] even though, according to the *Catechism of the Catholic Church*, "The use of drugs inflicts very grave damage on human health and life," and their illegal use is "gravely contrary to the moral law" (n. 2291).

Another major front in the cultural war involves sex. The

so-called "sexual revolution" of the mid-1960s didn't occur spontaneously; it was prepared for by the activism of Margaret Sanger and her followers, the "research" of Alfred Kinsey and his colleagues, and the promotion of social rebels like Hugh Hefner, who blamed "the comfort and prosperity of middle-class America for his urgent need to create a sexual revolution."[11] Hefner, the founder of *Playboy* magazine, and Jack Valenti, president of the Motion Picture Association of America, worked together to impose a movie ratings scheme on the film industry—which, when implemented in 1968, resulted in a drastic lowering of moral standards in Hollywood filmmaking, even though it had been promoted as a way of "improving" the movie-going experience for American audiences.[12]

The political, economic, and cultural transformation of American society is a major goal for many influential activists, such as the billionaire George Soros; as political commentator Bill O'Reilly warns in his book *Culture Warrior* that "His secular approach would drastically diminish Judeo-Christian philosophy. . . . We ignore him at our own peril."[13] Author Michael Vincent Boyer describes Soros as "the polished package version of Aleister Crowley, promoting the destruction of the traditional family, open and unfettered drug use, demonizing Jews and Christians, promoting legal prostitution, abolishing punishment for crime and initiating the rewriting of the American Constitution."[14]

There are many other secular humanists in American society, and as their influence continues to grow, the political and religious freedoms Americans have always taken for granted will come under increasing threat. Already a number of books by Christian and conservative authors has warned of the growing movement to restrict religious rights,[15] along with the possibility of something previously unthinkable in the United States: a persecution of Christians and other believers in traditional morality.[16] Heavenly messages supposedly given to alleged visionaries have also warned of such events.[17] Even if these dire predictions don't come about, Catholicism in America, according to sociologist David Carlin, will continue to face growing pressure from an ever-more secularized culture.[18]

The Church will, of course, survive such challenges, just as she has weathered every storm over the past 2000 years, but this is no guarantee that individual Catholics (and other Christians) will hold on to their faith and escape serious suffering. Our Lord's warning that "False messiahs and false prophets will arise and will perform signs and wonders in order to mislead, if that were possible, the elect" (Mk. 13:22) clearly applies in a religious sense to the time immediately before His Second Coming—but it may also be true of political, scientific, and cultural "messiahs" in our own day.

# The New Age Movement

The occult origins of the New Age Movement have already been discussed (in Chapter 9), but several additional points can be made. In his book *The Judas Syndrome*, Catholic author Thomas Colyandro writes,

> *The New Age movement is a prime example of how a combination of Enlightenment humanism, spiritual division and confusion, and the occult have joined forces not only to reject Scripture and Tradition but also the divine personhood of Jesus Christ and His Holy Spirit. New Age spirituality, which gripped the United States from the mid-1960s through the 1970s and into the early 1980s, sought to collect elements of cosmology, astrology, occultism, esotericism, pantheism, Kabbalah and some of the polytheistic tendencies of Asian religions into a loosely configured philosophical paradigm. . . . America was flooded with a neo-pagan universalism that penetrated the political system and restructured society away from its Judeo-Christian roots, in part by rejecting Scripture, Tradition, authority and doctrines like the Trinity as outmoded ways of thinking.*[19]

A former New Age leader, Randall Baer, calls the Movement a "Satan-controlled, modern-day mass revival of occult-based philosophies and practices in both obvious and cleverly-disguised forms,"[20] designed to mislead the unwary and draw them away from the Savior. Moreover,

> *Most New Age prophecy foresees a millennial transition time during which those who accept the message and mark of the "New World Order" become a part of the greatly proclaimed*

*New Age. In effect, as the Antichrist forces come to greater world power, a revamped and upgraded New Age-based philosophy is to be applied toward "purifying" the planetary populace of those who are not "ready" to make the next step into becoming a superior race of godmen.*[21]

(The sinister nature of the purification process referred to is, of course, reminiscent of Nazi Germany's efforts to "purify" itself of the "Jewish scourge," and of later historical instances of "ethnic cleansing." Recall also that New Age thinker Alice Bailey advocated even the use of nuclear weapons against troublesome religious groups.)

Many, if not most, New Age teachings and practices come from the occult; indeed, the "New Ager is led to seek knowledge that is forbidden outside the course of God's influence."[22] This step can be highly dangerous because of the true source of this knowledge:

*Assuredly, <u>The New Age Movement</u> is <u>Luciferic</u> to its very core. David Spangler, one of the most prominent <u>New Age</u> gurus, lays out one of the most basic teachings of the <u>New Age</u>:* **"Lucifer is the angel of man's inner light. Lucifer, like Christ, stands at the door of man's consciousness and knocks. Each of us is brought in some way to that point which I term, the Luciferic initiation. Lucifer comes to give us the final gift of wholeness. If we accept it, then he is free, and we are free. That is Luciferic initiation. It is the one that many people now, and in the days ahead will be facing, for it is an initiation into the New Age."**[23]

One cannot help but be dismayed, not only over the diabolical deception at work in the mind of such a New Age spokesman, but especially over the success he and others have had in peddling their spiritual poison—including to many who called themselves Christian. During his 1987 visit to the United States, Pope John Paul II warned very perceptively,

*Every age poses new challenges and new temptations for the people of God on their pilgrimage, and our own is no exception. We face a growing secularism that tries to exclude God and religious truths from human affairs. We face an insidious relativism that undermines the absolute truth of Christ and the truths of faith, and tempts believers to think of them as merely one set of beliefs or opinions of others. We face an alluring hedonism that offers a whole series of pleasures that will never satisfy the human heart. All these attitudes can influence our sense of good and evil at the very moment when social and scientific progress requires ethical guidance. Once alienated from Christian faith and practice by these and other deceptions, people often commit themselves to passing fads, or to bizarre beliefs that are shallow and fanatical.*[24]

When brought before the Jewish Sanhedrin, St. Peter testified to the Lordship of Jesus, declaring, "There is no salvation through anyone else, nor is there any other Name under Heaven given to the human race by which we are to be saved" (Acts 4:12). Nevertheless, the temptation to look elsewhere is always with us, and remains a key element in Satan's efforts to "lead the nations astray" (cf. Rev. 20:3).

This Luciferic scheme will not succeed. As Christian author and New Age expert Russell Chandler states, "The man-made building of a way to heaven is through technological achievement—whether by a lofty tower futilely straining toward transcendence, or by New Age psycho-technologies and states of altered consciousness. But these are doomed to failure. The proud tower rose only several hundred feet; the technologies extend only as far as the fallen human psyche."[25]

# The New World Order

The first time most Americans heard the term "New World Order" was when President George H. Bush mentioned it early in the 1990s. There is a proper sense in which a new organizing principle, or order, for the world would be a good thing: one in harmony with the plans of the Creator, based on Christian moral principles, and expressing true peace and mutual respect among all nations and peoples. However, the reality of the New World Order in question—regardless of its noble-sounding propaganda, its legitimate goals, and even the genuinely well-intentioned aims of many of its adherents—is quite different.

The Church has always recognized the grave dangers posed by a government grown too-powerful, whether on a national or global scale, and regardless of the scope of the crises or problems it is intended to address. In his encyclical *Deus Caritas Est*, Pope Benedict XVI warns:

> *The State which would provide everything, absorbing everything into itself, would ultimately become a mere bureaucracy incapable of guaranteeing the very thing which the suffering person — every person — needs: namely, a loving personal concern. We do not need a State which regulates and controls everything, but a State which, in accordance with the **principle of subsidiarity**, generously acknowledges and supports initiatives arising from the different social forces and combines spontaneity with closeness to those in need. . . . In the end, the claim that just social structures would make works of charity superfluous masks a materialist conception of man: the mistaken notion that man can live "by bread alone" (Mt. 4:4; cf. Dt. 8:3) — a conviction that demeans man and ultimately disregards all that is specifically human* (n. 28).

The Holy Father's reference to subsidiarity (defined in 1931 by Pope Pius XI as meaning "Nothing should done by a larger and higher institution that can be done equally well by a smaller and lower institution"[26]) echoed a Church teaching first enunciated by Pope Leo XIII in his 1891 encyclical *Rerum Novarum*—but, as has so often been the case throughout history, the wisdom of the Church has largely been ignored.

The movement toward a New World Order was an announced goal of Adam Weishaupt's Illuminati, and by the 1920s, "we began to see planned economic, political, and military changes in our world designed to bring us to the place of world government."[27] The science fiction writer H. G. Wells wrote a book titled *The New World Order*, and political leaders as diverse as Woodrow Wilson, Adolf Hitler, and Mikhail Gorbachev used the term. Gorbachev actually stated, "Tolerance is the alpha and omega of the New World Order."[28] Because the term began giving rise to fears and developing negative connotations, advocates generally no longer refer to a "New World Order" in public—but the agenda of those advocating a global financial system, one-world government, and even a one-world religion, remains unchanged.

Most of the more important advocates of this change are

members of groups such as the Council of Foreign Relations (CFR), the Trilateral Commission, the Bilderbergers, and the Club of Rome. According to Ted and Maureen Flynn,

> The people belonging to these powerful organizations are high-ranking United Nations officials, noted world leaders, noted politicians, bankers, World Bank and International Monetary Fund officials, clergy, members of the World Future Society, top-level Masons, and people either inadvertently or purposely promoting a one-world government.[29]

Indeed, the United Nations itself, along with the above-mentioned groups and various others, has "been moving us toward a global currency, global tax, global stock exchange, global central bank, and world government for a long time."[30]

In regard to some of the more important organizations, the CFR has been called a "shadow government" with a larger agenda known only to its high-ranking members;[31] the Trilateral Commission was created in 1973 to promote economic linkage among Europe, Japan, and the United States (as a preliminary step to a unified global economic system);[32] and the Bilderbergers, a group of international politicians and bankers who've held secret annual meetings, were formed in 1954.[33]

C. S. Lewis had once observed that "The safest road to Hell is the gradual one—the gentle slope, soft underfoot, without sudden turnings, without milestones, without signposts," and this is the path supporters of a New World Order are inviting us to follow, a replication of Antonio Gramsci's strategy on a larger scale; the overall agenda includes the use of skillful propaganda, the control of education, and the creation of "crises" as an excuse for ever-greater consolidations of power. As one author notes,

> The Gramscian strategy calls for the United Nations to force world governance. This is the purpose of their efforts to employ historical revisionism, attack the Judeo-Christian belief system, promote socialism, bring global taxation, the end of national sovereignty, a U.N. police force, and an International Criminal Court that would replace U.S. courts.[34]

These coordinated efforts are unfolding very gradually, for "Global governance will not march on Washington in the form of blue-helmeted troops. It is marching into our towns in the form of 'smart growth' proposals; into our schools in the form of 'tolerance' curricula; into our churches in the form of 'The National Religious Partnership for the Environment'; and into our government in the form of a parade of bills to promote everything from global taxation, to a Department of Peace inspired by UNESCO" (United Nations Educational, Scientific, and Cultural Organization).[35]

A major goal of the globalists is to lower the standard of living of middle-class citizens in the United States and other prosperous nations, so as to reduce their economic independence and their ability to oppose the move to a one-world government; the U.N. hopes to achieve a mass transfer of wealth from wealthier countries to poorer ones by means of programs like "Agenda 21," "Sustainable Development," and "The Biodiversity Treaty."[36] In his book *Earth in the Balance*, former vice-president Al Gore insisted that a "wrenching transformation" must occur if America was to be led away from "the horrors of the Industrial Revolution, and Agenda 21 (adopted at the U.N.'s Earth Summit in 1992) is a major part of this process[37]—a process involving a radical reshaping of American life.[38]

At the same time, international trade agreements (which can be beneficial if properly implemented) facilitate the transfer of wealth from one nation to another, and NAFTA and GATT are possible weapons for undermining national sovereignty. When this occurs, individuals suffer—for as author Ted Flynn explains,

> *Workers increasingly have no value except to increase corporate profits and power. The "third worldization" of the U.S. is making many people poor with a small elite in control. When people are kept poor and are forced to work harder for less money, they have less time and energy for politics.*[39]

Moreover, the growing poverty of the working class tends to make people more dependent on government (and less capable of resisting its encroachments on human rights and constitutional freedoms)—a trend foreseen by the great Catholic apologist Hilaire Belloc in his 1912 book *The Servile State*.[40]

At the same time, public education is being turned into a tool of the globalists, who realize that "The only hope they could ever have to cause Americans to accept their radical socialist dictatorship would be to control the education and values of at least one generation of children, having eliminated the influence of parents and their traditional values."[41] As early as 1949, a series of UNESCO booklets promoted the teaching of global governance to young children as part of this effort.[42]

Not only are government (i.e., public) school students being indoctrinated with humanist and globalist values; parental control is consistently undermined—particularly when Christian parents try to raise their children according to their religious beliefs.[43] Furthermore, the U.N. has also called for an international computerized information system that would further shape the thinking not only of young people, but of all global citizens. This system would "disseminate its politically correct data and pseudo-scientific risk assessments into every community, build consensus based on its visions, goals, values, and choices, then monitor individual and collective compliance everywhere—in homes, schools, and offices."[44]

Even more ominous, however, are reports of proposals to reduce the current world population to a more "sustainable" level. The U.N. has, for most of its history, promoted vigorous population control policies (and even bestows its annual "U.N. Population Award" to those who most successfully champion its policies in any given year). Furthermore, as Ted Flynn notes,

> In 1968, the Club of Rome concluded that civilization would collapse unless the death rate was increased and the birth rate lowered. Various investigators, like author John Coleman, report the Club of Rome developed a plan called Global 2000 to kill several billion people by 2050. Paul Erlich, famous for his work on the population threat, said it might be necessary to add "a sterilant to drinking water or staple foods" to sterilize the entire population, giving the antidote to a select few. The forced sterilization programs of India and China may be the wave of the future in a corporate controlled society.[45]

Additionally, there are numerous reports of chemtrails, in which aircraft deliberately discharge harmful chemicals while traveling across the sky—supposedly as part of something called Operation Cloverleaf, which is intended to reduce the world's population by at least 90%.[46]

In his book *Hope of the Wicked: The Master Plan to Rule the World*,

Ted Flynn lists the following goals to be achieved as part of the implementation of the New World Order:

- *the destruction of Western civilization;*

- *the dissolution of legal government;*

- *eradicating nationalism and every form of patriotism;*

- *reducing the economic freedom and status of American citizens by means of graduated income taxes, property taxes, inheritance taxes, and sales taxes;*

- *abolishing the right to private property, primarily by ever-larger taxation; and*

- *destroying the family, primarily through divorce, abortion, and homosexuality.*[47]

Achieving this long-range goal has always been a gradual process, but a convenient crisis (real or manufactured) could allow the plan to be accelerated. For instance, at the 1992 meeting of the Bilderbergers, former U.S. Secretary of State Henry Kissinger reportedly said:

> *Today Americans would be outraged if U.N. troops entered Los Angeles to restore order; tomorrow they will be grateful! This is especially true if they were told there was an outside threat from beyond, whether real or promulgated, that threatened our very existence. It is then that all peoples of the world will pledge with world leaders to deliver them from this evil. The one thing every man fears is the unknown. When presented with this scenario, individual rights will be willingly relinquished for the guarantee of their well-being granted to them by their world government.*[48]

Definite plans are being developed by political leaders in the United States, Canada, and Mexico to merge their three nations into one "regional global government" (with the "North American Community" their preferred term), as part of a penultimate step to a one-world government.[49] In this regard, the CFR's "Building a North American Community" task force reported that the borders between the three nations would be erased;[50] supposedly "All the infrastructure, laws, technology, police, armies . . . media, and governments are ready for this radical transformation.[51] When this occurs (probably as the result of a major disturbance or crisis),

". . . the Americas would all become one piece in a trilateral plan also encompassing Europe and Asia. Combining countries under more easily managed regional authorities, regionalization, is the key to governing the world."[52]

The movement toward a New World Order has serious consequences for Christians and the Church, and author Paul McGuire describes very well what's at stake:

> *The ultimate conspiracy is not merely a political, economic, or a social conspiracy. At its heart, it is a spiritual conspiracy and a rebellion against God. This conspiracy plays out in the physical universe in very practical ways. It has practical implications in the world of economics, religion, philosophy, politics, sexuality, the family, history, psychology, medicine, art, literature, music, film, television, and science.*[53]

The "de-Christianizing" of society is especially evident in Western Europe, where the newly-adopted constitution of the European Union deliberately avoids any reference to the continent's Christian culture and traditions; the document also expressly forbids the implementation of certain laws essential from the perspective of Catholic morality (e.g., prohibiting abortion-on-demand and same-sex marriages).[54]

Furthermore, the original poster officially promoting the European Parliament (eventually withdrawn due to numerous protests) showed the Tower of Babel, with the caption "Europe: Many Tongues, One Voice"—an apt symbol for a society ever more increasingly rejecting God. America is not jettisoning its Judeo-Christian heritage as rapidly as Europe, but the United States has become a major, and perhaps the most important, battleground in the ongoing effort to replace Christianity with a New World Order, featuring a one-world religion ultimately dedicated to the worship of Satan.

One of the greatest Catholics of the 20th century, St. Pio of Pietrelcina, observed that

> *Man is so full of pride that when he has everything he needs and good health, he believes himself a god, and superior to God Himself—but when something happens and he can do nothing, and others can't do anything about it either, only then will he remember that there is a Supreme Being.*[55]

Until that day of crisis arrives, when the world comes crashing down and all human efforts are of no avail, human pride will interpret Christian humility and obedience as utter folly—but, in the words of St. Francis de Sales, "The world considers us fools; we must consider it crazy."[56]

The growing movement to create a one-world government, and a new world religion, represent an unprecedented rebellion against God, and perhaps the gravest threat the Church has faced so far; some elite members of this conspiracy even believe they are preparing for an imminent world leader and "messiah"—the one identified by Scripture as the Antichrist. Even if this particular expectation is mistaken, and the Antichrist's actual arrival is still many years off, the Church will be severely tested in the near future—but again she will prevail.

In the words of St. Peter Canisius, "Let the world indulge its madness, for it cannot endure and passes like a shadow. It is growing old, and I think, is in its last decrepit stage. But we, buried deep in the wounds of Christ, why should we be dismayed?"[57] Additionally, in both the Old and New Testaments we find an even greater message of reassurance.

During a time of great peril for Jerusalem, the Lord, speaking through the prophet Isaiah, addressed Israel's enemies: "Form a plan, and it shall be thwarted; make a resolve, and it shall not be carried out, for 'With us is God!'" (Is. 8:10). Moreover, St. Paul, writing some 800 years later, proclaimed: "The message of the Cross is foolishness to those who are perishing, but to us who are being saved it is the power of God. For it is written: "I will destroy the wisdom of the wise, and the learning of the learned I will set aside" (1 Cor. 1:18-19). These scriptural promises still apply today, for God's Word does not lose its force (cf. Jn. 10:13); no matter how cleverly-conceived and carefully-executed their plans, the architects of a New World Order will be no more successful than the architects of the Tower of Babel.

# NOTES TO CHAPTER 12

[1]   C. S. Lewis, *The Screwtape Letters* (Macmillan Paperbacks Edition, 1973), p. x.

[2]   Pope John Paul II, *Memory and Identity: Conversations at the Dawn of a Millennium* (Rizzoli International Publications, 2005), pp. 47-48.

[3]   *Ibid.,* p. 48.

[4]   *Ibid.,* pp. 120-121.

[5]   George Weigel, *God's Choice: Pope Benedict XVI and the Future of the Catholic Church* (Harper Collins, 2005), p. 140.

[6]   James Hitchcock, "Disentangling the Secular Humanism Debate," *Whose Values? The Battle for Morality in Pluralistic America,* ed. Carl Horn (Servant Books, 1985), p. 24.

[7]   Rosemary Ellen Guiley, *The Quotable Saint* (Checkmark Books, 2002), p. 55.

[8]   David Kupelian, *The Marketing of Evil* (WND Books, 2005), pp. 11-12.

[9]   Paul McGuire, *The Day the Dollar Died* (M House Publishers, 2009), pp. 73-74.

[10]  Michael Vincent Boyer, *The Hollywood Culture War* (Xlibris Corporation, 2008), p. 413.

[11]  *Ibid.,* p. 402.

[12]  *Ibid.,* pp. 30ff. According to the author, Valenti's "Voluntary Ratings System" would "forever divide the American family and moviegoing audience into age-restricted groups. The underlying effect, and perhaps the true intent, was to enable 'dark,' 'cutting-edge,' and 'rogue' filmmakers to produce largely 'adult' films with the legitimate Seal of Approval from the MPAA" (*ibid.*), p. 30.
     Not surprisingly, "Not only was Valenti's change a [moral and social] disaster, its effects were immediately catastrophic at the box office. In 1965, weekly movie attendance averaged 44 million viewers. In 1969, the year after Valenti established the Ratings Scheme, weekly attendance dropped to only 17.5 million, a mass exodus of more than sixty percent of the American movie-going audience. Many moviegoers simply never returned to the theater after 1968's orgy of X-rated and R-rated films flooded the box office" (*ibid.*), p. 32.

[13]  *Ibid.,* p. 148.

[14]  *Ibid.,* p. 359.

[15]  See, for instance, Rev. Donald E. Wildmon's *Speechless: Silencing the Christians* (Richard Vigilante Books, 2009), Bill Donohue's *Secular Sabotage* (Faith Words, 2009), and Gus R. Stelzer's *The State Against Religion* (Acorn Press, 2001).

[16]  See, for instance, Janet L. Folger's *The Criminalization of Christianity* (Multnomah Publishers, 2005), David Limbaugh's *Persecution: How Liberals Are Waging War Against Christianity* (Regnery Publishing, 2003), and Don

McAlvany's *Storm Warning* (Hearthstone Publishing, 1999).

[17] John Leary, for instance, is one of numerous alleged visionaries who've supposedly been warned by Our Lord, and by Our Lady or other saints, of a coming time of religious persecution in the United States. His alleged messages are available in a series of books published by Queenship Publishing and titled *Prepare for the Great Tribulation and the Era of Peace.*

[18] David Carlin, *The Decline & Fall of the Catholic Church in America* (Sophia Institute Press, 2003), pp. 245ff.

[19] Thomas Colyandro, *The Judas Syndrome* (St. Benedict Press, 2010), pp. 95-96.

[20] Randall Baer, *Inside the New Age Nightmare* (Huntington House, 1989), as quoted in Ted and Maureen Flynn, *The Thunder of Justice* (MaxKol Communications, 1993), p. 240.

[21] *Ibid.,* p. 243.

[22] Rev. Lawrence J. Gesy, *Today's Destructive Cults and Movements* (Our Sunday Visitor, 1993), p. 116.

[23] Stephen Mahowald, *She Shall Crush Thy Head* (MMR Publishing, 1996), p. 120.

[24] Address at St. Mary's Cathedral in San Francisco (Text by Vatican via U.S. Catholic Conference), as quoted in Gesy, pp. 113-114.

[25] Russell Chandler, *Understanding the New Age* (Word Publishing, 1988), p. 303.

[26] Pope Pius XI, *Quadragesimo Anno,* as quoted in Timothy G. McCarthy, *The Catholic Tradition* (Loyola University Press, 1994), p. 115.

[27] McGuire, p. 56. The author adds, "Even as far back as 1961, detailed plans were developed by the U.S. Government about how to effectively bring about a world government" (ibid.).

[28] *Ibid.,* p. 15.

[29] Ted and Maureen Flynn, *The Thunder of Justice* (MaxKol Communications, 1993), p. 266.

[30] McGuire, p. 35.

[31] *Ibid.,* pp. 97-98.

[32] *Ibid.,* p. 150. In his autobiography *With No Apologies,* former U.S. senator Barry Goldwater wrote, "In my view the Trilateral Commission represents a skillful, coordinated effort to seize control and consolidate the four centers of power—political, monetary, intellectual and ecclesiastical. All this is to be done in the interest of creating a more peaceful, more productive world community. What the Trilateralists truly intend is the creation of a worldwide economic power superior to the political governments of the nation-states involved. They believe the abundant materialism they propose to create will overwhelm existing differences. As managers and creators of the system they will rule the future" -- as quoted in Ted Flynn, *Hope of the Wicked* (MaxKol Communications, 2000), p. 14.

[33] Ted Flynn, *Hope of the Wicked: The Master Plan to Rule the World* (MaxKol

Communications, 2000), p. 9.

[34] McGuire, p. 152.

[35] Henry Lamb, "Stuck Before You Know It," *WorldNetDaily.com.*, January 12, 2002.

[36] McGuire, p. 87.

[37] Tom DeWeese, "Sustainable Development: The Root of All of Our Problems," *The DeWeese Report* (August 2009), pp. 1-2. The author notes that "The Sustainablists insist that society be transformed into feudal-like governance by making *nature* the central organizing principle for our economy and society. To achieve this, Sustainablist policy focuses on three components: global land use, global education, and global population control. . . . private property is incompatible with the collectivist premise of Sustainable Development" (*ibid.*).

   Also, in a companion article in the same issue, "Forcing International Agendas Through Local Mayors," Mr. DeWeese warns, "According to the U.N.'s Biodiversity Assessment Report, items for our everyday lives that are NOT sustainable include: *Ski runs, grazing of livestock, plowing of soil, building fences, industry, single family homes, paved and tarred roads, logging activities, dams and reservoirs, power line construction, and economic systems that fail to set proper value on the environment (capitalism, free markets). . .*" (*ibid.*), p. 1.

[38] Nancy Levant, "Globalized America—Not a Pretty Sight," *NewsWithViews. com*, August 18, 2005. According to the author, Agenda 21 "expects the world's people to be relocated into what it calls 'human settlements.' . . . The super trade corridors also [will] have mass transit, bike, and pedestrian systems and trails. Human settlements, industries, and corporations will relocate and grow along the super trade corridors. Old roads will be dismantled. . . . they can force all jobs and businesses into business and trade corridors, and they can remove rural and wilderness roads. . . . there has been an on-going, international plan to bring civilian mobility rights, as well as most others, to a halt."

[39] Flynn, p. 186.

[40] Mark Steyn, *America Alone* (Regnery, 2006), p. 112. The author notes that Belloc "understood that the long-term cost of welfare is the infantilization of the population. The populations of wealthy democratic societies expect to have total choice over their satellite TV packages, yet think it perfectly normal to allow the state to make all the choices in respect of their health care. It's a curious inversion of citizenship to demand control over peripheral leisure activities but to contract out the big life-changing stuff to the government" (ibid.).

[41] Flynn, p. 308.

[42] McGuire, p. 83. The booklets were titled *Toward World Understanding*, and claimed "The success of the teacher in bringing up his pupils is to be good citizens of the world. As long as the child breathes the poisoned air of

nationalism, education in world-mindedness can only produce precarious results" (*ibid.*).

[43] *Ibid.*, pp. 9-10. According to the author, "Based on cases in the European Union that have happened in Germany, Christian parents will not be allowed to home school their children or teach them Biblical principles, such as sexual morality, purity, and marriage" (p. 9). Moreover, "Teenage and pre-teenage girls can get an abortion during the school day and the school is not legally allowed to inform the parent. Under the U.N. Convention of the Rights of the Child, parents will not be allowed to tell their children they cannot watch pornography or require their own children to read the Bible or go to church" (p. 10).

[44] Berit Kjos, "An International Information System," 1998, 2006, www.crossroad.to/text/articles/nis1196.html.

[45] Flynn, p. 351.

[46] Rev. Joseph M. Esper, *Spiritual Dangers of the 21st Century* (Queenship Publishing, 2009), p. 47. In 2005, the *Las Vegas Tribune* reported that chemical trails over Las Vegas—which were appearing every weekend—contained the known carcinogen ethylene dibromide, and a similar report was made by station KSLA News 12. Moreover, one alleged visionary was supposedly told that "Our adversary is dropping germs, toxins, poisons, insect eggs, deadly larvae from chemtrails," and alleged visionary John Leary claims he was told by Jesus that weapons grade bacteria are being spread over the U.S. population by this means, leading to chronic coughs, year-round flu symptoms, allergies, sinus problems, and other illnesses—all for the purpose of spreading diseases and weakening immune systems.

[47] Flynn, p. 361.

[48] Geoff Metcalf, "Freedom on the Line," *WorldNetDaily.com*, October 29, 2001.

[49] McGuire, p. 6.

[50] *Ibid.*, p. 151.

[51] *Ibid.*, p. 8.

[52] Flynn, p. 174.

[53] McGuire, p. 23.

[54] Colyandro, p. 80.

[55] Guiley, p. 218.

[56] Paul Thigpen, *Quotes from the Saints* (Servant Publications, 2001), p. 252.

[57] Jill Haak Adels, *The Wisdom of the Saints* (Barnes & Noble, 1987), p. 26.

# Chapter 13

# The Coming Antichrist

*The devil who had led them astray was thrown into the pool of fire and sulfur, where the beast and the false prophet were. There they will be tormented day and night forever and ever.* (Rev. 20:10)

In one of His many confrontations with His opponents, Jesus said, "I came in the Name of My Father, but you do not accept Me; yet if another comes in his own name, you will accept him" (Jn. 5:43). There are relatively few direct scriptural references to the Antichrist;[1] some scholars interpret this verse from St. John's Gospel as an indirect reference by Our Lord to the "man of iniquity". The implication is that he will be an illegitimate "savior," or a false messiah, coming without any true authority, yet able to deceive many into serving and following him.

No one knows the name of the Antichrist (in spite of numerous attempts over the centuries to identify him[2]), nor the time of his appearance on earth. The late Jesuit scholar Fr. Vincent Miceli, in his book *The Antichrist,* had a very insightful passage on this point that deserves to be quoted at length:

> *Concerning the exact name of the Antichrist, [St.] Irenaeus says that it is a secret kept by God until the man of sin arrives. He warns his readers not to try to guess the name from the number of the beast 666 [cf. Rev. 13:18]. He tells us that those who saw and spoke with St. John in person were also warned by the beloved disciple not to play the guessing-game or the numbers-game with the name of the Antichrist. Irenaeus adds that those who fix on a certain name for the Antichrist from*

*their own speculations will be easily deceived by him when he arrives under his own name. They will not be aware that he has yet come and hence the Antichrist will easily seduce them for they will not be on their guard against him. Moreover, the Holy Spirit will not give us the name of the Antichrist ahead of time, but only when we must know it. The Antichrist is not worthy to be heralded ahead of time by a special name announced by messengers from heaven. Such divine revelations of special names for the coming of servants of God into history are made in the cases of certain holy prophets and of the Son of God, all of whom were destined to bring salvation to men and glory to God. Since the Antichrist is to come suddenly and disappear suddenly, as if he had never existed, God has not revealed his name ahead of time.[3]*

Thus, there is no practical purpose to be served in trying to guess or discover the name of the Antichrist in advance.

In regard to the day of his arrival, St. Augustine wrote, "In vain, then, do we attempt to compute definitively the years that may remain to the world, when we may hear from the mouth the Truth Himself [cf. Mt. 24:36] that it is not for us to know this."[4] This observation is echoed by the *Catechism of the Catholic Church*, which cautions that Christ's "eschatological coming could be accomplished at any moment, even if both it and the final trial that will precede it are 'delayed'" (n. 673).

The *Catechism* has relatively little to say about the Antichrist himself, telling us that

*Before Christ's second coming the Church must pass through a final trial that will shake the faith of many believers. The persecution that accompanies her pilgrimage on earth will unveil the "mystery of iniquity" in the form of a religious deception offering men an apparent solution to their problems at the price of apostasy from the truth. The supreme religious deception is that of the Antichrist, a pseudo-messianism by which man glorifies himself in place of God and of His Messiah come in the flesh* (n. 675).

We're also instructed that "The Antichrist's deception already begins to take share in the world every time the claim is made to realize within history that messianic hope which can only be realized through the eschatological judgment" (n. 676)—in other words, every utopian scheme to create a "heaven on earth" is in some way a prefiguring or "trial run" of the Antichrist's eventual three-and-a-half year reign (cf. Dn. 7:25; Rev. 12:14) before the end of the world.

In the same way, the historical precursors of the Antichrist prefigure his reign, and thus can reveal to us something of his character: not enough to foretell his identity or the time of his coming, but perhaps sufficient to recognize him when he does finally arrive—or even, assuming he initially makes great efforts to hide his true character by pretending to be a servant of humanity, to provide us with a description or "checklist" of telltale characteristics and warning signs.

Because evil has no existence in and of itself, but is only a negation or corruption of the good, it makes sense to begin this undertaking from a particular direction—namely, a review of what Scripture tells us about the nature of our Savior. By definition, antichrist figures are literally "anti-Christ": that is, not only rooted in hostility toward Jesus, but also His opposite in terms of personality, character, and values. Thus, we can learn something about the antichrist figures of history—and, more importantly, about the future Antichrist himself—by comparing them with the incarnate Lord.

We begin with several New Testament passages in which Jesus describes Himself:

- *"I am meek and humble of heart"* (Mt. 11:29). This contrasts with those historical figures legendary for their extreme arrogance and cruelty (Herod, Nero, Attila, Stalin, Mao, and others), and with those motivated by intense pride (Arius, Rousseau, Voltaire, Napoleon, and Hitler, among others). When he comes, the Antichrist will pretend to be humble—for, as Machiavelli noted, the appearance of humility is very useful for a leader—but it will only be an act (and God's grace will allow His people to see through it).

- *"I came down from Heaven not to do My own will"* (Jn. 6:38). In contrast, all the historical precursors of the Antichrist were intent on furthering their own ambitions (including those religious figures, such as Arius, Luther, and Calvin, who confused their own will with God's). The "Will to Power," Nietzsche's dictum that supermen must not submit to any authority outside themselves (especially divine authority and the "slave morality" of Christianity), is the antithesis of Christ's example of humble obedience—an example the Antichrist and his followers will likewise scorn.

- *"I am the light of the world"* (Jn. 8:12). As Our Lord noted, there are persons who prefer the darkness because of their evil deeds (Jn. 3:19-20), and we see this in the lives of those who promoted the darkness of sin and death (Blavatsky, Crowley, LaVey, and other Satanists), and also of those who feared the light and persecuted everyone who bore witness to it (the Roman emperors and other persecutors of the Church). The Antichrist will claim to be a savior of the oppressed, finally enlightening the world and freeing it from the "darkness" of Christian religious "superstition," but in fact, his kingdom itself will be plunged into darkness (Rev. 16:10) as an indication of God's irrevocable judgment.

- *"I am the Good Shepherd"* (Jn. 10:11). Jesus is truly devoted to the unity of His flock, and willing to lay down His life for the sheep. This is in marked contrast to those who divided the flock of Christ (Nestorius, Donatus, Pelagius, the "Reformers," Henry VIII, and Elizabeth I), those who served as false shepherds (John XII, Alexander VI), and those who, instead of giving their lives for their people, sacrificed millions for their own ambitions (Lenin, Stalin, Hitler, Mao, Kim Il Sung, Pol Pot). The Antichrist will pretend to be concerned for the suffering and lowly (again following the advice of Machiavelli), but he will have in mind solely his own interests—and those of Satan, his lord.

- *"I am the way, the truth, and the life"* (Jn. 14:6). Our Savior promises that those who take up their cross (cf. Lk. 9:23-24) and follow the straight and narrow path (cf. Mt. 7:13-14) of discipleship will enter into eternal life, but over the last few centuries, many have tried to lead humanity astray by their lies and anti-life philosophies (Rousseau, Voltaire, Darwin,

Blavatsky, Crowley, Kinsey, Sanger, Hefner). A focus on this world will be an important part of the Antichrist's promises, along with a denial of divine judgment and eternity—and, tragically, many people will follow him to their own destruction.

- *"I am the alpha and the omega"* (Rev. 22:13). Our Lord describes Himself as the beginning and end of all things, and the measure of all that is good and worthy of eternal life. This contrasts with those who attempted to create new calendars so as to obliterate Christian feasts (the French revolutionaries and Comte), those whose efforts to create lasting monuments to themselves have crumbled (as in Hitler's "Thousand Year Reich," which lasted only twelve years), and those whose ephemeral achievements ended up having no lasting value (too many to enumerate). The Antichrist, imitating the pride of Lucifer (cf. Is. 14:12-15), will exalt himself even above Almighty God, but will end up being "thrown alive into the fiery pool burning with sulfur" (Rev. 19:20).

  God's Word in Scripture is "living and effective, sharper than any two-edged sword . . . and able to discern reflections and thoughts of the heart" (Heb. 4:12)—and thus, a reliable guide to uncovering the true character of the Antichrist and his precursors, for "everything is naked and exposed to the eyes of Him to Whom we must render an account" (Heb. 4:13). Jesus' words about Himself not only describe His own character and mission, but also warn us what expect of the one who will wage war on His Church (cf. Rev. 12:17). Further useful information and comparisons are given in these passages about Jesus:

- *Jesus is the One Who came to serve, not be served* (Mk. 10:45). This has not been true of many of the precursors of the Antichrist; quite a few of them (the emperors of Rome, the wicked popes and religious leaders, the various monarchs and dictators) had large entourages, and numerous servants, quick to respond to their every expressed order or desire. This will especially be true of the Antichrist, for virtually the whole world will follow him in fascination (Rev. 13:3).

- *Jesus is the Faithful Witness* (Rev. 1:5), the One Who proclaims the truth even to the point of shedding His blood for our salvation. In contrast, many antichrists have been unfaithful: in marriage (Weishaupt, Freud, Sanger, Kinsey); in fulfilling their religious duties (the heretics, John XII, Alexander VI); and in remaining true to their Catholic upbringing (Julian, Henry VIII, Sanger, Hitler). Jesus is the same yesterday, today, and forever (Heb. 13:8), and His word is completely trustworthy (1 Th. 5:24). This will not be true of the Antichrist, who will deny the truths of salvation (1 Jn. 2:22) and who, along with his false prophet, will deceive the inhabitants of the earth (Rev. 13:14).

- *Jesus is the One Who judges justly, in accord with the Father's Will* (Jn. 5:30). The Savior of the world never rejects anyone who comes to Him (Jn. 6:37), but He does not force anyone to follow Him or worship Him (cf. Jn. 6:66-67). However, as Our Lord pointed out, worldly rulers make their authority over their subjects felt (Mk. 10:42). This was certainly true of all the political antichrists from Pharaoh to Pol Pot (and sometimes manifested in egregious injustices and abuses of power), and will most especially be true of the one who will receive authority for forty-two months over "every tribe, people, tongue, and nation" (Rev. 13:5,7).

- *Jesus is the One Who has a perfect and complete understanding of human nature* (Jn. 2:25), unlike Darwin (whose theories denied our creation by God), Freud (who taught that all human needs revolve around sex), Marx (who claimed religion is merely the opiate of the people), Nietzsche (who asserted that "supermen" are beyond moral judgment), and the architects of a New World Order (who believe that, under their direction, humanity's coming effort to construct a new Tower of Babel will be successful and beneficial to humanity). The Antichrist will have a certain understanding of human nature—in the sense of a natural shrewdness that will allow him to exploit human fears and desires; however, his denial that we are made in the image and likeness of God (Gn. 1:27), and thus subject to divine authority, will lead the human race into much suffering and agony (Rev. 16:9,11,21).

- *Jesus in His poverty had no place to lay His head* (Lk. 9:58). In contrast, many antichrist figures (emperors, monarchs, and dictators) built or stole numerous palaces and estates for their own use. There were some persons who welcomed Jesus and His disciples into their homes (Lk. 10:38; 19:6), but He warned His followers they would also face hatred and rejection (Mk. 6:11; Jn. 15:18-20). Not only will the Antichrist receive the adulation of much of humanity (Rev. 13:4) and gain control over the world's wealth and finances (Rev. 13:16-17); he will also intensify the persecution of the Church (Rev. 13:7), imprisoning and martyring many (Rev. 13:10), and forcing the remaining followers of Christ to leave their homes and go into hiding. However, the Lord Jesus promises a special place in His Kingdom to those who remain faithful in the coming persecution (Rev. 7:14).

- *Jesus was scorned and rejected* (Is. 53:3), *a prophet without honor* (Mt. 13:57), *and a true King Who did not seek His own glory* (Jn. 8:49). Many of the antichrists (the Roman emperors, Hitler, Stalin, Mao, Kim Il Sung) created personality cults for themselves, thereby receiving widespread adulation and even worship. This will be especially true of the Antichrist, to whom Satan (the dragon) will give his authority (Rev. 13:4). However, when the devil, the Antichrist, and the false prophet assemble the kings and armies of the earth at Armageddon (Rev. 16:13-16), they will be utterly defeated by the true "King of kings and Lord of lords" (Rev. 19:16-21).

Thus, Scripture gives us much information not only about Jesus Himself, but also—indirectly—much insight into the character of the antichrists, past and future. Some of these figures clearly embraced this accursed role (Blavatsky, Nietzsche, Crowley); others would have been shocked and dismayed to learn they would one day be so identified (the heretics and the "Reformers"). Still others, thankfully, later repented of their part in attacking or weakening Christ's Church (Cromwell, and apparently Weishaupt, Napoleon, and Engels).

Few, if any, of the historical precursors of the Antichrist had normal and enjoyable personal lives; many, if not most, of them had violent or terrifying deaths. All of them represented, to one degree or another, a serious threat to Catholicism, and all of them failed in their efforts to destroy the Church or prevent her from fulfilling her mission. This undeniable truth, however, will not dissuade the final and ultimate Antichrist from attempting—as Satan's last doomed act of defiance against God—to achieve what none of his predecessors could accomplish.

The prophecies of various saints and mystics over the Church's history supplement the teaching of Scripture and Tradition, giving us additional information on what the Antichrist will be like, what he will do, and what fate awaits him. For instance, St. Cyril of Jerusalem (d. 386) revealed, "Antichrist will exceed in malice, perversity, lust, wickedness, impiety, and heartless cruelty and barbarity all men that have ever disgraced human nature,"[5] and St. John Damascene (d. 770) taught, "Antichrist shall be an illegitimate child, under the complete power of Satan, and God, knowing his incredible future perversity, will allow the devil to take a full and perpetual possession of him from his very sinful conception."[6] The saint further added, "He will practice the most consummate hypocrisy, deceiving the Jews and all his followers. In proportion as he shall advance in age, knowledge, vice, and power, his ambitions will become excessive."[7]

According to St. Thomas Aquinas (d. 1274), the Antichrist

*is the head of all the wicked because in him wickedness is perfect. . . . As in Christ dwells the fullness of the Godhead so in Antichrist the fullness of all wickedness. Not indeed in the sense that his humanity is to be assumed by the devil into unity of person . . . , but that the devil by suggestion infuses his wickedness more copiously into him than into all others. In this way all the wicked that have gone before are signs of Antichrist.*[8]

St. Thomas also noted that his pride will make him truly "anti-Christ:"

*The crime of Antichrist is duplex: he is against God and puts himself against Christ. In opposing God, he puts himself above the true God, in place of all false gods and even denies the participation of humans in the godhead. The pride of Antichrist surpasses that of all his predecessors and like Caesar and the King of Tyre [cf. Ez. 28:1-10], he will say he is God and man, and so represented he will sit in the temple.*[9]

This teaching was echoed by Richard Rolle of Hampole (d. 1349), who wrote, "Antichrist will appear and exalt himself above pagan deities and the Trinity."[10]

The holy German priest Ven. Bartholomew Holzhauser (d. 1658) wrote that the Antichrist "will begin work in the East, as a soldier and preacher of religion, when thirty years old,"[11] and Sr. Jeanne le Royer (d. 1798) also stated that the Antichrist would begin his public life at that age.[12] According to the theologian Franciso Suarez (d. 1617),

> Antichrist will be born of Jewish extraction, and will profess the Jewish religion; not through real devotion, but through hypocrisy, in order more easily to persuade the great majority of that mysterious race to receive him as their Messiah. He will have two important objects in doing this. In the first place he will mimic Jesus Christ; in the second place, he will thus obtain the enthusiastic support and the wealth of the Jews, and through this material advantage be able to open the way to his ambitions for high dignities and human power. . . .[13]

Just as the pagan priests of ancient Egypt sought to undermine the message of Moses and Aaron by their false miracles (cf. Ex. 7:11-12,22; 8:3), so will the coming man of deception work false signs and wonders. St. Zenobius (d. 285) predicted, "Antichrist shall work a thousand prodigies on earth. He will make the blind see, the deaf hear, the lame walk, and the dead rise. . . ,"[14] echoing the words of the bishop and martyr St. Methodius (d. 255):"This enemy of religion will use a diabolic art to produce many false miracles, such as causing the blind to see, the lame to walk and the deaf to hear. Those possessed with demons will be exorcised. He will deceive many and, if he could, as Our Lord has said [cf. Mt. 24:24], even the faithful elect."[15]

St. Hildegard (d. 1179) had explained the nature of the Antichrist's supposed miracles:

> His arts will be practiced upon all the elements, but chiefly upon man will he exhaust his infernal power. He will seem to take away health and restore it; he will drive out devils and raise the dead. How so? By sending some possessed soul into a dead body, to move it for a time. But these resurrections will be of short duration. At sight of these things, many will be terrified

*and will believe in him; and some, preserving their primitive
faith, will nevertheless court the favors of the Man of Sin or fear
his displeasure. And so many will be led astray. . . .*[16]

St. Thomas Aquinas elaborated on this point: The works of
Antichrist may be called lying wonders either because he will
deceive men's senses by means of phantoms, so that he will not
really do what he seems to do; or because if he works real prodigies
they will lead those into falsehood who believe in him. . . . His
miracles may be said to real just as Pharaoh's magicians made real
frogs, but they will not be real miracles because they will be done
by the power of natural causes.[17] St. Cyril of Jerusalem foretold
that the Antichrist "shall through his great power, deceit and
malice, succeed in decoying or forcing to his worship two-thirds
of mankind; the remaining third part of men will most steadfastly
continue true to the faith and worship of Jesus Christ."[18]

The prophet Zechariah had described a basket filled with
wickedness (Zech. 5:8-11) being placed in the land of Shinar,
another name for Babylon. Fr. Frederick Faber (d. 1863) understood
this passage as meaning the Antichrist's kingdom would begin
in Babylon, an idea earlier expressed by Ven. Maria of Agreda (d.
1665), who wrote:

*Finally the delegates of certain nations, the Jews, the Turks
and Tartars will beg him to personally free them from their
unbearable yoke. He will now declare himself ready to
fulfill their wishes, while at the same time he will arouse the
neighboring nations to revolution. The Jews will finally bring
him a costly crown and a kingly garment, as well as a sceptre,
and declare him their freely elected king. The kings of the
world, who will hear of this, will laugh at it and not pay any
attention to this little horn [cf. Dn. 7:8]. In the meantime he
will build a powerful army and take up residence in Babylon,
where a magnificent palace will be built for him. Many Jews
will then stream to Babylon.*[19]

She also predicted that before long, the Antichrist
*will seek to enlarge his kingdom. He will, therefore, occupy
with his troops various surrounding districts in Asia. Then,
like a storm wind, he will appear in Egypt with his army and
conquer this country as well as Ethiopia. He will then endeavor*

*to make himself loved by the subjugated nations by a friendly
behavior, and by exacting a very small tribute from them. He
will declare everywhere that he is destined to be the Savior of
all the oppressed. He will not in the least let it be known that
he strives for a world kingdom.*[20]

These victories will allow the Antichrist to enter Israel in
triumph; according to Richard Rolle, "Coming to Jerusalem, he
will proclaim himself Christ and at first feign to be holy. . . . The
Jews will welcome him."[21] Further information is given in the
prediction of St. Zenobius: "Swollen with pride, Antichrist shall
enter in triumph the city of Jerusalem, and will sit on a throne to
be adored as if he were the Son of God. His heart being intoxicated
with arrogance, he will forget his being mere man, and the son of
a woman of the tribe of Dan. He shall seduce many credulous
persons through his deceitful errors. . . ."[22]

Ven. Bartholomew Holzhauser predicted, "The Jews, knowing
from the Bible that Jerusalem will be the seat of the Messiah, will
come from everywhere, and accept Antichrist as the Messiah."[23]
Also, in the words of St. Ephrem, "Antichrist will use worldly
goods as bait. He will entice many Christians with money and
goods to apostasize. He will give them free land, riches, honor
and power."[24] This "pseudo-generosity" will also be extended to
world leaders in a successful attempt to gain their allegiance, for
according to St. Mechtilde (d. 1299), "Antichrist will, through base
and false stratagems, and with presents of gold and gems, attain
influence over worldly princes. These will look up to him as the
Lord and God."[25]

Rabanus Maurus (d. 856) foretold that the Antichrist would
make Jerusalem the capital of his world empire, a prophecy
echoed by St. Anselm (d. 1109), who stated, "Antichrist will rule
the world from Jerusalem, which he will make into a magnificent
city."[26] The seer John of the Cleft Rock (d. 1340) prophesied that a
new pope—referred to by St. Malachy as Peter the Roman—would
be elected at the beginning of the Antichrist's reign,[27] an event
which the servant of Satan will perceive as a grave threat to his
rule; therefore, in the words of Ven. Bartholomew Holzhauser,
eventually "Antichrist and his army will conquer Rome, kill the
Pope and take the throne."[28]

In speaking of the "mark of the Beast" that the Antichrist and his false prophet will force upon everyone (Rev. 13:16-17)—except those Christians who hide from him so as to continue serving Christ—St. Hildegard said, "The mark will be a hellish symbol of Baptism, because thereby a person will be stamped as an adherent of Antichrist and also of the devil in that he thereby gives himself over to the influence of Satan."[29] Regarding the scriptural reference to the healing of what appeared to be a mortal wound to the Beast (Rev. 13:3), the saint also added that the Antichrist "will appear to be crucified and rise from the dead. All in all Christians will be astounded and in grievous doubts while [the followers of] Antichrist will be confirmed in their false faith."[30]

The Church will suffer severely at the Antichrist's hands; St. Anselm foretold that the Antichrist "will prohibit under pain of death the offering of the Holy Sacrifice of the Mass,"[31] forcing it to be held in secret. Moreover, John of the Cleft Rock predicted:

> He will massacre the priests, the monks, the women, the children, and the aged. He will show no mercy, but will pass torch in hand, like the barbarians, yet invoking Christ! His words of imposture will resemble those of Christians, but his actions will be those of Nero and of the Roman persecutors.[32]

St. Hildegard warned that "The executioners will not permit the Christians to win the martyr's crown easily for they will endeavor to prolong their pain until they renounce their faith. Yet some will receive a special grace from God to die during the torments."[33] These torments, St. Mechtilde added, will include, for some of those refusing to worship the Antichrist, being boiled or burned alive.[34]

The Book of Revelation tells us that, during the latter part of the Antichrist's reign, many chastisements will be inflicted by God upon the earth, including fearsome locusts (9:3ff); plagues of fire, smoke, and sulfur caused by fierce beasts of war (9:18); ugly and festering sores on those who accepted the mark of the Beast (16:2); the waters of the earth turned into blood (16:3); scorching heat (16:8-9); and a horrible and terrifying darkness throughout the Antichrist's kingdom (16:10-11). He, however, will not, according to St. Hippolytus, sympathize with the suffering of his people, nor have any desire to help them (if that were possible)—much to their intense regret.[35] Moreover, two witnesses from Heaven (traditionally identified as the Old Testament figures Enoch and Elijah[36]) will have the power to prevent rain from falling, turn water into blood, and inflict various other plagues, for 1260 days (11:3-6), during which they will testify to the truth and expose the Antichrist's wickedness.

The Antichrist will finally succeed in killing the two witnesses, and then forbid their corpses from being buried; his followers will rejoice in his victory, but—after three days—life will return to the two faithful servants of God. They will rise up to Heaven, filling the people of the earth with great fear (11:7-13) and, according to the seer Dionysius of Luxemberg (d. 1682),

> will actually confuse Antichrist. In order that the nations will not abandon him, he will lift himself up with great majesty into space on Mt. Olivet, with the purported intention to cast down the prophets who have ascended into heaven. But, in this moment Christ will strike him down. The earth will open and swallow him and his prophets alive. Then a large part of Jerusalem will fall into ruins from the earthquake.[37]

To this, St. Thomas Aquinas added, "Antichrist will be destroyed by the spirit of the mouth of Christ. That is, by the Holy Spirit or by Christ's command in that Michael [the archangel] will kill him on Mt. Olivet whence Christ ascended into Heaven, just as Julian was extinguished by the divine hand."[38] Similarly, the visionary Michaula of Saba (whose prophecy was printed in 1619), stated that, when the Antichrist, with demonic assistance, rises toward Heaven, "at the command of God, the Archangel Michael will cast him down to earth by a stroke of lightning."[39]

St. Hildegard predicted that "the planned ascent into Heaven will have been prepared by the artful employment of ingenious devices, and the moment at which the event was to have taken place, leading to his destruction, will produce a cloud that will spread an unbearable odor. Through this many people will again come to their senses and to understanding."[40] She added,

> The time is at hand. The abyss is opening; the king of the kings of darkness is watching; the Beast is watching with his subjects, who will proclaim him "savior of the world." He will rise superbly into the air, hoping to reach the sky; but the breath

*of the Archangel Michael will kill him. He will fall back and the earth will shake without ceasing for three days. It will then open its womb full of fire and the Beast and his followers will be admitted into the eternal abyss of the inferno.*[41]

According to Sr. Jeanne Le Royer, the Antichrist's defeat will occur exactly fifteen days after the ascension into Heaven of Enoch and Elijah. Her detailed description of the event is worth quoting at length:

*The day of retribution will now begin, because, being full of the spirit of Lucifer, with the greatest presumption and self-love he will consider himself God, and in his haughtiness he will endeavor, together with his followers, to solemnly arise to Heaven to the throne of God. The Almighty has already prepared St. Michael with power and justice and charged him to oppose Antichrist in the heavens. When the demon group with Antichrist in their midst arrives, St. Michael will descend from Heaven with great speed upon them, being filled with holy indignation. With his appearance great fear surges through the proud army. A terrible voice sounds forth from the mouth of St. Michael as the earth opens: "Be gone you cursed! Down into the deepest abyss of Hell!" A bolt of lightning from the cloud casts Antichrist and his cohorts into the fearful abyss of fire and flames with such force that the deepest foundations tremble and all Hell resounds. With the fall of Antichrist will come severe earthquakes, thick darkness will cover the Earth, the ground will open in thousands of places under the feet of the inhabitants and cities, towns, castles and an immense number of people will be swallowed up. One-half of that immense crowd on Mt. Olivet will be cast in the abyss with the Antichrist. The ocean will move frightfully and waves rise heavenward overflowing the coast and inundating the Earth. All these calamities are only to frighten the remaining into accepting the Grace and Mercy of God.*[42]

The deluded followers of the Antichrist who remain alive at that point will have one final chance to repent. The centrality of divine mercy is, in fact, the very reason for the Antichrist's terrible fate, as John of the Cleft Rock explained:

*That which makes the decree of the Lamb so implacable, is*

*that Antichrist dared to claim to be a Christian and to act in the Name of Christ, and if he did not perish, the fruit of the Redemption would be lost, and the gates of Hell would prevail against the Savior.*[43]

We do not know when the Antichrist will come, nor when his three-and-a-half year reign will end—but there can be no doubt that it *will* end, and that his efforts to destroy the Church will not succeed. The passages quoted above vividly describe his total and inevitable defeat. Though the Antichrist will for a brief time, unlike anyone else in history, literally rule the entire world, his doom—like those of all his predecessors in evil—is absolutely certain, and in him Our Lady's prediction that God "has thrown down the rulers from their thrones" (Lk. 1:51) will be fulfilled in the most complete and irrevocable manner possible.

Scripture tells us that Satan's condemnation and punishment is unavoidable (Is. 27:1; Mt. 16:18; Jn. 14:30, 16:11; Eph. 6:10-17; 1 Pt. 5:10; Rev. 20:10), and this means that the Antichrist—as a mere servant of the devil—will certainly not be able to prevail against the Church. He will, however, be very dangerous to those whose faith is built on a weak foundation (cf. Mt. 7:26-27), or who allow Satan to steal it away (cf. Mk. 4:15). That's why it's essential for Christians to recognize the grave threat he'll represent, for he and other servants of the devil will attempt to mislead even the elect, if that were possible (Mk. 13:22).

If we were to summarize the Antichrist's character, we might say that he will be as **ruthless** as Antiochus IV and Attila the Hun; his **paranoia** will match or exceed that of Stalin, and his **cunning** will be like that of Herod, Machiavelli, Weishaupt, Rasputin, and Gramsci. Additionally, the Antichrist's **perversity** (sexual and otherwise) will be reminiscent of Crowley and Kinsey; he will have the **hypnotic speaking ability** of Hitler, and the **moral depravity** of Nero, John XII, and Alexander VI. In his **misplaced religious idealism,** the Antichrist will resemble Mohammed, Calvin, and Lenin; moreover, Marx, Blavatsky, and Crowley will serve as representations (though on a very small scale) of his **satanic commitment.**

The Antichrist will be more **narcissistic** than Stalin, Mao, Kim Il-Sung, and all the other figures who demanded or encouraged personality cults—though his will be on a much vaster scale. He will have the **inner spiritual emptiness** of Darwin and Sartre, though he will fill it in part with the same **anti-Christian animus** we see in some of the French revolutionaries, in Nietzsche, and in Marx and many of his disciples. The Antichrist will manifest that sense of self-satisfaction, or an **intellectual haughtiness**, witnessed in Rousseau, Voltaire, and Freud, among others.

Lastly and most importantly, the Antichrist will demonstrate the arrogant **pride of Lucifer himself.**

It was pride which led the greatest of all the angels to rebel against God, causing him to be cast out of Heaven (Rev. 12:7-9), and pride will also prove to be the Antichrist's undoing,[44] for "God resists the proud, but gives grace to the humble" (Jas. 4:6; cf. 2 Pt. 5:5). The most humble of all creatures is, of course, the Virgin Mary, who identified herself as the "handmaid of the Lord" (Lk. 1:38) and declared herself to be blessed by Him in her lowliness (Lk. 1:48). As a result, she has become the "woman clothed with the sun" (Rev. 12:1), against whom the devil wages his utterly unsuccessful war (Gen. 3:15; Rev. 12:14-16).

Scripture scholars generally agree that the Woman of Revelation 12 represents not only the Virgin Mary, but also the Church herself—and in this sense, we have the assurance that Christ's one, holy, catholic, and apostolic Church will not be overcome—neither by the devil, nor by his Antichrist. Jesus has promised that the Church, as His Bride, will share in His final victory over all evil (Rev. 21:1ff), and then, in the words of the hymn, "the great Church victorious shall be the Church at rest."[45]

## NOTES TO CHAPTER 13

1    The word "antichrist" occurs only in 1 Jn. 2:18,22; 1 Jn. 4:3; and 2 Jn. 7. The "man of sin" mentioned by St. Paul in 2 Th. 2:3-12 is undoubtedly the same figure, as is "the beast that comes up from the abyss" mentioned in Rev. 11:7, 13:1ff. Many biblical scholars also see the arrogant "little horn" of Dn. 7:8,24-25 as an additional reference to the Antichrist.

2    Some historical figures identified in their own day as the Antichrist include—with varying degrees of plausibility—Nero and some other Roman emperors, Luther, Calvin, certain popes, Napoleon, Hitler, Stalin,

Henry Kissinger, Saddam Hussein, Ronald Reagan, and Barack Obama.
Literary attempts to name the Antichrist, by their very nature, allow
for more creativity. For instance, in his 1907 novel *Lord of the World*,
the scholarly English priest Robert Hugh Benson identifies the fictional
Antichrist as Julian Felsenburgh, and in my own novel *After the Darkness*
(Queenship Publishing, 1997), I give him the symbolic name Josiah Daniel
Tirsch (with "Tirsch" being an anagram for "Christ," and each of the three
names having six letters—thus, 6-6-6).

[3]  Rev. Vincent P. Miceli, S.J., *The Antichrist* (Roman Catholic Books, 1981), p. 55.

[4]  Paul Thigpen, *Quotes from the Saints* (Servant Publications, 2001), p. 18.

[5]  Edward Connor, *Prophecy for Today* (Apostolate of Christian Action, 1956, 1963), p. 62.

[6]  Ted and Maureen Flynn, *The Thunder of Justice* (MaxKol Communications, 1993), p. 260.

[7]  Connor., p. 63.

[8]  *Ibid.*

[9]  *Ibid.*, p. 65.

[10]  *Ibid.*, p. 66.

[11]  *Ibid.*, p. 68.

[12]  Rev. R. Gerald Culleton, *The Reign of Antichrist* (TAN Books & Publishers, 1974), p. 155.

[13]  Connor, p. 67.

[14]  *Ibid.*, p. 61.

[15]  Omar V. Garrison, *The Encyclopedia of Prophecy* (Citadel Press, 1978), p. 167.

[16]  *Ibid.*, p. 133.

[17]  Connor, p. 64.

[18]  *Ibid.*, p. 62.

[19]  *Ibid.*, p. 69.

[20]  *Ibid.*

[21]  *Ibid.*, p. 67.

[22]  *Ibid.*, p. 61.

[23]  *Ibid.*, p. 68.

[24]  *Ibid.*, p. 62.

[25]  Culleton, pp. 133-134.

[26]  Connor, p. 63.

[27]  Culleton, p. 136.

[28]  Flynn, p. 256.

29  Culleton, p. 129.

30  *Ibid.*

31  Emmett Culligan, *The Last World War and the End of Time* (Elbee Press, 1966), p. 131.

32  Culleton., p. 136.

33  *Ibid.,* p. 129.

34  *Ibid.,* p. 134.

35  Stephen A. Foglein, *The Age of "One Fold and One Shepherd" Is Coming* (Two Hearts Books & Publishers, 1994), p. 215.

36  This identification was made by St. Hippolytus, St. Benedict, St. Hildegard, St. Mechtilde, and St. Robert Bellarmine, among others. See my book *After the Darkness* (Queenship Publishing, 1997), pp. 436-437, for a more thorough examination of this point.

37  Connor, p. 71.

38  *Ibid.,* p. 66.

39  *Ibid.,* p. 68.

40  Culleton, pp. 129-130.

41  Garrison, pp. 64-65.

42  Culleton, pp. 155-156.

43  *Ibid.,* p. 137.

44  The great Russian author Vladimir Soloviev, who was born Orthodox but died in 1900 as a Byzantine Catholic, wrote a very perceptive novel titled *Tale of the Antichrist.* Soloviev described the Antichrist in a very surprising way: a man of noble character free from every tendency toward greed, lust, anger, self-indulgence, and virtually every other moral weakness. Soloviev's antichrist even admired Jesus Christ. He had only one sinful flaw: an overwhelming sense of pride and self-importance—and that alone was sufficient to lead him to his destiny of disaster and doom. Cf. Livio Fanzaga, *Wrath of God: The Days of the Antichrist,* trans. A. J. O'Brien (Roman Catholic Books, 1997), p. 35.

45  Samuel J. Stone, "The Church's One Foundation," verse 3.

# Conclusion

*The beast was caught and with it the false prophet*
*who had performed in its sight the signs by which he*
*led astray those who had accepted the mark of the*
*beast and those who had worshipped in its image.*
*The two were thrown alive into the fiery pool*
*burning with sulfur.* (Rev. 19:20)

As noted in the Introduction, St. Hildegard observed that "The devil performs his craftiness through the work of people,"[1] and throughout history, he's never lacked for willing servants. In the preceding chapters we've seen very clearly that Satan's characteristics are all manifested in his antichrists: hatred, a spirit of division, cruelty, perversity, deception, and, in fact, all the seven deadly sins—especially pride. We've also seen that the fate of each antichrist is ultimately one of failure, ruin, and disgrace, for the Church—following in the footsteps of her Lord—suffers, but is never conquered; she stumbles, but always rises again, more beautiful, powerful, and glorious than before.

The century just ended was undoubtedly the most bloody, the most violent, and, indeed, in many ways the most wicked in all human history; evil manifested itself more strongly and clearly than ever before. However, even though the shadow of Satan seemed to poison and darken the decades of the 20th century in an unprecedented way, the light of God's grace continued to shine brightly, illuminating the way of salvation for those seeking to find it. In reflecting upon the limits God places on iniquity, Pope John

Paul II stated:

> It can seem that the evil of concentration camps, of gas chambers,
> of police cruelty, of total war, and of oppressive regimes—evil
> which, among other things, systematically contradicts the
> message of the Cross—it can seem, I say, that such evil is more
> powerful than any good. Yet if we look more closely at the
> history of those peoples and nations who have endured the trial
> of totalitarian systems and persecutions on account of faith, we
> discover that this is precisely where the victorious presence of
> Christ's Cross is most clearly revealed.[2]

Jesus is "the Lamb that was slain," the One Who alone is worthy "to receive power and riches, wisdom and strength, honor and glory and blessing" (Rev. 5:12), and only those whose names are written in His book of life will enter into the eternal life and joy of God's Kingdom (Rev. 21:27). This is the greatest possible news for all the children of God—but at the same time, a terrible judgment upon the wicked. Our Lord's parable of the weeds among the wheat (Mt. 13:24-30, 36-43) teaches us that while the good and the evil exist together in this world, a very different fate awaits each group—and He warns us that "whoever has ears ought to hear" (Mt. 13:43).

Opposition to the Gospel seems perhaps more widespread and violent than ever before—but God has not forgotten His people, nor will He overlook the sins of those who persecute them. As Jesus warns, "Behold, I am coming soon. I bring with Me the recompense I will give to each according to his deeds" (Rev. 22:12). Thus, as St. Bede observed, "The evil should always be anxious as regards their wretched works, since even each of their thoughts lies open to the view of the strict Judge."[3] All who cling to their sins and place their hopes in this life are choosing for themselves an eternity of horror and regret, for "the world and its enticement are passing away—but whoever does the will of God remains forever" (1 Jn. 2:17).

The Church will continue to be victorious over every earthly challenge, and will withstand every demonic assault, because of her loving union with Christ—for love "bears all things, believes all things, hopes all things, endures all things; love never fails" (1 Cor. 13:7-8). As St. Hilary of Poitiers noted in the 4th century, "It is the peculiar property of the Church that when she is buffeted, she is triumphant; when she is assaulted with argument she proves herself in the right; when she is deserted by her supporters, she holds the field."[4] Over 1500 years later a similar observation was made by G. K. Chesterton, who wrote:

> *Christianity has died many times and risen again; for it had a God Who knew the way out of the grave. But the first extraordinary fact which marks this history is this: that Europe has been turned upside down over and over again; and that at the end of each of these revolutions the same religion has again been found on top. The Faith is always converting the age, not as an old religion but as a new religion.*[5]

God is able to make all things new (cf. Rev. 21:5), and so the Church is thus renewed in every age; each of her members is able to echo the words of the Blessed Virgin Mary in proclaiming that "the Mighty One has done great things for me, and holy is His Name" (Lk. 1:49).

Jesus has chosen to give His Mother a central role in His Church's victory over evil, and indeed, in the words of St. Louis de Montfort,

> *The most fearful enemy that God has set up against the devil is Mary, His holy Mother. From the time of the earthly paradise, although she existed then only in His mind, He gave her such a hatred for His accursed enemy, such ingenuity in exposing the wickedness of the ancient serpent and such power to defeat, overthrow and crush this proud rebel, that Satan fears her not only more than angels and men but in a certain sense more than God Himself.*[6]

The saint also warned that "Satan, knowing that he has little time—even less now than ever—to destroy souls, intensifies his efforts and his onslaughts every day,"[7] but assured us that the devil is unable to do any real harm to those who entrust themselves to the Mother of the Savior.

Sr. Lucia, the Fatima visionary, stated in a 1957 interview that "The devil is about to wage a decisive battle against the Blessed Virgin, and a decisive battle is where one side will be victorious and the other side will suffer defeat."[8] She also noted that Our Lady had informed her and her two cousins (the other visionaries of Fatima) that "God is giving two last remedies to the world: the Holy Rosary and the devotion to the Immaculate Heart of Mary."[9] On her deathbed, Jacinta, the youngest of the three visionaries, reminded Lucia, "Make it known that the Sacred Heart of Jesus wishes that the Immaculate Heart of Mary be honored with Him. People must ask for peace through the Immaculate Heart, for God has entrusted the peace of the world to her."[10]

Mary, as the Queen of Peace, is able to bestow great blessings from her Son—especially those of a religious and spiritual nature. In her classic work *Mystical City of God*, the 17th century mystic Ven. Mary of Agreda wrote:

*It was revealed to me that through the intercession of the Mother of God, all heresies will disappear. This victory over heresies has been reserved by Christ for His Blessed Mother. In the last times the Lord will especially spread the renown of His Mother: Mary began salvation and by her intercession it will be concluded. Before the Second Coming of Christ, Mary must, more than ever, shine in mercy, might and grace in order to bring unbelievers into the Catholic Faith.[11]*

The visionary also added that "the powers of Mary in the last times over the demons will be very conspicuous. . . and it will be a time of great joy when Mary, as Mistress and Queen of Hearts, is enthroned."[12]

This wonderful assurance is echoed in the words of Ven. John Henry Newman, who stated,

*No one has access to the Almighty as His mother has; none has such merit as hers. Her Son will deny her nothing that she asks; and herein lies her power. While she defends the Church, neither height nor depth, neither men nor evil spirits, neither great monarchs, nor craft of man, nor popular violence, can avail to harm us; for human life is short, but Mary reigns above, a Queen forever.[13]*

The woman of Revelation 12 underwent great suffering and persecution (12:2, 13-16), but the dragon did not prevail against her. In the same way, the Holy Catholic Church, under the loving and powerful protection of Our Lady, may have much to suffer, but will always successfully withstand every assault by her enemies, and in the end will conquer the gates of hell itself. This is Our

Savior's promise (Mt. 16:18), and "this hope will not leave us disappointed" (Rom. 5:5).

## NOTES TO CONCLUSION

[1]   Rosemary Ellen Guiley, *The Quotable Saint* (Checkmark Books, 2002), p. 61.

[2]   Pope John Paul II, *Memory and Identity: Conversations at the Dawn of a Millennium* (Rizzoli International Publications, 2005), p. 19.

[3]   Guiley, p. 77.

[4]   Paul Thigpen, *Quotes from the Saints* (Servant Publications, 2001), p. 36.

[5]   G. K. Chesterton, *The Everlasting Man* (Dodd, Mead, 1926), p. 312.

[6]   St. Louis de Montfort, *True Devotion to Mary*, chapter 1, #52, as quoted in Guiley, pp. 64-65. The reason for this, the saint explains, is not because Mary is more powerful than God, but because she is infinitely *less* powerful than Him—and thus, for Satan to be defeated by her inflicts a terrible injury on his overwhelming pride.

[7]   Guiley, p. 65.

[8]   Mark Fellows, *Sister Lucia: Apostle of Mary's Immaculate Heart* (Immaculate Heart Publications, 2007), p. 160.

[9]   *Ibid.*, p. 161.

[10]  Professor Courtenay Bartholomew, *Her Majesty Mary: Queen of Peace* (Queenship Publishing, 2002), p. 290.

[11]  Thomas W. Petrisko, *Call of the Ages* (Queenship Publishing, 1995), pp. 448-449.

[12]  *Ibid.*, p. 449.

[13]  Paul Thigpen, *A Dictionary of Quotes from the Saints* (Servant Publications, 2001), p. 148.

# Other Queenship Publishing books by Rev. Joseph M. Esper

*Christian, Yes—But why Catholic?*
*Helpful Ideas on Explaining & Defending Your Faith*

*After the Darkness:*
*A Catholic Novel on the Coming of the Antichrist*

*Catholicism in Crisis,*
*Satan's Assault on the Church &*
*The Coming Triumph of the Immaculate Heart*

*With Mary to Jesus,*
*Our Surest Path to Heaven*

*Spiritual Dangers of the 21st Century*